C000133550

MYSTERIES OF THE NORMAN CONQUEST

MYSTERIES OF THE NORMAN CONQUEST

UNRAVELLING THE TRUTH OF THE BATTLE OF HASTINGS AND THE EVENTS OF 1066

ROBERT ALLRED

FRONTLINE
BOOKS

MYSTERIES OF THE NORMAN CONQUEST
Unravelling the Truth of the Battle of Hastings and the Events of 1066

First published in Great Britain in 2022 by

Frontline Books
An imprint of
Pen & Sword Books Ltd
Yorkshire - Philadelphia

Copyright © Robert Allred, 2022

ISBN 978 1 39908 803 9

The right of Robert Allred to be identified as
the author of this work has been asserted by him in accordance
with the Copyright, Designs and Patents Act 1988.

A CIP catalogue record for this book is
available from the British Library

All rights reserved. No part of this book may be reproduced or
transmitted in any form or by any means, electronic or mechanical
including photocopying, recording or by any information storage and
retrieval system, without permission from the Publisher in writing.

Typeset in 10.5/13 pt Palatino
by SJmagic DESIGN SERVICES, India.

Printed and bound in the UK by CPI Group (UK) Ltd.

Pen & Sword Books Ltd incorporates the Imprints of Aviation, Atlas,
Family History, Fiction, Maritime, Military, Discovery, Politics, History,
Archaeology, Select, Wharncliffe Local History, Wharncliffe True Crime,
Military Classics, Wharncliffe Transport, Leo Cooper, The Praetorian Press,
Remember When, Seaforth Publishing and Frontline Publishing.

For a complete list of Pen & Sword titles please contact

PEN & SWORD BOOKS LTD
47 Church Street, Barnsley, South Yorkshire, S70 2AS, England
E-mail: enquiries@pen-and-sword.co.uk
Website: www.pen-and-sword.co.uk

Or

PEN AND SWORD BOOKS
1950 Lawrence Rd, Havertown, PA 19083, USA
E-mail: Uspen-and-sword@casematepublishers.com
Website: www.penandswordbooks.com

Contents

This book is dedicated to my loving wife, Kim Van, and our sons, Austin and Jordan, for all of your love and support through all the years, through good times and not so good ones as well.

Acknowledgements

I must thank all of the dedicated professionals who have gone before me in solving the mysteries of the Norman Conquest, from medieval times until the present day. Among the unheralded heroes are John Grehan, at Pen and Sword Books for his sound advice in helping me make this into a publishable book. Also to be thanked are Pen and Sword editor Stephen Chumbley and editorial facilitator at Pen and Sword Lisa Hoosan. Then there are the numerous troupers in public, academic and private libraries who helped me track down and obtain the many sources utilised in conducting this investigation. I must, of course, thank my wife, Kim Van, and our sons, Austin and Jordan for all of their assistance – spiritual and tangible. I must also include a sincere thank-you to Isidro Diaz for his contributions in crafting the maps appearing in this work. My gratitude extends to that anonymous editorial assistant who first reviewed my submission to Pen and Sword Books and who forwarded it to John Grehan, who was the proper man to provide the assistance required to make the publication of *Mysteries of the Norman Conquest* possible.

Thanks for all.

List of Illustrations

1. This is Duke William's impressive fortress in Falaise, Normandy. The author has benefitted from an unplanned weight-loss regimen after just five weeks, out of eight, of hikes at historical sites in England, from the south-east coast to Hadrian's Wall. A very accommodating family of German tourists, using the author's camera, took the photo.
2. Where the Viking fleet beached at Riccall, looking south-west. The Vikings would have begun beaching their 325 ships here, then farther along the east shore of the River Ouse as far as today's 'Landing Lane', where the Norwegian King Harald Hardrada, and King Harold Godwinsson's brother, the former Earl Tostig, are thought to have come ashore.
3. Fulford Marsh along the River Ouse. This flooded area is not as deep as it seems, particularly at low tide. The Norse *Heimskringla* ('Chronicle of the Kings of Norway') tells us that the Vikings flanked and outflanked the Anglo-Saxons at the ford and along Germany Beck by wading across here, then bursting out from the woods ahead and to the right.
4. The Viking side at Fulford. Looking west along the glacial moraine on the south or 'Viking' side of Germany Beck. The beck (small stream) is on the right. Straight ahead in the distance (past the clump of trees in mid-frame), the ford, and just beyond and to the right, the woods from which the Vikings erupted, outflanking the Anglo-Saxons. This caused the Anglo-Saxons who would have been in the shield wall in the foreground to turn and flee to save themselves.
5. Shallows at Stamford Bridge ford. Looking upstream from where the bridge likely stood in 1066, scores of yards east-north-east

of today's more modern bridge. It is here that the Anglo-Saxons swarmed across, some on foot, others on horseback.

6. The old and crumbling castle at Pevensey, built upon the ruins of an ancient Roman fort, is where Duke William and his nobles and knights spent their first night in England. It is roomy enough inside the walls to also shelter the horses, while the bulk of the army would have camped all around, where the ships were beached.

7. This huge old tree in St Mary's Tract was likely broken in half by the occasional powerful storms to strike southern England. Tropical storms have made landfall in south-east England in 2004, 2006, 2008 and 2021.

8. The author stands at about the spot where, as tradition has it, Duke William stood as he directed the battle. Battle Abbey is visible on the ridgetop in the background. Unfortunately for many historians, and English Heritage, the battle actually took place off-camera – to the right, with only the final phase, where the Norman knights drowned in the 'Malfosse', taking place about where the author stands.

9. The leaves, pollen, dust, and twigs floating atop the flooded areas along the lower reaches of the trail around the traditionally-accepted battlefield make them seem to be solid ground, until one approaches very closely, and crouches down to observe the 'forest floor', as the author did when taking this photograph.

10. This is the gate on Powdermill Lane, looking toward where the author stood on the historically reckoned battle site. However, as the author shows in the text, the battle was actually fought to the rear of where this photo was taken.

11. The author not only found an ancient (hoar), twisted, struggling apple tree near where King Harold fell, in St Mary's Tract, he harvested about a dozen apples and shared them with his flatmates at the University of Sussex. (They were tangy and a bit sweet – not as sour as anticipated.)

12. The 'scenic meadows' break up the woods on both sides of the valley now holding the Southeastern Railway line. It is believed by some, including the author, that 'Scenic Meadow', or 'Scean Leagh' (Anglo-Saxon for 'scenic meadow') was corrupted to form what the Normans called 'Senlac', a name now assigned to 'Battle Hill.'

13. This was but one of many huge old trees the author encountered in St Mary's Tract, near to the A2100 and continuing near the Southeastern Railway line, where the Anglo-Saxon shield wall held the 'fosse,' or fortified 'ditch' until late in the battle, when the Normans at last broke through and won the day.

MAP 1

Fulford: The armies meet at Germany Beck. The Vikings seem to be checked. The Anglo-Saxons press the attack at the ford, where the Vikings briefly turn back while their main thrust – along the River Ouse, across the marsh and into the woods on their left – breaks through and bursts from the woods. Not shown: the Anglo-Saxon army is surprised, outflanked, routed, and hastily retreats to the relative safety of the walls of York. The outline shows the municipal limits of today's Fulford.

MAP 2

Stamford Bridge: The Viking army approaches from the south-east on the heights when they see the Anglo-Saxons rapidly advancing from the north-west on the high ground across the River Derwent.

Seeing that he is being attacked by a large force, the king of the Vikings sends an advance guard to block the bridge while the Viking army and its allies form a hedgehog defence on the heights, at what is now known as Battle Flats.

King Harold sends his mounted men in a dash across the ford just upstream from the bridge, along with the main body of infantry, while he accompanies a mounted column as they attack the bridge. There, after a brief struggle, King Harold and the second mounted group complete the encirclement of the Vikings.

Not shown: The Anglo-Saxons and Vikings engage in a bitter, drawn-out fight, reducing and eliminating the Viking army, killing Earl Tostig and King Harald Hardrada of Norway. Then, too late, a Viking relief force arrives, only to be defeated in turn. As dusk falls, the Anglo-Saxons pursue the few surviving Vikings all the way back to their ships, beached at Riccall.

The outline shows the town limits of modern Stamford Bridge.

MAP 3

Hastings, Phase One: Each side being aware of the presence of the enemy, advances – the Normans from the south-east along the Hastings-to-London ridgetop road; the Anglo-Saxons from the north-west at their rallying point near 'the hoar apple tree' on Caldbec Hill.

The Anglo-Saxon 'shield wall' blocks the road as the Normans fan out, discovering that their flanking movements are blocked by marshes to the east, and a ravine to the west, which the Anglo-Saxons have 'fortified' with sharpened stakes driven into the ground along the top of the slope on the northern edge of the narrow valley there.

MAP 4
Hastings, Phase Two: The Norman right flank remains checked behind marshes while the Norman main body is also stalled by a stout Anglo-Saxon defence on the ridgeway; but the Norman heavy infantry and cavalry press the attack on the left, across the 'fosse' or fortified 'ditch' (narrow, steep-sided valley or ravine). Seeing the threat, King Harold shifts from his initial command position on the high point just south of what is now the Marley Lane traffic circle, and advances into the present-day St Mary's tract. As he does so, he sends reinforcements – likely including many of his personal guards, his Huscarls – to fortify and extend the Anglo-Saxon battle lines toward the south-west.

MAP 5
Hastings, Phase Three: The Norman heavy infantry and cavalry – after an all-day fight of repeated attacks – finally break through. Some of the cavalry swings wide, coming to grief in the flooded terrain at the southern edge of what has been the historically-accepted battlefield site below Battle Abbey. Meanwhile, Duke William and other knights close in and kill King Harold. Not shown: As evening falls, the Anglo-Saxons try to mount a last stand, likely at the present day St Mary's Church, across from Battle Abbey, as the scattered survivors flee, many of whom are pursued and killed by Norman cavalry.

MAP 6
Hastings Today: The deployments of the armies are shown in relation to a few modern features of the town of Battle.

By Way of Introduction: Prelude and Preliminaries to Investigating the Battle of Hastings

I was eight years old when I first heard and read about the Norman Conquest of England. The year of the Conquest, I learned, was 1066. It would be a fateful year for a man – Harold Godwinsson, Earl of Wessex – become King Harold II, his family and his countrymen, as it would be for another man – William, Duke of Normandy – become William the Conqueror and also for his family and his countrymen. The events of 1066 would eventually influence the history of the entire planet.

But learning all of that about the Norman Conquest and 1066 would come later for me and continues to this day, as it does for many people: professionals and scholars with advanced degrees; investigators who can be regarded as amateurs in status but some of whom possess the curiosity and/or skills and capabilities of the most experienced and learned professional historians; archaeologists; and researchers who are fascinated by subjects other people might find obscure, remote and mundane, but which nevertheless have a continuing impact on the majority of the people of this world; and, finally, curious fledglings such as I am.

When I first read of the Battle of Hastings, which was the military culmination of the historic events of 1066, like any eight-year-old, I thought it would be interesting to visit the site of the battle, described as being 'on Senlac Hill'. It would be 60 years before that fleeting fantasy became a reality for me.

In my final semester of (belated) study for my undergraduate degrees at the University of California at Berkeley in 2016, I was extended an invitation to study the history and environment of southern England.

Taking the opportunity, I attended summer classes for eight weeks at the University of Sussex, at Falmer, on the outer rim of Brighton. Hastings is only a comparatively short, hour-long train journey eastward from Falmer, barring strikes or other relatively rare problems. So, on my earliest day free of classes or other obligations, within the first week, I set forth to Hastings.

I had been prepared to accept the 'official' version of the events of 1066, even though and also as a child, I recognised that history is just that – 'his story' – and that the reporting of the outcome of the battle and of the overall Conquest would derive, either partly or in its entirety, from the perspective of the victor, Duke William – become William the Conqueror – and the Normans. So I would, again, strive to be objective in analysing the point of view of the 'official' historians while remaining curious about the viewpoint of the losers of the conflict – King Harold II and his Anglo-Saxons.

During the three years leading up to my brief sojourn in southern England I had been pursuing degrees in American Studies and Political Economy at the University of California at Berkeley. Therefore, I had been somewhat ignorant about distant events and developments in other areas of knowledge and other parts of the world, while I focused on and read about, for example, American Indian Reservations and commentators in the realm of political economy such as John Locke, etc. So, as I entered the tourist information office in Hastings I was cheerfully informed by a gracious lady there that, according to some experts and investigators – such as television presenter Tony Robinson – the exact site of the Battle of Hastings had recently been cast into some doubt.[1] This was news to my up-to-that-point academically-distracted mind. Nevertheless, I vowed that as I journeyed to Battle Abbey, supposed site of the combat, at the aptly-named town of Battle, I would try to be not too sceptical. I would carefully look into precisely what the official version would have to say prior to formulating any possible but as yet unlikely alternate scenarios regarding the exact locations or other factors relating to the historical events of 1066.

In that I was already in Hastings and had planned to visit the castle ruins there, I asked directions from the kind lady at the tourism office who had pierced my ignorance of the recent controversy and alerted me to the 'location of the battle at Battle' counter-view. I followed her directions regarding how to get up the bluffs to the castle, until I found a very unpretentious doorway almost hidden between two shops on a winding, slightly touristy little lane below the heights, upon which I had been able to see the castle ruins since walking 'downtown', literally 'down to town', from the train station – the city 'centre' being on lower ground, near the seashore.

Entering the anonymous doorway, I went up a very long flight of steps. (I had been warned about there being '100 steps', but I quit counting at the number 80, which was far from the top. I had thus, inadvertently, begun my weight-loss and fitness programme (unplanned and unanticipated) while journeying around England on trains, buses and on foot, in my quest to 'uncover the mysteries of 1066'.) The very long flight of steps was followed by another and yet another – the last one slightly shorter – until I was upon the gently rolling grassy slope above the white cliffs of chalk that rim many of the southern and south-eastern shores of England. I turned toward the castle ruins, went overland past the funicular 'railway' that I could have taken up but declined to do so – partly due to the fact that I had just spent about an hour and a half on trains and in part to simply enjoy the outdoors and the climb – and made my way, now a bit downslope, to the entryway through the crumbling bastion's walls. I paid my fee and entered the castle grounds – maintained and managed by English Heritage.

I already knew that the castle was a later, stone-crafted replacement for the motte and bailey, prefabricated wooden fortification the Normans had quickly assembled in 1066. About half of the now disintegrating castle, made of coast-side flint set into mortar, has, over the centuries, fallen into the sea or, more accurately, onto the seashore as the chalk cliffs below it, too, are even now being eroded away by wind and waves. It – like many other old castles, churches and abbeys – is now a simultaneously impressive yet forlorn place. One can still sense the feeling of raw power it must have generated among those who occupied it, while also reminding you of the sense of isolation and even loneliness it would have imposed on those who lived and worked within its walls. The day I visited Hastings Castle was sunny and breezy, with the brightness and fresh air creating a more cheerful atmosphere, unlike the all-too-common days in southern England with its oceanic climate, when the grey gloom of low clouds or even fog made what were refreshing breezes on a sunny day become cold blasts off the English Channel, which is but a chill and choppy branch of the tumultuous North Atlantic Ocean. It was here that Duke William and his Normans and their allies set up their eastern bastion on the narrow strip of coast they then controlled after their initial landings on the island nation at Pevensey. Having surveyed and toured the location and the castle itself and viewed the brief film about the place in the small theatre there, I continued by bus on to the town of Battle, where the key conflict of 1066 occurred.

Before reporting on my going to the generally accepted site of that historic contest, we must step back and review the events leading up to 1066, the invasions of England that year and the decisive fight at Hastings/Battle. However, prior to that, we must first take a look at what others have had to say about the actual site of the fighting and offer a preview of my perspectives on those ideas and the conclusions I have drawn after visiting various locations in the area where the combat is thought to have taken place and my readings of historical source documents.

What Others Have Had to Say About the Actual Battlefield Site

In recent years, not just the television documentary by Tony Robinson but other works prior to that programme have questioned exactly where the Battle of Hastings was fought and the authors of those books have reached widely different conclusions, all based on the same or nearly identical evidence.

The completion of this book is the result of fortunate circumstances. After I had queried several publishers when all I had were my preliminary notes and one expressed a willingness to review it after I had completed the work, I promptly set about 'finishing' it, of course. But this book was not quite in a finished form, yet. In the meantime, the publisher in question itself fell into a 'questionable' category and decided instead to become a 'hybrid' operation, whereby regular publishing agreements were largely if not almost entirely replaced by 'cooperative agreements', which meant that authors must pay – instead of being paid – for the publication of their books. Back to square one, almost.

In my subsequent querying effort regarding my now 'completed' manuscript, several publishers, while turning me down, suggested that I contact the Pen and Sword publishing house, to which, naturally, I had already sent a partial submission. Fortunately for this book and its writer, one of the 'gatekeepers' on the Pen and Sword staff forwarded my query to editor and distinguished military-affairs authority John Grehan. Mr Grehan, who, along with writing collaborator Martin Mace, had published a book some years previously,[2] *The Battle of Hastings 1066: The Uncomfortable Truth – Revealing the True Location of England's Most Famous Battle*. Mr Grehan was subsequently kind enough to offer some sound advice and guidance on how to make this book better and, consequently, marketable. In his thoughtful and thorough mentorship, he informed me that I must do a better job of defending my thesis regarding the actual site of the Battle of Hastings against competing theories, including his own. He listed three must-read – and must-comment-upon – books in his communications with me. They include: *The Battle of Hastings at Sedlescombe*, by Jonathan Starkey and Michael Starkey;[3] *Secrets of the Norman Conquest*, by Nick Austin;[4] and the aforementioned *The Battle of Hastings 1066: The Uncomfortable Truth – Revealing the True Location of England's Most Famous Battle*, by John Grehan and Martin Mace.

Each of these books makes a strong case for the Battle of Hastings being fought at locations other than the traditionally accepted site at Battle Abbey. I believe my thesis is stronger, but I will not attempt to ridicule or disparage the theories of these other observers – only to refute some of their assertions as I defend my own views and to strengthen my arguments in favour of my alternate scenario.

Before continuing with my critiques and refutations, I feel compelled to report that upon first reading them, Mr Grehan thought it seemed as if I were fawning over him and his writing partner and urged me to be brutal in ripping into his book's contents. I now present my reasons for offering my thoughts about these other works in the manner in which I proceeded.

The books were delivered from England at my California residence with the Starkey brothers' writings arriving first, then Mr Austin's and, finally, the work of Messers Grehan and Mace. Long ago, I worked as an assistant to a published author who ran a writers' workshop in Hollywood, California, where I gained a great deal of experience reading, critiquing and providing assistance to writers – mostly fiction and screenwriters – as they improved their work. This does not mean that I am able to always critique my own work objectively – a common human failing. However, I do believe I am able to offer valid criticisms and praise concerning the books in question here.

I found the book by the Starkey brothers to be challenging to read overall in general, partly because the authors chose to barely lay the foundations of many of their arguments before promptly declaring them to be establish fact as they moved on to build what was, to me, a tenuous set of assertions that did not properly warrant what I considered to be their hasty and unfounded conclusions.

Mr Austin's book suffered from the same faults, but to a lesser degree. Still, I found his book to also be a chore to read, due to a writing style similar to that of the Starkey brothers.

After wading through the previous books, I found the writing style and professionalism of Mr Grehan and Mr Mace to be a refreshing relief. Moreover, as I observe later in these pages, the theory they present is closest to my own. While reaching geographically-opposite conclusions regarding the site of the Hastings fighting, their scenario does not call for discounting so many generally-accepted facts concerning the place where the Normans landed, where they travelled and camped, from whence the Anglo-Saxons approached and the circumstances and places of the armies coming together in combat. The Starkey brothers and Mr Austin want us to believe that so many sources – some of which recorded their review of the facts of the Battle of Hastings shortly after it occurred – were partly, or even mostly, in error. They resorted to what are, to me, elaborate and fantastic constructs in their attempts to move England's most famous battle up to miles from Battle Abbey, which is where most scholars and historians have placed it for nearly 1,000 years. In brief, it is all just too much to accept logically.

I will now look at each of these books in turn. The Starkey brothers assert that the actual site of the Battle of Hastings is in fact located at Sedlescombe, some two to three miles east-north-east of Battle Abbey. Mr Austin believes the fighting on 14 October 1066 was waged at Crowhurst, just about two miles south-south-east of the generally historically recognised location. Misters Grehan and Mace contend that the Battle of Hastings was fought very near to the currently accepted location just beyond Battle Abbey, with their theory that the fighting actually occurred on the slopes of the adjacent Caldbec Hill, about 1,000 to 2,000ft just to the north-north-east. To me, they made a much more credible presentation of the facts as they saw them and, also to this writer, I simply conclude that they are just plain wrong, for many reasons I will point out during my presentation of my theories. I make my own case in this book for the struggle to have happened almost contiguous to the Battle Abbey grounds, but to the south-east and possibly extending just slightly onto the lower part of the so-far acknowledged battlefield site – specifically, just off Powdermill Lane (the B2095), the Hastings-to-London Road (the A2100) and the Marley Lane and Station Approach avenue to the Southeastern Railway platforms. All of these locations are also within, roughly, about 1,000 to 2,000ft of the Abbey and its neighbouring supposed site of the fighting.

I will initially address some of the arguments presented in the three books cited in turn, and will further refer to them as my argument progresses throughout this work, with some further summations near the end of my coverage of the subject. For now, I will take us back to describing the overall setting and historical background of the Norman Conquest before addressing the issues raised in those other books.

Chapter 1

Why The Norman Conquest Matters

Prior to the Norman Conquest, England, while for a time leading up to the fateful year of 1066 becoming heavily influenced by Norman clergymen and immigrants, remained primarily a 'Nordic' or north-facing country, as far as culture, society, trade and politics were concerned. But the successful invasion by William the Conqueror changed all of that. Henceforth, England or at least its newest incorporation of an imported ruling class of Latinised, French-speaking Northmen-become-Continentals, would face south – toward the Continent. Henceforth, England would increasingly become more attached to the Roman Catholic Church as many English – or Anglo-Norman – lords, including the king, Richard the Lionheart, partook of the adventures and plundering made available after 1095 by the Crusades.

England's detachment from the Nordic world and increased attachment to the mainstream of European culture on the Continent would intertwine the fates of both that island nation and its mainland counterparts. With regard to France, the once-conquered English island would turn around and exact a sort of revenge by ruling over much of the French homeland for many decades. Eventually, England's Continental focus would embroil the formerly more insular nation in international intrigues extending as far as the Balkans and would, over time, lead to England looking further afield, until the British Empire became the most extensive the world had ever seen, before or since. It can be argued – and the argument is valid – that without the Norman Conquest England might have strayed onto a less consequential historical path, becoming more focused on Scandinavian and North Atlantic concerns and not assuming its world-class status obtained by all of the machinations and complications of participating in the cultural, economic and political affairs of its Continental neighbours such as France, Spain, the German states and others farther afield. In short, William the Conqueror not only acquired England as an extended Norman province, he unknowingly – for such a future could hardly have been foreseen, whether by William or anyone else – thrust an island nation lying on the outskirts of a peninsula of peninsulas in Western Europe to the centre of the world stage, albeit before the international drama of imperial conquests of a grander nature had even been contemplated by a people whose world view extended hardly past neighbouring and nearby northern islands, waters and lands.

Chapter 2

Anglo-Saxon England – the Background

For those who need to be acquainted with or reminded about English history, what follows is a relatively compact review to set the events leading up to 1066 within a more easily digestible historical context. Even those who have become jaded by a thorough inundation in the facts of this period of English history may benefit from some of the reminders that follow.

The centuries prior to the Norman Conquest had been more than turbulent – and that is an understatement. This was especially so regarding the eleventh century. One thousand years earlier, the Romans had conquered almost all of Britain – that is present-day England proper, exclusive of Scotland and Wales – making it the Roman province of Britannia. But with the collapse of Rome after 410 AD came the invasion, conquest and resettlement of the same territories of old England itself – again exclusive of Scotland and Wales – by the Anglo-Saxons. Eventually, Britannia became known in the Old English language as 'Engla-land', so named in part after the people who were the companions of the Germanic Saxon conquerors – the tribes of the Angles, who migrated from what is now southern Denmark.

Anglo-Saxon England settled into almost half a millennium of relative peace and prosperity, until marauding Viking (Norse – Norwegian, Swedish and Danish and later Norman) seafaring raiders discovered the easy pickings of often gold Church artefacts to be found at remote monasteries such as at Lindisfarne. Viking raiders struck that island monastery off the more isolated northern shores of the main English island on 8 January 793, according to *The Anglo-Saxon Chronicle*.[1]

After about a century of attacks and invasions by Viking raiders, some to later become Viking settlers, the many small kingdoms of

3

Anglo-Saxon England began to fall to the Norse conquerors one by one, until only the southern English kingdom of Wessex stood between the Vikings and their complete conquest of old 'Engla-land'.

To place the events of 1066 into their proper historical context, it is necessary to look at not only the roots of Viking (Norwegian and Danish) inroads into England but to also delve into the complications of Norman involvement in English (Anglo-Saxon) dynastic and therefore political developments dating back to just prior to the year 1000.

The seeds of 1066 were sown almost a century earlier, when a teenaged monarch, Edward (The Martyr), was assassinated and the then 10- or 12 year-old (birth dates reliant on now lost old church records are often unknown today) Æthelred II (The Unrædy – meaning, in Old English, 'unwisely counselled'; but later, when – due to subsequent revised spelling standardisations – rendered as 'Unready', to become a double entendre, also indicating that he was not up to the task of kingship, as held by many of his countrymen at the time). It was widely believed then that the accession of the child-king to the throne in the year 978 was part of a plot instigated by his mother, Ælfthryth (the first Anglo-Saxon king's wife to be crowned queen of England) – stepmother of the slain Edward. This fitted in well with the labyrinthine and even Byzantine plots, manoeuvres and machinations among Anglo-Saxon, Viking and Norman nobles, rulers and their families – and all other nobility and royalty around the world at the time – that were befitting a modern-day soap opera.

The primary significance of Æthelred II's reign is that he was unable to rally enough support among the divided English to resist the conquest of the Anglo-Saxon territories of England then being vanquished by the Viking Danes. After several defeats at the hands of the Danes and many missteps, his (unwise?) counsellors decided to place the Danish Viking Swein Forkbeard on the English throne on Christmas Day 1013, driving Æthelred II into exile across the English Channel, in his queen, Emma's* homeland of Normandy. This move thus magnified the involvement of

---

* Upon their marriage, Emma became known as 'Ælfgifu', which means 'elf's gift'. Ælfgifu was a very common appellation among Anglo-Saxon women at that time. There is uncertainty among some observers as to whether it was merely a given name or a title awarded to women of high social standing or both. I believe it was both – first given as a compliment, then becoming an indication of formal or informal rank and then presented by parents to their otherwise 'low-born' daughters to indicate, at least, their very high expectations for their female offspring (https://www.bl.uk/people/queen-emma).

Normandy's noble lineage in Anglo-Saxon England's political affairs. Emma's father was Richard I of Normandy; her mother, Gunnor, was also herself a Dane. Moreover, Emma's great-grandfather was the Viking Rollo, founder of the Viking colony-to-become-dukedom of the Normans. Fate soon intervened, however: Swein died within 10 weeks and Æthelred's (yet unwise?) counsellors invited him to return and resume his kingship, which lasted until his death in 1016.

Upon his return from exile in 1014, Æthelred II had pledged to grant the Saxon manor of Rameslie to the Benedictine Abbey of Fécamp in Normandy, out of gratitude because his Norman brother-in-law, Richard II, had given him shelter in his country. Later, Æthelred II's widow, Queen Emma, would in turn marry his successor, the Danish King Canute, and she thereafter obtained the manor for the Norman abbey in 1017.[2]

Æthelred II's son, Edmund II (Ironside) had been resisting the Danish invasion since 1015. After his father's death, the leaders in London elected him to sit on the throne, but the royal council of nobles and senior churchmen of England as a whole – the Witan or Witenagemot – chose the invading Dane Canute, son of Swein Forkbeard, as king. Edmund Ironside resisted Canute's forces, but was defeated in battle at Assandun, with the loss of much of England's Anglo-Saxon nobility. The two would-be monarchs of the entire country concluded a pact: Canute would reign in the northern and eastern parts of England. In the south and west, Edmund Ironside would rule over the sole remaining but large earldom of Wessex, with the proviso that when one of the two died, the other would become ruler of all the land. Edmund Ironside died within the year (1016). Some observers suspected Edmund's death was possibly the result of assassination as he was yet young and evidently physically fit.[3] However, the opposing school of thought regarding Edmund's death considered the possibility of illness or wounds suffered at the Assandun fight.[4]

King Canute

During the armed struggle for control of England, Canute had already demonstrated his ruthlessness and renowned Viking cruelty in abruptly abandoning his English allies and mutilating and putting ashore hostages before sailing off with his own force on a sudden expedition to Denmark to secure his position there. Even those who adhered to Canute's cause such as the Northumbrian Earl Uhtred were not immune from treachery and he was murdered in his own hall after pledging his

5

loyalty to the Viking contender for the throne. Upon his accession to kingship, Canute at first continued in his ruthlessness, appointing the Norwegian Viking Eric of Hlathir to replace the assassinated Uhtred; and he was behind the deaths of Edmund II Ironside's brother, Edwig, and many other prominent Englishmen. However, Edmund's infant sons – Edward the Exile and Edmund Atheling – both marked for death, were safely escorted to asylum in Hungary. King Canute had other Anglo-Saxons sent into exile and appointed the Viking chieftain Thorkell the Tall as earl of East Anglia.[5]

However, Canute had earlier met and consorted with Ælfgifu (not Emma but another of the same name), daughter of an ealdorman of Northumbria who had been murdered by King Æthelred II's (unwise?) counsellors in 1006. Ælfgifu of Northumbria bore Canute two sons – Sweyn and Harold. This union and, probably more substantially, the influence of Wulfstan, Archbishop of York, eventually led to Canute mellowing and by 1018 Anglo-Saxon earls ruled in the former kingdoms-become-earldoms of Wessex and Mercia. The troublesome Thorkell was outlawed in 1021. Canute's Danish inner circle gradually diminished in number until his three most influential advisers included just one Dane.[6]

The Danish king and his English subjects concluded an agreement at Oxford, described as being 'according to Edgar's law'. (Edgar 'the Peaceful' was the father of Edward the Martyr and Æthelred II, where our encapsulated history herein began.) The treaty was drafted in the writing style of the previously noted Archbishop Wulfstan, who also crafted Canute's body of laws, which were primarily based on earlier English legal traditions. It is probable that Wulfstan also inspired King Canute to emulate the ruling style of the best English kings, especially Edgar. Thus did Canute prove to be an effective monarch who kept internal peace and brought prosperity to the land.

King Canute supported and generously donated to the church and his pilgrimage to Rome was inspired by religious fervour almost as much as diplomatic considerations. Because Canute required an English power base for support against outside domestic threats, he married Æthelred's widow, Emma. He also evidently hoped to forestall machinations by Emma's brother, the Norman Duke Richard II, in support of the claims of her sons by the late English king, who were yet in refuge in Normandy, to the Anglo-Saxon throne. Canute even enlisted Anglo-Saxon forces to secure his own claims in Denmark when he went there in 1019 to assume the kingship after his brother died. He was again distracted in Denmark when the outlawed Thorkell the Tall stirred up unrest there in 1023.

In 1026, Canute's appointed regent in Denmark, Ulf Jarl – who was married to Canute's sister, Estrid – rebelled and allied with the kings of Norway and Sweden in their conflict with Canute as king of Denmark. Despite Canute's subsequent defeat in Sweden, at the Battle of the Holy River, a treaty not unfavourable to the king of now both England and Denmark was signed. Ulf died soon after, with the Scandinavians asserting that Canute was the cause of his passing. King Canute next instigated a successful rebellion against Norwegian King Olaf II Haraldsson in 1028 and then replaced him. Now king of England, Denmark and Norway, Canute left Norway in charge of his appointed regent there, Haakon Ericsson and when Ericsson died his consort Ælfgifu (yet another woman of the same name/title) and her son Swein continued to rule on Canute's behalf, but were so unpopular they fled to Denmark in 1035 just a short time before Canute's death.

In England itself, however, peace reigned during Canute's time on the throne, except for a brief foray into Scotland in 1027 to gain the submission of the three Scottish kings. England benefitted from Canute's obtaining lower tariffs and tolls from European princes for English merchants and for pilgrims travelling to Rome. English commerce also profited from Canute's control of the Danish trade route to the Baltic. Denmark benefitted from Canute's good relationship with the Holy Roman Emperor Conrad II, whom he had met at the emperor's coronation during Canute's pilgrimage to Rome in 1027. Conrad granted the lands of Schleswig north of the Eider River to Denmark during the arrangements for the emperor's son, Henry, to marry Canute's daughter, Gunhild.

King Canute is, I believe, unfairly remembered for ordering the tide to not come in; but I agree with others in their assessment that his command has been taken too literally and that, instead, likely influenced by his pilgrimage to Rome, he actually intended to demonstrate to some of his overly devoted followers that he was not a god and that his edict to the tides would not come to pass because he was in fact a mere mortal. With his death, King Canute's time of relative stability, though spawned in brutal bloodshed, came to an immediate end.

Upon Canute's death in 1035, Harold Harefoot – his son by Canute's consort, the earlier-mentioned Ælfgifu of Northumbria – claimed the throne. His half-brother, Harthacanute, could have been rightly presumed to be, literally, the legitimate heir – being the son of Canute and his formally wed wife, the now former Queen Emma (who was also the widow of Æthelred II and the mother of yet two other potential claimants to the kingship – Harold Harefoot's and Harthacanute's half-brothers Alfred the Atheling,[†] and Edward). The Witan disagreed on the grounds that Harthacanute, then abroad fighting to secure his kingship of Denmark, was too preoccupied there to adequately serve as king of England. Harold Harefoot (meaning 'fleet of foot', due to his hunting and running abilities) was proclaimed King Harold (the First).

Emma's son by King Æthelred II, Alfred the Atheling, landed in Sussex in 1036 and attempted to make his way to London to claim the throne; but he was lured astray by a staunch supporter of Harold I – the Earl of Wessex, Godwin. (After all, Harold I's father, Canute, had made Godwin the first earl of Wessex in 1018.) Alfred was deceived by Godwin, bound, blinded with hot pokers and left to die of his wounds in a monastery near Guildford. More than 200 of his Norman bodyguards were also captured and killed on a hillside close by. There would be a long-lasting and lingering resentment and hatred among some Anglo-Saxons, many Normans and those Danes who had become more and more Englishmen for Earl Godwin for this crime.[7]

Besides engineering the murder of Alfred the Atheling, Harold I also banished Alfred's and Harthacanute's, mother, Emma, into exile. Harthacanute had not been sitting still over the contended usurpation by Harold I and was raising an army in Denmark for his return to England to claim the throne when, just weeks ahead of the scheduled invasion, Harold I died, in 1040.

When Harthacanute, accompanied by his mother Emma and an invasion force aboard about sixty warships, landed in England, he was immediately acclaimed as the new king. Harold I was buried in Westminster Abbey, but King Harthacanute ordered that Harold I's body be disinterred, beheaded and thrown into the River Thames. However, Harold Harefoot's stalwarts recovered his body parts and had them re-buried at St Clement Danes in London.[8] Emma was able to convince Harthacanute to bestow better treatment on his remaining half-brother than Harold I had granted to Alfred the Atheling. Harthacanute in 1041 allowed Edward (soon to become king himself, as Edward the Confessor) to return from his long exile in Normandy.

The following year, during a wedding celebration, Harthacanute, while toasting the good health of the bride, collapsed and died at the age of 24. Harthacanute had been the fourth and final Danish king of England.

---

† 'Atheling' denoted the status of a prince who was a qualified potential legitimate heir to kingship.

1066 Prelude – The Reign of Edward the Confessor

Next came the lengthy interlude of Edward 'the Confessor'[‡] during the almost two dozen years leading up to that pivotal year of 1066. He attained the throne on 3 April 1043, at the age of about 40 (his year of birth is estimated as being between 1001 and 1005). The rule of Edward the Confessor was one of relative stability, so far as his kingship and retaining it were concerned. It was also a period of abundant uncertainty, confusion and intrigue, much of which was caused or contributed to by Edward himself. In this, he was only partly to blame as upon his accession to the throne he had a very limited following, other than the desire of the Witan to return the crown to an Anglo-Saxon head. However, Edward's Englishness was tempered, or diluted, by a strong component of Norman genes (recalling that his mother's father had been Duke Richard I of Normandy) and in outlook due to his 25 years in exile in Normandy as well.

In recognition of his tenuous hold on the throne, Edward vastly increased his power base by relying on that most potent of English earls at the time, Godwin of Wessex. In 1045 Edward married Godwin's daughter, Eadgyth (Edith). Despite his marriage and his heavy reliance on Earl Godwin's advice and support, Edward is thought to have harboured a great but secret hatred of the earl for his aforementioned suspected part in the death of Edward's brother, Alfred the Atheling.[9]

Edward seemed unable at times to accurately judge the feelings of his English subjects and he largely negated his alliance with Earl Godwin of Wessex by appointing a Norman, Robert of Jumièges, Archbishop of Canterbury and also by placing many other Normans in positions of prestige and power. These missteps, as far as England's Anglo-Saxons were concerned, made him seem diffident and suspect with regard to his English over his Norman loyalties.

While Edward's mother, Emma, had returned to England from her own exile, he remained distant and reserved toward her due to his resentment at her having married the Danish successor Canute after the death of Edward's father, King Æthelred II. He was also without doubt severely stung and still hurting over his mother's preferences for both of his Danish half-brothers – Harold I and Harthacanute – over

---

‡ Edward was known as 'the Confessor' by his subjects due to his perceived piety and purity of soul.

himself and his murdered brother, Alfred the Atheling, despite the fact that it had been she who had prevailed upon Harthacanute to allow Edward's return to England in 1041. Their rift continued until Emma died on 6 March 1052.

However, in keeping with the spirit of the times, by 1049 events began to push Edward's reign into turmoil. In 1046, Earl Godwin's oldest son, Swein, had taken it into his head to abduct the abbess of Leominster, Eadgifu, apparently with the intent of marrying her and acquiring her Leominster estates. The king denied Swein permission to marry her and Eadgifu was returned to her abbey. Amid the uproar regarding this outrageous crime, Edward stripped Swein of his earldom and awarded his lands to the cousin of Eadgyth and Earl Godwin's second son, Harold Godwinsson (and also Swein) – Beorn. Swein settled in Flanders, then, in 1049 reappeared to ask for reinstatement and the return of his landholdings, some of which had also been given to Harold Godwinsson. At Earl Godwin's urging, King Edward was considering allowing Swein's 'rehabilitation'. Swein had meanwhile persuaded cousin Beorn to ride with him to meet with Harold Godwinsson at the latter's stronghold at Bosham and to then proceed to plead Swein's case to the king, but on the way Swein murdered Beorn. For this crime Swein was again condemned and once more fled to Flanders; but, on this occasion it was not Earl Godwin but his close friend, Bishop Ealdred of Worcester, who mediated with King Edward and, incredibly, Swein was once more reinstated.[10]

As Edward's exasperation with Earl Godwin and his family increased, the earl's influence waned and the king moved closer to his Norman allies. The king's sister, Goda, was married to Count Eustace of Boulogne – a neighbour to Normandy – who decided to visit his brother-in-law in England. Eustace and his entourage stopped off in Dover and his retainers offended the local citizens by appropriating free lodgings for themselves. There was a clash and an Englishman, having been wounded, killed one of the Normans (or, more properly near-Normans) in self-defence. Eustace and his men surrounded the Anglo-Saxon man's home and killed him and an additional half-dozen local men. The inhabitants of Dover chased the near-Norman Frenchmen out of town and Eustace promptly complained to his royal brother-in-law in London, who accepted his version of what had happened, summoned Earl Godwin and ordered him to punish the town's residents. Godwin refused and he and his sons Swein and Harold raised an army and insisted that Eustace and his men be turned over to the Godwins for them to exact revenge.

However, the northern earls, seizing on the opportunity to weaken the all-powerful Godwin, sided with the king. A truce was arranged, the Witan outlawed Swein, and Godwin and Harold were summoned to appear before them. Godwin and Harold asked for safe conduct, which was denied, and they declined to attend. The assembly passed a sentence of banishment and Earl Godwin and Harold had their estates confiscated. Taking advantage of Earl Godwin's moment of weakness, King Edward forsook his marriage to the earl's daughter, Eadgyth, on the grounds that she had produced no heirs. Edward then took the added steps of seizing Eadgyth's property – estates and jewellery – and consigning her to the custody of a convent.[11]

It is significant that at this time – when the leading house of Anglo-Saxon England had fallen into disfavour with King Edward – that Duke William of Normandy decided to visit and is reported to have obtained the king's promise that William would be his successor, despite the fact that the final say in the matter would not be Edward's but rather the Witan's. It is also relevant to recall that the Witan would often if not usually resort to practicality over formality and choose a king who could best serve the country, irrespective of 'legitimacy', as had been done in the choice of Harold I over the legitimate heir, Harthacanute.

Of course the Godwins were not content with the loss of their wealth and power. They raised an army and returned to England in 1052 in force, ready to do battle. In the meantime, many of those Englishmen who had previously been unfamiliar with or not accustomed to the inroads of Edward's Norman appointments to positions of power in both church and state began to see the Godwin family in a different light and rallied to their cause. Fearing a civil war, the Witan lived up to its reputation for wisdom and advised Edward to return the lands and titles of the Godwins. The king did so and even took back his wife and restored her wealth and her title as his queen.[12]

Then, in 1053, Earl Godwin died. According to one tradition (by the twelfth-century writer Aelred of Rievaulx, as cited by David C. Douglas),[13] Edward's secret hostility toward Earl Godwin boiled over and, at a banquet at Winchester, he challenged the earl regarding his possible involvement in the king's brother's – Alfred the Atheling's – death. Earl Godwin is said to have declared his innocence, adding that if he were guilty of such a crime, 'May this morsel of bread be my last'. Whereupon he put a crust of bread into his mouth, then evidently fell into a seizure, choked and died. An alternative view is that the earl had merely suffered an ill-timed (as far as establishing his innocence is concerned) stroke. The date was 15 April 1053. All that medieval historical recorder Master (Robert or Richard?) Wace had to say about the event was, '. . . I know that Godwin in the end choked himself, while eating at the king's table during a feast'.[14]

Godwin's oldest son, Harold, remained in good graces and he immediately inherited his late father's wealth, influence and prestige. *The Anglo-Saxon Chronicle*'s report on Earl Godwin's death was:

> In this year was the king at Winchester, at Easter; and Earl Godwin with him and Earl Harold his son and Tosty [Tostig, Earl Godwin's other son]. On the day after Easter sat he with the king at table; when he suddenly sunk beneath against the foot-rail, deprived of speech and of all his strength. He was brought into the king's chamber; and they supposed that it would pass over: but it was not so. He continued thus speechless and helpless till the Thursday; when he resigned his life, on the seventeenth before the calends of May; and he was buried at Winchester in the old minster. Earl Harold, his son, took to the earldom that his father had before and to all that his father possessed . . .[15]

The *Chronicle*'s account seems more likely, despite the fact that the more entertaining version was penned by a namesake of my own – despite spelling variations.[16]

Then, in 1064, there was a curious interlude which was to have major repercussions, on both sides of the English Channel. Master Wace describes what happened in a manner that is sympathetic to the cause of Harold and the English, for he says that the most powerful earl in the house of Godwin decided to travel to Normandy to try to secure the release of the hostages Edward the Confessor had given up to Duke William years previously:

> Harold, pitying the hostages, was desirous to cross over into Normandy, to bring them home. So he went to take leave of the king. But Edward strictly forbade him and charged and conjured him not to go to Normandy, nor to speak with duke William; for he might soon be drawn into some snare, as the duke was very shrewd; and he told him, that if he wished to have the hostages home, he would choose some messenger for the purpose.[17]

Wace then goes on to quote another source for a differing version of the inception of the following events:

'I cannot say how the truth may be,
I but tell the tale as 'twas told to me'.

Benoit de Sainte-More sends the Archbishop of Canterbury to William, at Edward's desire, to convey his intention of leaving the inheritance of the English crown to the duke.

L'arcevesque de Cantorbire,
Li plus hauz hom de son empire,
Out en Normendie tramis,
Les anz avant, si cum je vos dis,
Por afermer ce qu'il li done,
Tot le reaume e la corone.

And Harold's mission is described as being expressly intended, in the following year, to confirm the same bequest:

Por estre plus certains e meres,
E qu'il n'i sorsist encombrier,
Resout l'ovre plus esforcier.
Heraut, qui quens ert del pais,
Trestot li plus poestéis
Que nul des autres del reiaume,
Ce lui tramist al duc Guillaume,
Que del regne enterinement
Tot qui a la corone apent
Li feist feuté jurée,
Eissi cum ele ert devisée:
Veut qu'il l'en face serrement
Et qu'il l'en donge tenement . . .[18]

Master Wace also presents an opposing view of how Earl Harold's mission across the Channel came about: 'But another book tells me that the king ordered him to go, for the purpose of assuring duke William, his cousin, that he should have the realm after his death. How the matter really was I never knew and I find it written both the one way and the other.'[19]

Wace continues with his account of Harold's adventures and misadventures in Normandy: 'Whatever was the business he went upon or whatever it was that he meant to do, Harold set out on his way, taking the risk of what might fall out.'[20] He then adds a little fatalistic

13

wisdom: 'What is fated to happen no man can prevent, let him be who he will. What must be will come to pass and no one can make it nought.'[21]

Wace then elaborates:

> He made ready two ships and took to the sea at Bodeham [Bosham – on his inherited estates]. I know not how the mischief was occasioned; whether the steersman erred or whether it was that a storm arose; but this I know, that he missed the right course and touched the coast of Pontif [Ponthieu], where he could neither get away, nor conceal himself. A fisherman of that country, who had been in England and had often seen Harold, watched him; and knew him, both by his face and his speech; and went privily to Guy, the count of Pontif and would speak to no other; and he told the count how he could put a great prize in his way, if he would go with him; and that if he would give him only twenty livres, he should gain a hundred by it, for he would deliver him such a prisoner, as would pay a hundred livres or more for ransom. The count agreed to his terms and then the fisherman showed him Harold. They seized and took him to Abbeville; but Harold contrived to send off a message privily to duke William in Normandy and told him of his journey; how he had set out from England to visit him, but had missed the right port; and how the count of Pontif had seized him and without any cause of offence had put him in prison: and he promised that if the duke would deliver him from his captivity, he would do whatever he wished in return.[22]

Wace says that Count Guy attempted to hide his captive away in Beaurain.

> But William thought that if he could get Harold into his keeping, he might turn it to good account; so he made so many fair promises and offers to the earl [this should be read as 'count'] and so coaxed and flattered him, that he at last gave up his prisoner; and the duke thus got possession of him and gave in return to the count Guy a fair manor lying along the river Alne [Eaulne].[23]

William of Poitiers adds that Duke William also threatened Guy by making military preparations – probably the main reason the count relented and released the prisoner.[24]

Wace describes what happened after Earl Harold was 'ransomed' to Duke William:

William entertained Harold many days in great honour, as was his due. He took him to many rich tournaments, arrayed him nobly, gave him horses and arms and led him with him into Britanny – I am not certain whether three or four times – when he had to fight with the Bretons. And in the meantime he bespoke Harold so fairly, that he agreed to deliver up England to him, as soon as king Edward should die; and he was to have Ele,[§] one of William's daughters, for his wife if he would; and to swear to all this if required, William also binding himself to those terms.[25]

Master Wace then details the elaborate arrangements Duke William made to commemorate Harold's oath-swearing:

To receive the oath, he caused a parliament to be called. It is commonly said that it was at Bayeux[¶] that he had his great council assembled. He sent for all the holy bodies [relics] thither and put so many of them together as to fill a whole chest and then covered them with a pall; but Harold neither saw them, nor knew of their being there; for nought was shewn or told to him about it; and overall was a phylactery, the best that he could select; *OIL DE BŒF*,[**] I have heard it called. When Harold placed his hand upon it, the hand trembled and the flesh quivered; but he swore and promised upon his oath, to take Ele [one of William's daughters] to wife and to deliver up England to the duke: and thereunto to do all in his power, according to his might and wit, after the death

§ According to Ordericus Vitalis it was Agatha, another daughter. He adds a pathetic story as to her falling in love with Harold and dying of grief at her disappointment . . . The story of her attachment to Harold is inconsistent with the date of 1053, usually assigned to William's marriage, as his daughter would not be more than 11 years old at Harold's visit. The date, however, of the marriage is uncertain. According to Benoit de Sainte-More, it was part of the agreement that Harold should not only have '*Aeliz la proz e la sage*', but with her '*del regne une moitie*' ('Chivalrous, honest, brave-valiant-courageous, of the wise' and 'one-half reigns'). These passages, when translated (on-line) from the Old French, seem to indicate that Duke William held Earl Harold in high esteem, praised his honesty and promised that his proposed Norman marriage-mate would co-reign with him – Harold; but to co-reign over what – England? Nothing is said by him (Benoit) of any contrivance as to the relics on which the oath was administered.

¶ Orderic Vitalis puts the scene at Rouen and William of Poitiers at Bonneville-sur-Touques. The latter places the event before the expedition to Brittany; which, except on Wace's authority, is not known to have occurred more than once.

** 'Either from its figure or the ornaments upon it.'

of Edward, if he should live, so help him God and the holy relics there! Many cried 'God grant it!'[††] and when Harold had kissed the saints and had risen upon his feet, the duke led him up to the chest and made him stand near it; and took off the chest the pall that had covered it and shewed Harold upon what holy relics he had sworn; and he was sorely alarmed at the sight.[26]

So, here we see just how deceitful Duke William was in duping then Earl Harold into making a solemn oath upon religious relics hidden beneath a pall.

Wace next continues: 'Then when all was ready for his journey homeward, he took his leave; and William exhorted him to be true to his word and kissed him in the name of good faith and friendship. And Harold passed freely homeward and arrived safely in England.'[27]

Also with regard to the supposed oath that Earl Harold swore to Duke William: It is worth observing that Eadmer (English ecclesiastic, theologian and historian, c. 1060–c. 1126),[28] states that he, Eadmer, '. . . considered that Harold swore under constraint and did not consider himself bound by any such oath'.[29]

It is also worth noting that Wace concedes that Earl Harold returned to England with one of the hostages Duke William had held but released to him for his safe return.[30] This was Haakon, grandson of the late Earl Godwin. This is in accordance with the Anglo-Saxon view of Harold's mission – not that it was to reaffirm Edward the Confessor's pledge to bestow the kingship on Duke William, which, according to Anglo-Saxon law and tradition, would not have been the king's choice but that of the Witan. Instead, the purpose of Earl Harold's mission to the Continent was evidently to obtain the release of hostages held by Duke William.

---

†† *'Ki Dex li dont!'* It is unnecessary to observe how variously these events have been told. In the words of William of Malmsbury, *'Lectorem premonitum velim, quod hic quasi ancipitem viam narrationis video, quia veritas factorum pendet in dubio'*. The accounts of Thierry, Sir Francis Palgrave and Depping may be referred to as those of the latest writers. In Wace we are following the story of a Norman, as told at a Norman court: but on the whole there is little in his history that is at variance with probability or with the best evidence on the subject. It will be observed that he does not go the full length of some of the Norman historians, in pretending that the English nation gave any formal assent to Edward's views as to the disposition of his kingdom in favour of his kinsman William. So, here we also see that even the pro-Norman William of Malmesbury does not insist that the English – the Witan – agreed with the notion that Duke William should become king of England.

Following this interlude, there was great progress on the part of Earl Harold upon his return to England, as, over time, the young earl would further increase his standing and power.[31] In this, Harold's opportunity to prove himself as a military leader had already come in 1063, when the Welsh king, Gruffydd ap Llywelyn, instigated raids and larger armed incursions into the western and south-western earldoms of Mercia and Wessex.

Harold and his younger brother Tostig adopted an aggressive, two-pronged approach to resolving the problem. Tostig led a land force into the Welsh king's seat of power while Harold brought a seaborne force along the coast, rolling up their forts. When Tostig and Harold captured their capital and neutralised the Welsh coastal strongholds, the subjects of Gruffydd ap Llywelyn signalled their – literal – capitulation, by sending Harold the head of their king well as the figurehead of his ship.[32] In this campaign Earl Harold demonstrated his inclination to rely on a rapid advance to quickly confront and crush opposition forces – a strategy that would serve him first well, then badly, in 1066.[33] It was in the Welsh campaign that Harold Godwinsson sealed his reputation as the chief military leader and key supporter of Edward the Confessor, which helped him greatly when the bedridden king died on 5 January 1066 and he was named as his successor and promptly proclaimed King Harold II by the Witan. The selection of Harold by Edward is clearly shown in that great medieval illustration of the story of the Norman Conquest – the Bayeux Tapestry, which, having been commissioned by the Norman victors, must hold considerable weight because this bequeathal is depicted in the Tapestry despite the fact that it conflicts with the Norman reading of the situation. This bestowing of succession is also acknowledged in *The Anglo-Saxon Chronicle*: 'But the prudent king had settled the realm on high-born men – on Harold himself, the noble earl; who in every season faithfully heard and obeyed his lord, in word and deed; nor gave to any what might be wanted by the nation's king.'[34] Moreover, even in the heavily pro-Norman account of William of Poitiers, he concedes that death-bed bequests held overriding validity in Anglo-Saxon tradition and law.[35]

However, here church politics also came into play for, according to Wace, Harold's kingship was consecrated by Archbishop Stigand of Canterbury – a post he had assumed after the Norman Robert of Jumièges fled to the Continent. Unfortunately for Stigand, he had also been given the pallium by the 'Anti-Pope', Benedict X and had therefore, *ipso facto*, been excommunicated by Pope Leo IX, and his excommunication was renewed by the popes Nicholas II and Alexander II. This led to the taint of illegitimacy hanging over King Harold's reign from the very start, at least in Norman eyes. All of this despite the fact that the Worcester and York traditions assert that King Harold's consecration was given by Bishop Ealdred of York.[36]

We have now reached the pivotal moment – the history-packed year of 1066, which decided the fates of so many people in not only England and Normandy but also affecting the futures of the Viking lands of Norway, Denmark and Sweden. So, it is time to return to this author's preliminary investigations at the town of Battle, near Hastings, East Sussex, England.

Chapter 3

The First Trip to Battle

Arriving by train on that first of my several visits to Battle, some six miles inland from Hastings, in East Sussex, I visually surveyed the 'lay of the land' from the approach (alongside the street aptly named Station Approach) beside the railway embankment from the site of the train station, and the location and shape and gradients of the hillsides and embankments of Senlac Hill as I trudged along the few blocks up to Battle Abbey. Actually, even before that, while still on the train, I had been observing what to me already had been a possible route of advance for the Normans – beside but not upon the ridge crest that extended from Hastings Castle. I had been foreseen in my anticipation regarding a ridgeway by the authors of the book who reckoned that the actual site of the Battle of Hastings was at Sedlescombe – the Starkey brothers, who assure us that a ridgetop road was likely due to the fact that since 'time immemorial' the inhabitants of England travelled atop ridges to avoid the island's many streams and marshlands in low-lying valleys. On page 12 of their book they provide a map showing a likely track through the woods from the site of Hastings Castle to the town of Battle. That ancient trail was improved and expanded into a coach road in the 1840s, according to Nick Austin, who believes the Hastings battle was fought at Crowhurst. It extends, and extended, to beyond Battle, following Hastings Road, becoming Battle Hill, both being the modern-day A2100 route from Hastings to Johns Cross, north of Battle, where it rejoins the current A21, from which it had diverged at Baldslow, at outlying Hastings. About the road names: some roads have many names, so, whenever practical, I will refer to the A2100 as just that, because it enters the Battle area as Battle Hill, then becomes Lower Lake, Upper Lake, High Street and, at the northern end of the town, continues on its course as London Road, citing its ultimate destination, which is why Duke William was, presumably, using it as his route of march that historic day in 1066.

The main focus of my travels to Battle, Battle Abbey, Hastings and other locations related to the Conquest and the events leading up to and including 1066, was to survey and move across the actual terrain myself – as often as possible on foot; to take photographs – of which I took more than 2,000; to speak to people from the area; and to gather locally-available printed materials. But, probably most important of all, I attempted to comprehend what might have been going through the minds of the leaders at the battles (actually, there were three, with King Harald Sigurdsson, also known as 'Harald Hardrada' – meaning hard ruler or harsh counsellor – of Norway getting involved in a major and crucial way – but more about that later); their sub-commanders; their supporters and their detractors; the lesser leaders – nobles, knights, elite troops; and the masses of average men who constituted the bulk of the armies involved in the trio of fateful battles that year.

Encountering the impressive structure of Battle Abbey itself, I switched to photographer mode and recorded as many images as possible while still maintaining at least a modest progress into the abbey reception room, where I bought a couple of printed items, paid my admission fee and asked the helpful young man whose name tag identified him as 'Richard', behind the counter to show me, on the brochure I had been given, exactly where he – and, presumably, English Heritage, who would likely have briefed their employees on the subject – thought the Anglo-Saxons (or 'the English' as they are often referred to) and the Normans had been deployed for the opening stage of the battle. The young man cheerfully complied, outlining the official view with some deft arcs with his pen and sent me on my now slightly more doubtfully-viewed way; for a problem had already presented itself for me: my just-completed trek up to the abbey from the railway station confirmed for me with absolute certainty that, if the official view were to be accepted, the Anglo-Saxons would, at least in part, have had their left flank and backs to the most likely route of advance of their Norman enemies, along the aforementioned likely ridgeway (now the A2100). Also, the Normans would, in turn, have had to abandon their easiest avenue of approach and assault, by complying with the best hopes of the Anglo-Saxons in obligingly detouring downhill and then wheeling and attacking them uphill toward the most favourable defensive position for the English – along the ridgetop. But I tried to shrug my doubts aside as I entered the display pavilion with its excellent short film about the battle and a series of fine exhibits of replicated Anglo-Saxon and Norman weapons and accoutrements.

Leaving the pavilion, I began my tour along the abbey's 'Conquest Trail'. As is often my custom, however, I quickly deviated from the pre-arranged suggested route of advance to take in the view along the 'Battle Terrace', from which the Anglo-Saxons would have looked down upon and over the supposed battle site and observed the advancing Normans and their supporting troops. (The Normans had brought along allies from France, Flanders and Brittany.)

Despite my earlier scepticism, the 'lay of the land' of the theoretical battle site made sense, if one accepted that the Normans, French, Flemish and Bretons had not continued to advance along the ridge crest – taking the path of the current A2100 and had instead deviated left – toward, over or along Powdermill Lane (also known as the B2095) – and attacked the Anglo-Saxon right flank on that part of the ridge now known as 'Senlac Hill'. Why they could conceivably have done that will be addressed later; for now, I am recording my first impressions in order to demonstrate how I have built my case that the battle may have, in fact, not occurred on the premises of Battle Abbey, at the least in large part, at most not at all.

The first surprise I encountered was found just a few dozen yards down the trail, where I had stopped often to camera-record the view of the hypothetical battlefield from the edge of the woods there, looking through the few trees scattered along what would have been the all-important – according to historic accounts dating from the time of the battle – Norman left flank. There, the woods, which had been behind me as I faced onto the open fields of the imagined battle site, flowed onto the edge of the supposed battlefield. My photographs focused on the thickening growth of trees and brush downhill from the trail and, as I tightened my camera's view of the underbrush, I was startled to realise that the 'ground' beneath the vegetation there was actually stagnant water coated with a thin layer of pollen, dust and leaves. This, I supposed, was likely the site of the 'marshy ground' that was to play an important part in the latter phases of the Battle of Hastings, as reported by participants and historians alike.

I am an experienced, life-long hiker and a cautious one, too. I had respectfully kept to the 'Conquest Trail', outlined by brown-painted wooden two-by-fours and rocks lain along each side, except to take one or two steps over the boundary to set my backpack atop a stump to retrieve my camera and throat lozenges from it. I immediately became more cautious and vowed to remain increasingly vigilant should I again venture even just one or two paces off the marked trail; falling into a muddy bog would not make for a great time – all the more so as every day of my tight schedule had already been well planned in advance; any injury-causing accidents or mishaps would set the entire project back hours or even days.

Returning to my initial tour of the Battle Abbey grounds, I proceeded along the 'Conquest Trail' while taking photographs of the increasingly wooded and flooded terrain to my left as the pathway led farther downhill, deeper into the woods and onto more flooded territory, until the trail itself curved left and circuited the lower end of the alleged battle site. There, the trail builders were forced to resort to using some obviously intentionally elevated terrain or 'berms', with culverts through them on the way, making short bridges along that 'causeway' to traverse the 'marshy ground' cited by the battle's participants and subsequent chroniclers as having made a major impact at the outcome of the struggle that fateful day in 1066. Indeed, as the trail circled around the bottom edge of the supposed battlefield, the marshy area became even more flooded on not just the uphill side, facing toward what is generally thought to have been the Anglo-Saxon battle line, from the pathway itself, but even more so 'below' (to the south-west of) the 'Conquest Trail', forming what can only be described as a small lake, not just a pond.

Having read accounts of the battle for many decades, I was familiar with the fact that the 'marshy ground' was to the left side of the Norman advance; however, yet another surprise, greater in some ways, confronted me as I rounded the lower extreme of the supposed battle site, just before ascending a not-very-steep slope on what is conjectured to have been the Norman right flank – the swampland and even another small lake extended to the north-east, toward what is alleged to have been the Anglo-Saxon position. In fact, the pre-recorded 'talking tour' that is provided to each visitor claimed that a spot just behind and to the right of that second, more right-hand, small lake or large pond, from the Norman point of view, was likely the very place from where Duke William (he wasn't 'The Conqueror' yet) supposedly reviewed and directed the battle, at least for a time. However, had he done so, the flooded or at least marshy ground and lake would stand between him and most of his troops – an awkward situation, at least. In fact, the 'marshy ground' was not confined to the left side of the battlefield but instead extended almost all the way across the rear of the imagined Norman initial deployment just before the fighting began in earnest.

I was later to learn that the small lake (New Lake) was a later creation, dug out and dammed to hold water for livestock and crop watering. But to create the lake, water seeping from the ground just uphill from and at its site would have formed 'marshy ground' there and, even if not a lake, that would have placed more muddy soil and standing – or, at least, seeping – water underfoot at that location, in the middle of and even to the right of (from the Norman perspective) the imagined battlefield, too. Moreover, had Duke William been there, whether on foot or horseback, he would have been well within range of Anglo-Saxon archers, of whom there were more than a few; he would also have been close enough for Anglo-Saxon warriors on the ridgetop to cast their spears at him as well. Even the unarmoured and lightly armed Anglo-Saxon slingers would have been able to hurl their stones at the duke. This would have been a far from optimal position from which to command the battle.

After having my photo taken in front of that small lake by some cooperative tourists, I again deviated from the recommended path, this time to the (Norman) right and followed a set of tyre tracks up the hill and a little away from the abbey and the presumed battle site, veering toward the trees on what would have been the extreme Norman right flank as they proceeded up the slope. (Had they done so, in fact.) There, following the tyre tracks, I encountered a cottage where the couple of herds-folk who minded the sheep that grazed on the abbey grounds lived, some more trees in a not-very-thick wood, then a farm gate that led, I supposed, then later confirmed, onto the bordering Powdermill Lane/B2095, which will loom, to a larger or lesser degree, depending on how one views my ultimate conclusions, in this somewhat revised estimation of the history of the Hastings battle at Battle.

I should note at this point that had the Normans in fact advanced along, crossed, then passed below the upper reaches of the slight ridge upon which Powdermill Lane runs and onto the officially recognised site of the fighting, they would have voluntarily given up the advantage of being on the higher ground at and along the aforementioned Powdermill Lane and instead descended to the area of the open fields and wet terrain, below Battle Terrace, where the Anglo-Saxons would, theoretically, await their assault. From there, the Normans would have had to wheel right and attack uphill toward the enemy. All of this presumably unnecessary diversion and detouring would have been counter-productive. By discontinuing their march along and alongside the present-day A2100, then across Powdermill Lane, they would have abandoned a much better position from which to attack the exposed flank and rear of the supposed Anglo-Saxon line of resistance, as it was conjectured (and shown to me on the 'battle-site' brochure). Such manoeuvring made no tactical sense, on its face, but, as I was eventually to discover, there could be a fairly convincing case for such a move, at least in part, but most likely only in a very small part, due to another feature of the terrain I was not to discover till much later in my investigations of the entire local area.

Taking photographs all along the way, I veered back toward the 'Conquest Trail', now following the hypothetical Anglo-Saxon line of defence near the top of the ridge, stopping now and then to gauge likely vantage points for King Harold to oversee and direct his troops during the battle. I was later to discover that the most likely spot I had chosen was maybe half a football (American) field (about 50 yards or 44m) downhill and about two or three dozen yards to the left along what had been the high point of the theoretical Anglo-Saxon line. This 'high point' was the place where some experts, as well as English Heritage, reckon that King Harold fell toward the end of the fight. As will be shown later, I do not agree.

Upon completing the circuit of the presumed battle site along the 'Conquest Trail', I once more lingered upon Battle Terrace, as it is called – the alleged main line of resistance where the Anglo-Saxons would have positioned their 'shield wall' and I pondered yet again the 'lay of the land'. I was later to confirm a first impression regarding 'Battle Terrace': It was almost certainly a later built-up earthen construction to support the foundation of the south-western wall of Battle Abbey and is in all likelihood not a feature of the original terrain.

It was during the pensive moments when I rested upon a bench below the stone ramparts above that I wondered about the feelings of the men who went and fought there and if they and especially their fallen comrades would have thought it had been worthwhile for so many of them, on both sides, to lose their lives or well-being – physical and mental and their livelihoods and property (because the losers of any such conflict in those times would have had their landholdings, if any, confiscated by the victors as many of them would have become *persona non grata* and would probably have had to flee into exile, internal or overseas), all for the sake of which nobleman would become or remain king of England. I finally decided that the reckonings of the participants would have run deeper than that. For the Norman and allied invaders, honours, glory, titles and estates confiscated from the losers would be most in mind. For the Anglo-Saxons and the King Harold's Danish guards – his 'Huscarls' – defence of homeland and estates, families and communities from foreign rule or loss altogether, along with the chance of obtaining booty such as valuable chain-mail hauberks, weapons, even coins, from fallen enemies on the battlefield would have been the motivating factors. As with the invaders, for the defenders, too, honours, glory, titles and awards of royal properties or lands previously held in common out of the king's gratitude were anticipated. Likewise would be the case for the Norwegian Vikings; they too, sought booty and rewards, such as titles to land, as was also their custom at the time. For the fighting men involved, 1066 was more than just another socially-removed power struggle among three men who were, ultimately, possible or probable distant cousins – whether by blood or marriage – as so many European wars before and since have been throughout the history of this too often troubled part of the world.

Thus did my first visit to the conjectured battlefield at Battle draw to a close, for I had two trains to catch to deliver me to Falmer and the University of Sussex in time to get a good night's sleep before attending classes the next day. On my way to the train station, I again took in the sloping terrain and rises and dips along the way as I hiked back down High Street – the A2100 – and past the side roads of Marley Lane, then Powdermill Lane – each with its own roundabout – and I wondered about the partly-wooded area 'below' Powdermill Lane – almost opposite Station Approach, as doubts continued to nag me despite my vow to keep an open mind about the 'historical record' and the views of the experts in academia and at English Heritage. But, as I awaited the trains and rode the way back and later, as I lay in bed, I contemplated the reasons for my feelings of doubt. Again, the Anglo-Saxons would have faced away from and to one side of the most likely Norman route of initial advance along the top of the ridge from Hastings to Battle – unless, for some unknown reasons, Duke William had diverted his troops onto the now-accepted battlefield. But that made little sense, as evidenced then, because that would have placed him and his army at a greater disadvantage, having to charge uphill on a steeper slope than the relatively gentler gradient along the A2100. Not only that, the Normans and their Breton, French and Flemish allies would have had to thread their way between dangerous – or at least inconvenient – flooded and marshy ground to their left and even centre, with the Anglo-Saxons close at hand on their right flank as they deployed below the site of the current Battle Abbey. Upon seeing that the marshy and flooded land was so close to the Battle Terrace supposed position of the Anglo-Saxons, I immediately recognised that the defenders would have been pelting the Normans with spears, rocks, rocks tied to sticks and arrow shots, as contemporary or near-contemporary accounts and historical records indicate.[1] But these records also suggest that this happened only when the Normans and their allies were actually attacking and charging against the Anglo-Saxon shield wall, not as they deployed across the battlefield. Duke William was an experienced and skilled military commander. Why, I wondered, would he place his troops in such an awkward and dangerous situation prior to the battle, during which, it is recorded,[2] his troops were repeatedly driven back or made feigned retreats, toward or into marshes where they, and their horses for the Normans' mounted knights, would become bogged down or might even drown?

I decided to set my scepticism aside, as far as possible, as I turned my efforts to surveying the site of the initial battle of 1066, at Fulford, a healthy hike south of the city walls of York, in northern England. Before describing my travels and findings in Yorkshire, it is necessary to once more take a step back and review the events leading up to the involvement of the king of the Vikings – Harald Sigurdsson (Hardrada) of Norway – and the fights at Fulford and Stamford Bridge.

The Involvement of King Harald Sigurdsson (Hardrada)

According to the 'Heimskringla – The Chronicle of the Kings of Norway',[*] by the Icelandic skald (a poet who celebrates the pre-historic and historic deeds of heroic figures in the Scandinavian tradition) Snorri Sturluson,[3] after Harold Godwinsson became king, his younger brother, Tostig, did not take it well – believing he should have been made king

---

[*] Note that the Heimskringla ('The Circle of the World') was written by Sturluson in about the year 1220, in Iceland, so in places it suffers from being removed from the events it depicts in both time and distance – 154 years later and 1,013 miles away. However, while some may dismiss such accounts, over the past three-quarters of a century researchers and historians have placed greater value on oral traditions. Moreover, with regard to my own family, due to the fact that my great-grandfather joined the Union Army at the age of 14, I was able to hear American Civil War-era memories directly from his daughter – my grandmother (born in 1892); so, while we were about a half-century closer to those events than those related by Sturluson, as well as by Master Wace, regarding 1066, my grandmother's reminiscences were yet valid to me because they were only one generation removed and were confirmed by other sources, including official records. Therefore, I give Sturluson's and Wace's, reports more credence than the more sceptical among us.

instead because he had been in command of Edward's army (while Harold had commanded the navy); he believed himself to have been the king's principal adviser; he had been placed in charge of the land defence of England; he believed he had been overlord over all of the other earls, while Harold was merely in attendance by Edward's side at court.[4] As reported in the same source, Tostig went to Flanders, then to Denmark and, finally, Norway, looking for support in his effort to launch an expedition to England to dethrone Harold II. Sturluson says that Tostig convinced the Norwegian king that he, Harald Hardrada, was the rightful heir to the English throne because, Tostig said, the last Danish king of England, Harthacanute, had desired that he should have the crown (because Harthacanute's father, Canute, was 'your mother's – Hardrada's – brother', thus making the two men cousins).[5] After Hardrada objected that he would meet with much English opposition, Tostig assured him that he would arrange for a generally good reception for him in England.[6] Harald Hardrada then levied an army of half the available warriors in Norway and Tostig returned to recruit some of his followers in Flanders as both prepared to invade England.[7]

King Harald Hardrada was able to raise an army of an estimated 7,000 to 10,000 warriors and embarked them on some 300 ships. He was joined by Tostig's force of a few hundred men aboard about thirty ships. After stopping off in the then Norwegian-controlled Shetland and Orkney Islands to pick up reinforcements, the Vikings made landfall at the mouth of the River Tees and plundered the countryside until reaching Scarborough, which they burned to the ground. Thereafter, fearing total destruction if they resisted, other English towns in the area submitted to Harald Hardrada. After defeating an English force at the present-day Holderness, King Harald Hardrada reboarded the Viking fleet carrying his army and entered the mouth of the Humber at Hull, then took the branch of the Ouse toward York.[8] They proceeded up the Ouse about 60 miles before the river became too risky for them to continue along it toward York, so they beached their 300 ships and disembarked at Riccall (pronounced 'Rickle', rhymes with 'pickle'.) It is at this point that we'll resume with the author's travels, this time to the Yorkshire battlefields and other historic sights related to the events of 1066.

Chapter 4

The First of the Three Battles of 1066 – Fulford

Brimming with overconfidence, I had undertaken the 200+-mile railway journey from Falmer to York without making advance hotel reservations. This proved to be a mistake, but one with a fortunate outcome. While leaving the impressive old train station at York, I stopped to ask the man at the tourist information desk about reasonably-priced lodging for the night. He directed me toward the two most expensive hotels, so I asked a taxi driver, who only gave me vague directions to a local youth hostel. Back inside the train station, a more helpful platform attendant sent me to a nearby inn, where I learned that few to no rooms were available in York that night due to it being Graduation Week, as well as the height of the summer tourist season, but a very obliging clerk found a room for me at a competing hotel chain just a couple of miles south, on the outskirts of the next day's planned objective: the town of Fulford.

After a pleasant night's stay, I set off early the next morning, walking south from the hotel along the east side of the road – the A19 – noting that the land was flat and even, but then observing a slight elevation then dip in the terrain as I approached the locally renowned site of the battle, at a small stream known as Germany Beck (formerly spelled 'Bec'). Asking a Fulford resident as she walked past on the other side of the street, I was directed east, past a new construction site and toward the open country beyond. Before the beck ('bec' is an Anglo-Saxon word for a small stream) itself came into view, I observed a large excavator on caterpillar tracks digging into the ground alongside the beck, near the road through town, the A19, which bears a sign declaring that the Battle of Fulford occurred at that exact spot. I took some photos of the machine at work, then headed farther east, into the as-yet open country cut through by the relatively large ditch within which the beck runs. It is about 10 to 12ft deep and about 15 to 18ft wide at its steepest pitch, near its centre section – an adequate but not ideal position, as far as the local area is concerned, for the Anglo-Saxons to deploy in readiness to defend the city of York from the Norwegian Viking invaders, their king Harald Hardrada, their English allies and their treacherous leader, Tostig Godwinsson – the alienated and estranged brother of King Harold II. The Anglo-Saxons were led in the defence of York by the local earls – Morcar of Northumbria and his brother, Edwin of Mercia. The date was 20 September 1066.

It was due to the near-perfect intelligence of the area provided by Tostig, who had ruled over this part of England, Northumbria (before he had doubled the taxes for the people under his charge, causing him to be overruled and removed from his position and then banished by King Edward the Confessor), that the Vikings had determined to sail some three-score miles up the River Ouse. They knew the Viking fleet of about 300 ships could safely proceed until they reached the village of Riccall, some 20 miles south of York, where the water would become too shallow and the channel narrows too dangerously at low tide* for the Vikings to continue securely upriver aboard their ships.

Surveying Where the Viking Fleet Landed

Later that same day upon which I investigated the lay of the land at Germany Beck, I travelled by bus and on foot for a lengthy and at times circuitous trek over some occasionally rugged ground to two very important spots on the River Ouse. After having been directed there by a helpful receptionist at the Riccall Community Centre, I eventually stumbled upon the spot where the River Ouse remained deep enough, and wide enough, for the Vikings fleet to beach most of their ships in the mud and sandbanks there.

At that first location, I discovered that while the river still had enough depth, even at low tide, to accommodate the Viking ships, it would quickly narrow around a bend to the north-north-east at a choke point where the Viking ships would likely have had to proceed in single file.

The latter of the two sites is just outside the offices and carpark of the local environmental protection agency. After my hike from the bus

---

* This part of England is so flat relative to sea level that the tides have a decided effect on water levels, even in river courses so far from the sea.

stop in town and an exhausting and sometimes roundabout trek of two to three miles to the wider point of the River Ouse, cited above, I had spotted a vacant picnic table outside their offices and went inside to ask if I could take a break there. Not only did the director agree, he sent someone outside to offer me some refreshments. I asked the man sent out about the area and he shared more than a few very informative insights and some invaluable background information. Then he directed me to the end of the carpark, near the gate by which I had entered the grounds, where I found a plaque he had mentioned, which announced that Harald Hardrada and Tostig Godwinsson had themselves landed at that exact spot, where the River Ouse is not only narrower but shallower, all the more so when I visited there that day, at low tide.

I believe it is now necessary for me to digress for a brief description of a few of the beneficial aspects regarding some English traditions and habits that greatly aid the researcher and traveller when touring England, whether for business, studies or general recreation.

Throughout my hikes around England I was thankful for the ancient custom of preserving and honouring public footpaths. I had learned about them from my University of Sussex courses of the various landscapes and their history in the county of Sussex and southern England, which were presented by Geoffrey Mead, Ph.D.: people travelling on foot are allowed and even encouraged to cross private plots of land as long as they adhere to the public footpaths, which are clearly marked; do not diverge from them; do not trespass into private areas such as around homes; do not bother the livestock; do not litter, vandalise or commit other misdemeanours or crimes; so long as they close and latch livestock gates behind them; do not disturb residents with loud noise, etc.; and, in general, behave themselves, which almost all people in England evidently do when on their walking journeys. I availed myself of the public footpaths often and could not have completed the investigations required for the writing of this book without them and the hospitality and helpfulness of property owners; fellow hikers; occasional public servants such as employees of the Royal Mail, local police officers; roadway, sanitation and other maintenance workers; people at government offices; and other friendly and cooperative residents in many different parts of England.

It is at this point that I also realise that I am more than a bit overdue in stating that throughout my visit of eight weeks in England, I found the English people, without exception and without regard to culture, nationality or sub-nationality, complexion, evident religion, social status, income level, etc., to be soft-spoken, polite and helpful, and some were very generous in providing additional information and insights once they learned of the purpose of my visits and inquiries.

Another digression is in order at this point. As I stated before, I am a lifelong hiker and continue to walk several miles each day up until the time this is being typed – I will take a three-mile hike within the hour. However, I discovered on my trip that the English people can, literally, walk circles around me. When I had inquired about the distances and travel times, a typical response was given to me by an older woman who was a bit overweight and did not seem to me to be the type of person who walked much when she said, 'Oh, it's not far; just a 10-minute walk'. This was while on a visit to the shingle beach at Pevensey, on England's south coast. About 20 minutes later I was still walking and looking for the pub where she had told me to make the turn toward the water. It was just about 10 minutes after that when I was (finally) making the turn and the English Channel was in sight. Later, after surveying the beach and taking photos of the features of the shore near where Duke William had presumably sailed into the bay that had been there in 1066 (the land has since risen and the former coastline is now several hundred yards inland), I headed back toward the railway line, only to pass the very same woman who had given me the directions briskly going by in the other direction on the far side of the road, proving that she was, in fact, an avid walker and a very capable one at that, as her pace was as rapid or more so, than mine.

Getting back to the River Ouse at Riccall, the plaque proclaiming the landing site is, in my view, probably correct as I have long ago concluded that local custom, legend and lore regarding historical locations and events are more likely to be accurate than the scribblings of reporters, writers, researchers and academics who may have never even set foot anywhere in an area about which they are opining. This conclusion was confirmed by my travels to the various battlefields, castles, churches, cemeteries and abbeys connected in different ways to the events of 1066 I visited during my brief sojourn in England and foray into Normandy. Some who have written on this subject failed to get the facts of geography correct due to not having visited the places about which they chose to write and a few even misread (or didn't read at all) the many historical accounts, records, eyewitness reports, 'news' stories (in, for example, *The Anglo-Saxon Chronicle*) or even the writings of other 'outsiders' before making numerous and egregious reporting errors in their own writings. (In fact, reading the books recommended to me by John Grehan prevented me from making a few of the same mistakes.) So, how could the plaque near the environmental protection offices at the River Ouse at Riccall and the 'lay of the water' of the river almost a mile away both be correct with regard to the actual landing site of the 300 Viking ships?

As with determining the 'exact site' of a particular battle, the exact location of the landing of the Vikings must be a bit more vague than a single, precise point at the side of a river with a nearby plaque. Three hundred ships, even relatively smaller yet still ocean-going Viking rowing craft of about 55ft in length, take up considerable space. They would not have all, or even mostly, been driven onto the riverbank in one place. The location where the River Ouse is still relatively wide is about three-quarters of a mile to a mile from the site of the plaque. Obviously, if King Harald Hardrada and Tostig Godwinsson were in one of the lead ships that were beached at the location of the plaque, the remaining almost 300 ships would have been driven ashore behind them, reaching around the bend in the river for three-quarters of a mile or more.

In that these same 'smaller' Viking ships of 55ft in length also had a beam of 15–17ft, if we conclude that the ships were beached gunwale to gunwale – which they would not have been, allowing at least a couple of feet on either side for debarking and re-embarking – then 100 ships would have taken up 1,500ft of riverbank and 300 ships would have occupied 4,500ft, just over three-quarters of a mile of space along the river shore. These 'smaller' Viking ships could carry about 30 passengers each, making for a grand total of about 9,000 warriors, attendants, nobles, servants and clergymen, which is close to the estimates of some academics, historians and other experts regarding the events of 1066. Some ships were larger, though, being capable of transporting up to 100 warriors,[†] so, based on the number and size of the ships in the invading armada, some estimates of Viking strength that day of up to or even in excess of 10,000 fighting men are not unrealistic.

I was about to make an egregious error of the type I mentioned above when I realised that with the River Ouse at low tide and therefore

---

† Frank Barlow states (Introduction, *The Carmen de Hastingae Proelio of Guy, Bishop of Amiens*, p. lxv) that Viking ships of the time could transport about forty to fifty men each. *The Carmen de Hastingae Proelio* is considered by Barlow to be the 'urtext' – original or earliest version of a text, to which later versions can be compared – of other early accounts of the Battle of Hastings. Barlow specifies that this does not mean this epic poem is the one and only 'true' version of the story, only that all other works, even the earliest, owe their existence and at least some of their contents to said urtext.

probably impassable beyond the point where the plaque proclaimed that King Harald Hardrada and Earl Tostig had landed, I was not properly reckoning with the fluctuation of the tides. This made me realise that the Viking fleet could have proceeded further up the River Ouse at high tide, perhaps all the way to York or nearly so – at least to Fulford. Why the Viking king and the deposed English earl decided to disembark at Riccall would puzzle me only briefly because, in my next consultation with Google Earth images and maps, I saw that the historically-recognised landing site made sense for the Viking army to make landfall, organise for the attack and march up the route of the current A19 toward Fulford. Yet the question as to why they would disembark so far away continued to confound me until I recalled that King Harold II had already positioned at least a part, possibly a large part, of the Anglo-Saxon fleet at Tadcaster, on the River Wharfe. If Harald Hardrada and Tostig had learned of this, a great likelihood as there were some of Tostig's supporters probably remaining in Northumbria to provide such intelligence, then the wise move would be to leave the Viking ships near Riccall, below the junction with the River Wharfe. Otherwise, if the Vikings had sailed past the branching of the Wharfe, then the Anglo-Saxon fleet could have entered the River Ouse behind them, cutting them off from resupply and retreat if that should become necessary.

The Fulford Battle Site

Returning to the area of the Fulford battle, as with Riccall, the 'exact location' of what happened was spread over a wide area – extending almost a mile from the River Ouse, into which the Germany Bec(k) flows. This, too, is a reasonable assumption as 10,000 men, side by side, shields overlapping, if spread out in a shield wall, could have occupied about two or more feet of battle frontage each. However, historical accounts proclaim that King Harald Hardrada left about one-third of his men behind to guard the Viking ships, leaving roughly 6,500 men to advance toward York. So, 6,500 times 2 equals 13,000ft or just over two miles. But fighters engaged in actual combat were as often as possible thickly laid, with not just two but when possible three, four or even five ranks of men along the fighting front, plus clumps of reserve formations here and there, which 'shrinks' the probable length of the Viking shield wall to about 4,500ft – or just under one mile.

I discovered earlier that, as with Riccall, there is a plaque at the Fulford battle site, alongside the beck, in a small community park west of the A19, declaring that it is the precise location of the Anglo-Saxon counter-attack against the Vikings that very nearly granted them a victory over the invaders. The decisive phase of the battle probably also later took place there, just a few yards from the River Ouse and a bit farther inland, at the ancient ford across the beck.

Where the Germany Beck part of the battlefield that lies back to the east of the A19, I had originally continued along the northern (Anglo-Saxon) side for about a half-mile 'inland', also east, from the River Ouse, to a point where the beck splits, with the main channel proceeding eastward and with a side branch running north along and just a yard or two east of what I was told was an old Roman roadbed there. I turned north and progressed up that alleged old Roman side road for about a quarter of a mile, satisfying myself that the general lay of the land continued on approximately the same toward York. Doubling back south, taking photos all along the way, I returned to the junction of the beck's branches, noting that the open and sun-drenched land was a bit marshy there, even in warm and dry July weather. I then went back to the west again along the northern side of the ditch until I encountered a culvert-underlain earthen 'bridgeway' (a sort of short 'causeway') across the ditch onto the 'Viking side' to the south. I noted that the raised terrain at the uppermost lip on the south side of the beck – said ditch at its widest point there of about 40ft – was higher than that on the 'Anglo-Saxon' side by about 4 to 6ft, giving the Viking troops and their commanders a slightly better view and arrow- or spear-shot, to the north of their position in the 'middle section' of the battlefield overall. I crossed over to the south side of the beck there and turned west again toward the A19.

I proceeded down a temporary earthen 'roadway' for construction equipment to build the access road to the large meadow upon which the soon-to-be-built tract of housing on the far, northern, side of the beck was to be erected. That is where the Anglo-Saxon reserves had been held in readiness by Ealdorman Uhtred during the battle and across which the defeated English warriors fled later that day. I pressed on as far as I could into that lower terrain before being shooed off by construction workers who were probably concerned that I might end up underneath their heavy machines. As the land on both sides of the beck fell away to the west into a shallow, bowl-shaped depression, toward the location of the old stone bridge and the route of the current A19, it was evident from my observations that the ground does, in fact, become increasingly muddy there, even on the relatively dry July day of my excursion. I quickly retreated, travelling east again, stopping to take more photos of the beck and the slight ridge on its southern lip, which I later learned is the 'crest' of the 12,000-year-old glacial moraine below which Germany Beck now flows and upon which the Vikings charged forward to repel the attacks by the Anglo-Saxons in that middle stretch of the battlefield. I then circled around, now on the north side of Germany Beck again as I returned to the A19. This was the location of the drop in elevation from the slight rise I had encountered before, on my early-morning trek south along the A19 from the inn. This is the area of the old ford, under the current bridge – a shallow, bowl-shaped, muddy depression where a major phase of the battle likely occurred. Judging from the lay of the land and relying on a medieval account[1] of the battle, I determined that on that 20 September 1066, the Anglo-Saxon defenders had probably been able to briefly steal a march on the Vikings and had crossed the beck at the road's low point at the ford, but had, according to the 'historical record' as reported by Snorri Sturluson, been driven back by the Viking army pushing north toward York.[2]

I turned and went south again, traversed the bridge, then crossed to the west side of the A19 and entered the woods at the western end of the battle site. The ground continued its overall gentle descent, exclusive of the depression under the bridge at the old ford, toward the River Ouse, through gradually thickening woods. I believe I should at this point add some relevant observations about the woods and vegetation – then and now.

England has been inhabited for nearly a million years – first by an early human ancestor (Homo antecessor).[3] Since then, when England was linked to the Continent by a land bridge, there have been successive waves of habitation as the population was repeatedly driven back to the south by environmental changes – primarily the climate cycles of recurrent ice ages. During all of this time, many of England's forests, at least in the less remote parts and more so in the more heavily populated south, have been cleared, then re-established themselves, again cleared and time after time regrew. While it is impossible, without undertaking informed excavations and analyses of ancient plant remains and soils, to say definitely whether a particular place was forested or open land at a certain definite time, in general, the water retention of the soil, climate – short-term as well as long-term, soil acidity or alkalinity – or pH balance and soil types, as well as tree types, will dictate whether generally, over time, a tract of land will reforest or remain an open meadow or become a heath, at least for a while – long or short. So, again generally, it is sometimes possible to state the likelihood that one spot or another was grassland or woods within some expectations of probability and with the aforementioned and following caveats to apply.

The foregoing referred to the natural growth of woodlands, barring human interventions such as planting orchards, clearing for fields of crops, constructing motorways, railway beds or – most important as far as environmental impact is concerned – housing, industrial and/or commercial tracts. Therefore, given the likelihood that climate (bearing in mind that England in 1066 was in the middle of the Medieval Warm Period, sending temperatures 3 to 5 degrees higher than today), geography and the other variables stated above are roughly equivalent to those of 1066, it seems also likely that at the time of the battle at Fulford this particular part of the local landscape was about the same then as it is now – marshy and boggy in the wetter months, with thicker woods nearer the river than in some other areas even just a few yards inland. The factors of the relative wetness of the land near the river and the thicker tree cover there conspired against the Anglo-Saxons as the battle strategy of the Viking King Harald Hardrada took shape.

The Viking King's Opening Moves

The single, spare account of the battle comes to us from the only source available – the *Heimskringla* – by Snorri Sturluson.[4] 'King Harald now went on the land and drew up his men. The one arm of this line stood at the outer edge of the river, the other turned up towards the land along a ditch; and there was also a morass, deep, broad and full of water.'[5]

This is a bit confusing unless the reader has been to the site, as I have. Except for a slender opening along the shore of the Ouse there is solid ground in a thin strip, interrupted here and there by narrow channels leading from Germany Beck into the river. Just inland is a swampy area, with a shallow pond or small lake, which was packed with cattails at the time I was there. Of course, I can't speak to those plants being there in 1066, but it is likely they were there then as well. Beyond the very small swampland there is a bowl-shaped depression – the ford. (While it is now known as 'Fulford', the original name was 'foul ford', due to the odours emanating from the bowl-shaped depression that would have been muddy almost all of the time, being replenished with moisture from the beck and its adjoining swamp, as well as further perfumed by the droppings of draft animals and livestock.) Then, beyond the muddy ford, Germany

Beck extends east from the river. It yet retains a gentle crescent shape, the ends pointing slightly northward but, according to the maps in the book *The Forgotten Battle of 1066: Fulford*, by Charles Jones, the dip in the crescent was evidently a little more pronounced just over 950 years ago.[6] However, the overall general shape of the beck has little effect on our description of the battle – in either 1066 or today. Snorri Sturluson goes on to report what the English were doing:

> The earls let their army proceed slowly down along the river, with all their troops in line. The king's banner was next to the river, where the line was thickest. It was thinnest at the ditch, where also the weakest of the men were. When the earls advanced downwards along the ditch, the arm of the Northmen's line which was at the ditch gave way; and the Englishmen followed, thinking the Northmen would fly. The banner of Earl Morukare [Morcar] advanced then bravely.[7]

I think it is appropriate to take a look at some earlier information imparted by Sturluson to get a better perspective when considering his reporting. The *Heimskringla*, #87 begins with: 'Thereafter the king sailed to the Humber and up along the river and then he landed.' 'Thereafter' refers to this event as following the Viking defeat of an Anglo-Saxon force at 'Hellornes' (Holderness) following Harald Sigurdsson's destruction of Scarborough.[8] (A minor but understandable discrepancy is that the Vikings did not continue up the Humber but instead branched-off onto the Ouse.) Sturluson continues: 'Up in Jorvik [York] were two earls, Earl Morukare and his brother, Earl Valthiof and they had an immense army.' Here Sturluson is in error, confusing Earl Edwin of Mercia with a later, the final, earl of Northumbria, 'Valthiof' or 'Waltheof'. He goes on: 'While the army of the earls was coming down from the upper part of the country, King Harald lay in the Usa [Ouse].' So, according to Sturluson, Harald and his Vikings were lying in wait as the Anglo-Saxons advanced. The broad outlines of the battle can be taken as fairly accurate, despite the confusion of a detail or two, with regard to my reading of the text and all the more so in that Sturluson does describe the country accurately, again based on my personal observations of the battle site.

As we've seen, Sturluson then tells of the Vikings' deployment, after which he reports that: 'The earls let their army proceed slowly down along the river, with all their troops in line. The king's banner was next the river, where the line was thickest. It was thinnest at the ditch, where also the weakest of the men were.'[9] The relative 'thickness' of the deployments will have some bearing on the progress of the battle.

How the Battle at Fulford Unfolded – the 'Authentic Historical Record'

The actual start of the fighting, according to Sturluson, is found in the final two sentences of the *Heimskringla*, #87: 'When the earls advanced downwards along the ditch, the arm of the Northmen's line which was at the ditch gave way; and the Englishmen followed, thinking the Northmen would fly. The banner of Earl Morukare advanced then bravely'. This account says that the Viking line 'gave way' where 'the line was thinnest'. At first, it would seem that Sturluson means that the English pushed the Vikings back along the 'ditch' part of Germany Beck and they may have done so. However, in stating that 'The banner of Earl Morukare advanced then bravely', it would seem possible, if not probable, that the part of the Anglo-Saxon line at the ford itself also advanced, but this is, of course, unclear. This description is given despite the fact that Sturluson had earlier reported that the earls' banners were close to the river. Next, the Vikings made their move. Here the *Heimskringla*, #88 takes over: 'When King Harald saw that the English array had come to the ditch against him, he ordered the charge to be sounded and urged on his men.' So, here, Harald orders the counter-attack. The story proceeds: 'He ordered the banner which was called the Land-ravager to be carried before him and made so severe an assault that all had to give way before it; and there was a great loss among the men of the earls and they soon broke into flight, some running up the river, some down and the most leaping into the ditch, which was so filled with dead that the Norsemen could go dry-foot over the fen.' So, in this passage it is reported that the English 'broke into flight, some running up the river, some down and the most leaping into the ditch. . . ' This indicates that the Englishmen were driven into the river, which means they were the men closest to it; but also that the men – most of them – leapt into the ditch, which probably indicates the Germany Beck. The next part of the same sentence describes how many of the Anglo-Saxons died and also suggests where: '. . . which was so filled with dead that the Norsemen could go dry-foot over the fen'. Now piles of dead in the ditch so thick that the Vikings could tread on the bodies instead of wet ground is entirely plausible; however, the saga's use of the word 'fen' seems to indicate that the carnage so described was also located at the muddy ford itself. This is likely because of the word 'fen', which means: 'An area of low, flat, wet land in England: areas of marsh and fen'.[10] The use of this word here, instead of 'ditch', points toward a more marshy area, such as to be found at the muddy ford. It is interesting to note the use of this word, which is the same in Old Norse – the language used in the sagas, instead of 'ditch', which is nearly identical in Old Norse ('dicch'). That would make the comment about the number of dead men being so thick that one could step on their bodies without getting one's feet wet being worth remarking about, which the saga did. This is probably why the oral tradition preserving the record of the battle by still using this word would have been carried on for the 154 years between 1066 when the battle was fought and 1220 when the saga was penned. This, too, is conceivable if many hundreds of men fell in combat at the ford, which is not excessively large, as an inspection of a Google Earth image of where the A19 crosses the Germany Beck will show – about 200ft. Then, Sturluson's record falls victim to some evident exaggeration, likely on the part of the witness cited, 'Stein Herdison'.

The *Heimskringla*, #88 next reports: 'There Earl Morukare fell. So says Stein Herdison:—

The gallant Harald drove along,
Flying but fighting, the whole throng.
At last, confused, they could not fight,
And the whole body took to flight.
Up from the river's silent stream
At once rose desperate splash and scream;
But they who stood like men this fray
Round Morukare's body lay.

We know from subsequent accounts that Earl Morcar survived the fight at the ford; but the poem's insight into the progress of the battle describes it as an Anglo-Saxon 'flight' and adds that they fled up from 'the river's silent stream', which would be Germany Beck, which flows gently and silently. The description of the struggle degenerating into a desperate flight is in keeping with the fact that the English likely suffered heavy casualties, which, as will be shown in subsequent passages, is what results from an uncontrolled and panicked running-away, instead of a well-managed retreat.

I think it is necessary to mention at this point that few to no participants in medieval combat were anxious to engage in a fighting withdrawal or even to act as a rearguard to an orderly retreat as these tactics were very often if not nearly always fatal to the participants. As the Vikings advanced, the Anglo-Saxon shield wall would have begun to crumble, then collapse. But since this was happening at the ford and farther toward the riverside, the thicker woods there would have prevented the men still holding fast to the shield wall farther inland to observe this catastrophic development, until the fleeing Anglo-Saxons and their Viking pursuers burst from the woodlands and into the open, all rushing toward York, outflanking the as-yet intact shield wall to the east, along Germany Beck. Then, a slow 'withdrawal' became a sudden 'retreat' and the retreat quickly became a complete, disorganised rout; here's why.

It is difficult enough to survive in one-to-one combat in a melee battle – as was often the type fought in those days – at close quarters with a shield and spear, sword, battleaxe or club if one is relatively stationary or advancing and staying alert and focused on one's opponent, even if one is part of a shield wall. If a fighter must also 'walk backwards' while fighting, being sure to keep one's footing by not, for example, stumbling over a discarded weapon or a wounded or dead man, while keeping an eye on the men to either side to make sure they have not turned to flee, leaving one isolated, exposed and vulnerable to being overwhelmed by several opponents. These distractions could easily prove to be fatal. Once a battle line or shield wall is breached, especially if in several places, the situation usually almost immediately degenerates into a state of 'it's every man for himself' and 'to hell with the hindmost' as a formerly disciplined and organised fighting force disintegrates into a fear-driven mob trying desperately to escape a screaming horde of angry and vengeful enemies determined to kill as many men on your side as possible. It is at this point in any struggle when most of the deaths are inflicted on those trying to escape: One's back is unshielded and exposed to arrows, spears, hurled rocks and/or sword blows from closely pursuing enemies. In this case, the defeated warriors must, to survive, simply discard their shields and weapons and engage in a full-out run to save themselves. This is what likely happened at the end of the battle at Fulford.

How this situation came about is probably due to the fact that the initial Viking breakthrough near the river, in and beside the marshland and ford, was not at first visible to the men along the Anglo-Saxon line farther east, along Germany Beck, because the compact but relatively dense woodlands nearer the river would have hidden the worsening situation from view, until, too late, a fear-driven mob of defeated warriors, closely pursued by charging Vikings, suddenly burst from the tree line.

The description of the final stages of the battle is buttressed by the *Heimskringla*, #88's next passages: 'This song was composed by Stein

Herdison about Olaf, son of King Harald; and he speaks of Olaf being in this battle with King Harald, his father.' (This evidently refers to the preceding poem or 'song'.) The account then says, 'These things are also spoken of in the song called "Harald's Stave" –

Earl Valthiof's men
Lay in the fen,
By sword down hewed,
So thickly strewed,
That Norsemen say
They paved a way
Across the fen
For the brave Norsemen.

So, here again the saga confirms that the English 'lay in the fen' and were 'so thickly strewed, they paved the way across the fen for the brave Norsemen'. We also find once more here the witness's song composer's error that these were 'Valthiof's men'.

The final entries for the *Heimskringla*, #88 tell us: 'Earl Valthiof and the people who escaped, fled up to the castle of York; and there the greatest loss of men had been. This battle took place upon the Wednesday next Mathias' day [AD 1066].' This also reconfirms that the greatest losses had been when the English fled to escape. This chapter conveniently also informs readers of the exact date of the battle.

Looking back at the *Heimskringla*'s accounts, we can see that King Harald Hardrada drove the Viking counter-attack, which began with his strongest men in the thickest part of his line, where his banner was, at or near the river. Then, in stating that fought 'the whole throng', until 'At last, confused, the whole body took flight', that is, 'Up from the river's silent stream'. These passages indicate that Harald's army, beginning near the river, then driving through 'the whole throng', rolled up the English line, including those along the ditch – Germany Beck. Next, the entire Viking battle front would have charged the fleeing English, inflicting very many deaths as they drove the Anglo-Saxons back up to the walled city of York.

During the early stages of my research of this battle I encountered many descriptions of it that varied so much from Snorri Sturluson's account as to make them much less likely to be accurate than what he reported in his belated recording of the events. It is likely the oral tradition preserved in the poem's linguistic structure as a mnemonic technique held intact many if not most of the historical facts from generation to generation through retelling to retelling in the exact same form. Thus, the larger aspects of the fight at Fulford in Sturluson's account are likely to be fairly accurate, despite the discrepancies and relatively minor inaccuracies already cited above. It is for these reasons that I rely exclusively on Sturluson's account herein and not any reconstructions that were created, oftentimes without any attribution or even a minimum of supporting evidence and were composed even many more centuries later than the *Heimskringla*.

How the Battle at Fulford Developed – What the Viking Deployment and Terrain Tell Us

As Sturluson has reported, 'The king's banner was next the river, where the line was thickest'. Who would have been the men there, where the Viking deployment was 'thickest?' I'll pause for a moment here to analyse who at least some of these men were, in all likelihood.

I have participated in some mock sword combats[‡] wherein each person in the 'fight' is well-padded and provided with a sturdy and also well-upholstered helmet that gives very good cushioning against blows to the head and also excellent eye protection through tiny slits that are much narrower than the 'blade' of the 'sword' (more of a club, really) each 'combatant' is allowed to use. This was over 20 years ago or more, when I was yet in my 40s and to not quite 50. My opponent in one case in particular was a much larger man of about 35. In addition to the age factor, he outweighed me by dozens of pounds. During the 'fight', he would, when we were 'in a clinch', lean on me with his shield, pressing down on me for from a few seconds to about a third of a minute. Within several moments I was becoming more tired than I should have been, due to having to support his greater weight in addition to my own and that of my padding, helmet, 'weapon' and shield. At the time, I was also very active – swimming, hiking, lifting weights, doing outdoor work (as I still do, but not as much); I was in very good condition for my age, but I soon felt so tired that I was slowed in my actions and reactions, during the contest to a very considerable degree.

In addition, a much larger man could, as my opponent did, have not only mass and gravity but also momentum on his side. Anyone can demonstrate the effect of a taller and larger man swinging his sword, axe, club or other weapon down toward a shorter, smaller man. The blows fall heavier and faster when gravity adds momentum to the action.

---

‡ While attending science fiction and fantasy conventions and as an employee – roving security – at California's 'Renaissance Pleasure Faire'.

Taking a hammer and battering a nail down at waist level derives better results than hammering upward on a nail above one's head, unless one exerts extra force to drive the tool upward. In a fight, the shorter man also tires more quickly by having to fight gravity to impart extra inertia to his weapon's generally more upward blows. It is also important to note that it is the shield arm that tires before the sword arm. This is so because the shield arm generally is held in roughly the same position to block most blows, so the same few muscles become overworked. In time, this leads to the actions of the shield arm lagging, and leaves the shield movements slower and dragging behind the continued sharp action of opponents' sword slashes, thrusts and blows, particularly if one faces a series of enemy fighters, some of whom may be arriving at the battle line fresh from rotation and rest.

Moreover, when one is balancing on one's feet and manoeuvring during a fight, extra energy must be expended to regain and maintain one's balance and to adjust and readjust one's stance and movements each time a blow is struck against one's head or body that throws everything off-balance and out of synchronisation while attempting each step or other body movement. All of this adds to one's fatigue during the fight – whether actual or in mock combat.

So, with the above examples in mind, I conclude that King Harald Hardrada deployed not only his best fighters but also his largest men – most of whom were likely the same people – nearer to the river Ouse. It was likely these men who were also better able to ford the streamlets at the 'delta' where the Germany Beck branches as it reaches the Ouse. These larger men would also have the advantage of being better able to wade through the cattails of the swamp's pond or small lake that begins just a few yards or even feet at times, from the river, which plants presumably grew there in 1066 as well. These factors contribute to the later, largely fictional, reconstructions of the Battle of Fulford that declare that the Vikings first broke through along and near to the river bank. These conjectured events are not without merit and are only lacking in any sort of record, no matter how tenuous, as Sturluson's reports must be regarded. So, those other accounts are, ironically or perhaps not, likely partly to mostly to entirely accurate – with or without the logical analyses included here.

Another factor to be considered with regard to the terrain is that there is yet some 'marshy ground' about three-quarters of a mile to a mile farther to the east or 'inland' from the River Ouse and along the Germany Beck. (This is near where, I decided, the beck now splits, with a side-channel going northward, alongside the purported old Roman side road mentioned earlier.) It would make sense for the Anglo-

Saxon line to have been 'anchored' there, with less likelihood of being outflanked both due to the soggy ground and the fact that the Vikings would have been running out of men to deploy any farther 'inland' than at that point. The entire site of the battle is relatively flat, making it easier for the English, once they had discarded their weapons and shields, to outrun their Viking pursuers and make for the sheltering walls of York.

Before we depart from our account of the Fulford fight, we'll consult *The Anglo-Saxon Chronicle* to take a brief look – for but a brief look is all that is required – at its sparing report on the battle: 'But, ere King Harold [Harald Hardrada] could come thither, the Earls Edwin and Morcar had gathered from their earldoms as great a force as they could get and fought with the enemy. They made a great slaughter too; but there were a good number of the English people slain and drowned and put to flight: and the Northmen had possession of the field of battle.'[11] So, here, the *Chronicle* corroborates Sturluson's account, but without adding any new details.

I mentioned all of the aspects of a mass flight after the loss of a battle to buttress my speculation that it is likely that the Anglo-Saxon commanders, who survived the battle – Morcar and Edwin – agreed to surrender hostages to the Vikings five days later at Stamford Bridge because, in part, while many of their men also survived (I'm estimating that about one-third of their approximately 5,000 to 6,000 Anglo-Saxon fighters were killed during the fight at Fulford), many of those who yet lived probably had neither weapons nor shields, having left them on the battlefield. It would have been doubtful that York could still be properly defended due to a lack of enough men bearing arms (and shields) to protect the city walls until more weapons and shields could be produced and delivered to them.

King Harald Hardrada of the Vikings and his turncoat ally, Tostig Godwinsson, on the other hand, even though they knew that between 1,500 and 2,000 of York's defenders had been killed (being able to estimate by the number of bodies left on the field, plus their retrieval of probably about twice that number of Anglo-Saxon shields and weapons) they could not really be sure if there were reinforcements then available within or nearby the city. Both Harald and Tostig would have been anxious to neutralise York and get on with their anticipated conquest of not just the northern territories but all of England. Therefore, after accepting a few hostages from York, they agreed to meet five days hence, at Stamford Bridge, to receive even more hostages before continuing with their planned complete Viking subjugation of the island nation. But the Anglo-Saxons yet had a surprise in store for the Norwegian king and his warriors and rebellious Anglo-Saxon allies – a very big surprise.

44

Chapter 5

The Second of the Three Battles of 1066 – Stamford Bridge

The pivotal fight at Stamford Bridge is also dealt with most thoroughly in the *Heimskringla*, upon which we will again rely primarily to give as accurate an account of the battle as possible. We will also consult *The Anglo-Saxon Chronicle*.

Word of the landings and attacks from 14–17 August by Harald Hardrada and Tostig in the north had already, no doubt, reached King Harold II. But it was not until he had returned to London, after disbanding the Great Fyrd along the south coast, that he learned of the Vikings' progress upriver toward York. He immediately hastened north with the core of his army, gathering reinforcements along the way. Within days he was near York with his troops, at Tadcaster. There he was joined by men from the Anglo-Saxon fleet and, in unison with the Yorkshire men, by 25 September, King Harold managed to secretly move the Anglo-Saxon army and shore-deployed navy men to a point close to the Derwent River, which the Vikings were also approaching.

As an alternative obligation to the five-hide levy to be discussed later, hides were combined, up to 300 in number and named 'ship sokes'. Each of these required the delivery of sixty warrior seamen, plus a warship to be constructed, outfitted and supplied. In addition, there were 'Lithsmen' and 'Buscarls' – skilled seamen for hire. These seafaring mercenaries were paid for by either the earls or the king, depending on whether they were being deployed as either a regional or royal force. They would man the ships, then, if needed, would go ashore to fight as land troops. Thus, in later Anglo-Saxon times, levied as well as hired skilled sailors who also functioned as land fighters would provide a trained and experienced core, along with the Thegns and Huscarls, for the larger army of Hidesmen and Fyrdmen.[1] Therefore, it is likely the army King Harold II commanded that day was augmented by probably two-thirds of the warriors allocated to each ship from naval Hidesmen, plus hired seafaring fighters; and, in that the fleet likely was composed of hundreds, or at least scores, of ships, this would have been a considerable reinforcement for the upcoming battle. Moreover, with the inclusion of seaborne mercenaries we find even more evidence that King Harold II was able to enlist the aid of said hired seafarers to also fight ashore at Stamford Bridge, considerably augmenting his armed force there – enough to defeat the Vikings that day.

The Anglo-Saxon Chronicle reports the onset of the battle thusly: 'Thither came Harold, king of the English, unawares against them beyond the bridge; and they closed together there and continued long in the day fighting very severely.'[2] So, the *Chronicle* reports that King Harold and his army came against the Norwegians 'unawares' and 'beyond the bridge', which tells us that the Norwegians were not on both sides of the river but were rather across the bridge from the English as they approached.

Returning to the *Heimskringla* (#90), we find one of the earliest descriptions of the weather on the day when a historic battle was fought: 'The weather was uncommonly fine and it was hot sunshine.* The men therefore laid aside their armour and went on the land only with their shields, helmets and spears and girt with swords; and many had also arrows and bows.'† These facts set the scene for the coming events of the battle, which, again, commenced with the Anglo-Saxon army under King Harold II storming across the ford and over the bridge at 'Stanforda-bryggiur', as the Norwegian chronicler Snorri Sturluson refers to Stamford Bridge.

Snorri Sturluson then happens upon some potentially controversial content. He reports that 'King Harold Godwinsson came from the south

---

* 'Hot' in northern England today being at or higher than the mid-80s Fahrenheit, due to often high levels of humidity, making what would be otherwise 'mild' temperatures uncomfortable. Moreover, temperatures were about 2 to 4 degrees higher that century – amidst the 'Medieval Warm Period', from c. 950 AD to c. 1250 AD – which means it would have been around 90 degrees Fahrenheit and conditions probably 'muggy', due to the often high humidity on the island nation of England.

† The Vikings, accustomed as they were to the cooler climates of Norway and adjacent Scandinavian lands – Oslo is usually about 4 to 8 degrees cooler than the York area at that time of year – had therefore in all likelihood neglected to bring along from their ships their hauberks of chain mail, other armour and heavier weapons.

to the castle (York) with a numerous army and rode into the city with the good-will and consent of the people.'[3] It is not beyond reason to believe that Harold would *ride* into the walled city, suggesting that he was on horseback – a likelihood in that he was a nobleman and would, of course, be familiar with horseback riding and, otherwise, how could he have travelled up from London in just four days (this would have been Sunday, 24 September – the day before the battle at Stamford Bridge)?

Sturluson then tells us: 'Now as they [the Vikings] came near the castle a great army seemed coming against them and they saw a cloud of dust as from horses' feet and under it shining shields and bright armour.'[4] Here Sturluson again refers to York as 'the castle', but is clearly in error as Stamford Bridge is five miles away, to the east. But this passage also includes the first hint that the Anglo-Saxons arrived on horseback. Sturluson, in the *Heimskringla*, #92, says:

> Then King Harald [Hardrada] arranged his army and made the line of battle long, but not deep. He bent both wings of it back, so that they met together; and formed a wide ring equally thick all round, shield to shield, both in the front and rear ranks. The king himself and his retinue were within the circle; and there was the banner and a body of chosen men. Earl Tostig, with his retinue, was at another place and had a different banner. The army was arranged in this way, because the king knew that horsemen were accustomed to ride forwards with great vigour, but to turn back immediately.[5]

Here it is being reported that the English were attacking the Vikings on horseback; and Sturluson accurately describes the cavalry tactic of reining one's horse to a stop short of the enemy line or shield wall. What he does not say is that the mounted warriors would then hurl a spear or axe or make a bow shot, at the defenders and turn again and ride away, preparatory to rearming and repeating the manoeuvre. But, you might object and I expect many experts in medieval warfare and historians of the year of the Conquest will do so, that the Anglo-Saxons did not resort to the use of cavalry tactics but instead relied exclusively on mounted infantry – or dragoon – tactics, whereby the warriors would ride up near to a battle site, dismount, secure their horses, and then proceed to fight on foot. However, there is some evidence that the Anglo-Saxons could have occasionally or even often made use of cavalry tactics and possibly did so at least initially in the Battle of Stamford Bridge.

Unfortunately, the only 'direct', 'original' or 'first-hand' account of the battle is neither direct nor original or first-hand – the aforementioned report by Snorri Sturluson in his *Heimskringla* saga's history of the Norwegian kings. Besides being so far removed in both time and distance from the battle, the account of the fight at Stamford Bridge seems to and even obviously suffers from some confusion regarding that battle and the decisive struggle near Hastings just 19 days later. An example is to be found in the *Heimskringla*, #93: 'Now King Harald Sigurdsson [Hardrada] rode around his array, to see how every part was drawn up. He was upon a black horse and the horse stumbled under him, so that the king fell off. He got up in haste and said, "A fall is lucky for a traveller".' Now this anecdote mirrors, or at least resembles, the unfortunate landing of Duke William at Pevensey when he is described as slipping down onto all fours upon being the first to leap ashore. This caused consternation among his troops, until he relied on his quick wit to declare, 'By the splendour of God I have taken hold of my kingdom; the earth of England is in my hands!'[6] As Duke William made the proclamation, he is reported to have raised two fistfuls of soil overhead or so the story goes, for, if the composition of the land at the debarkation site was as it is today – composed of 'shingle' or rocks ranging in size from about that of a golf ball and up to the diameter of an ostrich egg – then scooping up two handfuls of shingle would be an awkward undertaking, but, in that the landing site was at an estuary then perhaps there was enough in the way of silt, mud and sand to make such a gesture an easier task.

While the relative near-duplication of these incidents could be a coincidence, I, for one, rarely accept the likelihood of coincidence and I prefer to believe that here Sturluson had been given a confused account that substituted events occurring at different times and places within a few weeks of each other 154 years before, in 1066. However, despite this and other possible and even probable errors on the part of Sturluson and/or his sources, there are so many references to cavalry being present at Stamford Bridge that I think it prudent to at least investigate the possibility – despite the possible or probably contrary opinions of many experts – of mounted combat having taken place on 25 September 1066.

Could the Anglo-Saxons Have Used Use Cavalry at Stamford Bridge, and Did They?

The evidence that the Anglo-Saxons had a tradition of using not just heavy infantry in shield walls and light infantry and archers as skirmishers, but also cavalry has been accumulating in recent years. In Frank Barlow's introduction to his coverage of the Battle of Hastings, he observes: 'The English, at least their elite troops, were mounted and some cavalry tactics were open to them.'[7] *The Anglo-Saxon Chronicle* also states that, beginning in AD 866, '. . . came a large heathen army into England and fixed their winter-quarters in East-Anglia, where they were soon horsed. . .'.[8] So, the Viking invaders obtained horses suitable for military use from the East Anglians, despite the fact that some historians claim that English horses were too small. Then, in 877: 'Meanwhile King Alfred with his army rode after the cavalry as far as Exeter. . .'[9] This declares as fact that King Alfred and his army 'rode after the cavalry' (not mounted infantry) of the Vikings. Later, in 1010, came the news: '. . . and the Danes remained masters of the field of slaughter. There they were they horsed; and afterwards took possession of East-Anglia . . . and the horsemen rode towards the ships . . .'[10] Again we see mounted Vikings after they were 'horsed' on English territory. In 1015: 'Ealdorman Edric then seduced forty ships from the king and submitted to Knute. The West-Saxons also submitted and gave hostages and horsed the army.'[11] So, here, as part of a going-over to the enemy, the English 'horsed the army' of the Danes. C. Warren Hollister makes numerous references to the possibility, probability and even likelihood that the Anglo-Saxons were familiar enough with the use of cavalry to have employed mounted combat at times themselves.[12]

What the above passages suggest, but may not prove entirely conclusively to some doubters, is that England possessed horses larger than the 'ponies' many believe only existed on English lands in earlier times. These would be 13 or 14 hands high, whereas a war horse, by today's standards, would be from 15 to 16 hands high. (A 'hand' is the average width of a man's hand – about 4in.) The fact is that, beginning with the Romans, larger breeds of horses had been imported from the European continent and there has been an abundance of larger horses in England ever since. However, in any case, according to an analysis by Richard Steckel, a professor of economics at Ohio State University, the height of an average Englishman decreased from an average of 68.27in (173.4cm) in the early Middle Ages, then increased in more recent times.[13] The average Anglo-Saxon was just 5ft 8¼in tall then, as opposed to 5ft 9in for Englishmen today. The three-quarters of an inch difference means a mounted Anglo-Saxon warrior would have required a slightly smaller horse, perhaps the difference of one-half to one hand of measurement. In other words, despite the fact that Anglo-Saxon England was well-stocked with larger horses, only a slightly smaller mount would have been required to achieve the same results today, as far as fighting on horseback is concerned.

As for indications and evidence of cavalry use in England brought to us by stone carvings, in a post at the blog, citing an unnamed author, writer Tom Cain wrote on 27 December 1997 that a Pictish standing stone, the Aberlemno Stone from the 700s, portrays not only Pict-Celtic cavalry but their Northumbrian enemies under the command of Ecgfrith also fighting on horseback at the Battle of Dunnichen in 685.[14] The cavalrymen are shown making use of throwing and thrusting spears and wearing chain mail fashioned for mounted combat – with split, knee-length skirts. How would the artisans who created this carving know the details of cavalry throwing and thrusting techniques and hauberks for mounted use if they had not seen them first-hand?

Cain goes on to cite from the same article regarding a funerary marker – the Repton Stone, likely in honour of Æthelbald, who preceded Offa (Æthelbald died in 757). The monument shows him as an equestrian warrior.[15] It is similar to a mounted combatant shown on the plate of the Sutton Hoo helmet and the Pliezhausen bracteates (beaten metal plates). The Vendel (Sweden) helmets, likened to the Sutton Hoo find, also, in one example, shows a Germanic-style mounted warrior; and, finally with regard to similar discoveries, Cain and his source cite what he calls 'amongst many', the Sockburn-on-Tees 'hogback' 'number nine'. This monument, dated from the mid-900s, also shows two mounted warriors who are armed with spears and shields and who are wearing Spanghelm-type helmets.[16] They are mounted on galloping horses and seated in saddles recalling those shown in the Bayeux Tapestry. Cain and his source assert that those who have analysed the 'hogback' stone refer to the saddles as being intended for mounted warfare, with high backs or cantles, even though there are no identifiable stirrups represented on the monument.[17] While stirrups and spurs made it easier for riders to control their mounts in combat, they were not indispensable; ancient cavalrymen functioned very well without them. Today's historical reenactors have demonstrated clearly that neither specialised saddles nor stirrups or spurs are needed to effectively deploy the couched lance, contrary to previously-held notions. In fact, the ability of riders to move more freely was essential for light cavalry to engage in either close-up or long-distance all-around combat; stirrups and spurs would hinder such manoeuvrability.[18] These illustrations make it clear, according to Cain, that these were cavalrymen, not dragoons. I could not locate an illustration of this pictograph, so I rely on the source – Tom Cain. However, I did locate a depiction of a mounted warrior leading an army and evidently engaged in combat on one of the Gotland Picture

Stones.[19] What all of these depictions indicate is that Scandinavians and Anglo-Saxons, at least occasionally, engaged in mounted combat.

We now turn briefly to the *Exeter Book* to see what one of its maxims has to say: 'An earl must ride upon a horse's back, the cavalry must ride forth together, the infantrymen must stand firmly . . .'[20] Why recite cavalry tactics if they were never used? Returning to *The Anglo-Saxon Chronicle*: 'A.D. 891. This year went the army eastward; and King Arnulf fought with the land-force, ere the ships arrived, in conjunction with the eastern Franks and Saxons and Bavarians and put them to flight. And three Scots came to King Alfred in a boat without any oars from Ireland . . .'[21] However, this passage, when rendered as it is into modern English, does not convey the implied meaning delivered in the original Anglo-Saxon or Old English, as follows: '892: Her for se here east, 7 Earnulf cyning gefeaht wið þam *radhere* [my italics] ær þa scipu comon, mid Eastfrancum 7 Seaxum 7 Bergerum, 7 hine geflymde. 7 þry Scottas comon to Ælfrede cynge on anum bate butan ælcum gereþrum of Hibernia . . .'[22] (Note that the years as reported at these websites differ, but the text does not.) What is important in the Old English/Anglo-Saxon version is that in the opening clause the words 'land-force' are translated as 'radhere', which, when rendered as the spelling variant of 'ræde-here', presents us with the definition: 'ræde-herees; m. A *mounted force, cavalry* Rædehere cerethi, Wrt. Voc. ii. 15, 76: cerethei, 130, 15. Of rádehere equitatu, Hpt. Gl. 525, 25. Alexandres næs ná má geslægen ðonne hundtwelftig on ðæm *rædehere* [my italics] in exercitu Alexandri centum et viginti equites defuere ors. 3, 9; Swt. 124, 21. Ægðer ge an gangehere ge on *rædehere* . . . (my italics again).[23] So, here again we find no other source than the original – Old English – version of *The Anglo-Saxon Chronicle* itself referring to an English army as being a mounted force or cavalry in the year 892.

Following on, remaining with *The Anglo-Saxon Chronicle*, in AD 894: '. . . When they were all collected together, they [the Anglo-Saxons] overtook the rear of the enemy [the Vikings] at Buttington on the banks of the Severn . . . [the raiding Northmen] slew the men whom they could overtake without the work and all the corn they either burned or consumed with their horses every evening . . .'[24] This passage finds the Anglo-Saxons overtaking a mounted Viking force, which they could not do without themselves pursuing the invaders on horseback; and, in turn, the Vikings overtook another group of Anglo-Saxons 'without the work' (a fortification), then, the Northmen (Vikings) either ate the captured corn there or were forced to consume their own horses, but this lattermost is not clearly established due to a vague sentence structure and wording. Again we see both sides resorting to horses in the campaign of this year, 172 years prior to the year of the Conquest. It is very unlikely that these traditions of horsemanship would have lapsed during that period of time, all the more so in view of the fact that they had been built-up over many preceding centuries.

At the website 'History and Hardware of Warfare – Anglo-Saxon Military Organization, Part III', Mitch Williamson, writing as MSW, reports that the *The Chronicon ex Chronicis* entry by John Worcester tells us that in 1055, just 11 years before the fight at Stamford Bridge, the Earl of Hereford, Ralph, a Norman settled in England, commanded that the Fyrdmen at the battle with the Welsh there fight on horseback 'contrary to their custom' ('*contra morem in equis pugnare jussit*').[25] Williamson adds that this entry is often used to refute the notion that the Anglo-Saxons used cavalry, but the entry merely states that mounted combat was against the usual practice of the *Fyrd*, but does *not* contend that fighting on horseback was unknown to mounted nobles or professional warriors such as Thegns, Huscarls, Hidesmen and / or hired mercenaries or even *some* Fyrdmen.

With the above-cited sources in mind, which are by no means anywhere near all of those now asserting that both Scandinavians and Anglo-Saxons resorted to at least the occasional use of cavalry, I will now present my case for allowing King Harold II and the English to attack the Norwegians at Stamford Bridge while mounted, as reported by Snorri Sturluson in his sagas of the Norwegian kings. Later, I will present my reasons for King Harold to decide to instead fight on foot at the battle near Hastings the following month.

Reconciling the Author's Hypothesis with Snorri Sturluson's Account

The *Heimskringla*, #90 informs us that: 'On Monday, when King Harald Sigurdsson had taken breakfast, he ordered the trumpets to sound for going on shore. The army accordingly got ready and he divided the men into the parties who should go and who should stay behind.'[26] All of this preparation, then the trek to Stamford Bridge, took some time. Even if the Vikings arose at dawn – which would have been about a half-hour before sunrise, at 05:56, with civil twilight commencing at 05:20 (before the advent of 'summer time', now become the new standard time in England). So, allowing for one hour to rise, don clothing, eat, gather weapons and go ashore, and another hour to meet with military commanders, address the troops, give instructions to leaders and followers alike and to saddle the horses; then to undertake the trek to Stamford Bridge from Riccall, which is 12.42 miles as the raven flies, but is a much more circuitous route along winding roads, across fields and fording streams, it would easily be midmorning before the Norwegian army arrived near the shore of the River Derwent. By then, King Harold II and the Anglo-Saxons were approaching, as Snorri Sturluson reports: 'Now as they [the Vikings] came near the castle a great army seemed coming against them and they saw a cloud of dust as from horses' feet and under it shining shields and bright armour.'[27] Here Sturluson tells us that the Vikings were still on the move when they spotted the English approaching; and, they saw a cloud of dust as if a mounted host came near and saw the sunlight reflecting off their armour and shields. The *Heimskringla*, #90 then reports: 'The king halted his people and called to him Earl Toste and asked him what army this could be. The earl replied that he thought it most likely to be a hostile army, but possibly it might be some of his relations who were seeking for mercy and friendship, in order to obtain certain peace and safety from the king.'[28] So, again, Sturluson says the Viking army was yet on the move and had to be halted by King Harald Hardrada, who then consulted with Tostig Godwinsson. After that: 'Then the king said, 'We must all halt, to discover what kind of a force this is'. They did so; and the nearer this force came the greater it appeared and their shining arms were to the sight like glancing ice.'[29] At the end of the *Heimskringla* #90, the waiting Norwegians realised that a very large English army was approaching and, judging from the dust cloud, on horseback and probably very rapidly.

At this point, I think it is appropriate to pause to investigate the terrain in and around the battlefield to get a proper perspective as unfolding developments in the fighting are reviewed.

The Site(s), and the Combat, at the 'Battle at Stamford Bridge'

As for my personal investigations of the purported sites and circumstances of the battle at Stamford Bridge, getting off the bus from York and alighting onto North Main Street in the town of Stamford Bridge, I was directed by the bus driver to a tiny, brick-lined 'plaza' or square, as being the site of the memorial to the battle there. I went and viewed the plaque affixed to the square brick column in the centre of the mini-plaza. It proclaimed, with disarming honesty, that the Battle of Stamford Bridge was fought 'in this neighbourhood'. Naturally, being sceptical about all claims of actual sites, I decided to investigate the 'lay of the land' in said 'neighbourhood' for later comparisons with maps purporting to accurately portray the more or less 'precise' location of the events of 25 September 1066.

First, I went into the compact and well-kept riverside park next to the monument square, being careful not to disturb a few people sitting singly at picnic tables to enjoy their lunches as I took photos of the millhouse and the shallows below the weir set across the River Derwent. Then, I turned and proceeded up and along North Main Street, the A166, toward the area between the old millhouse – which I assumed, correctly as I later reckoned, to be nearby the site of the original, small and narrow wooden bridge where a lone Viking warrior made his heroic last stand – and the Battle Flats area, which lies to the east-south-east of the Anglo-Saxon river crossing location.

On the way up the hill and along North Main Street as it slowly diverged away from the riverbank, I took photos of the as-yet remaining open field to my left, toward the River Derwent, with the exception of a few homes in a small housing tract on St Edmunds between North Main Street and the river. All along the way what I saw was a gradual slope down toward the river's edge. Just at the peak of the rise away from the river, forming a rounded, gentle ridgetop, North Main Street, as it becomes Roman Road, is met by a street almost as large – Burton Fields Road – that seemed to curve toward then also slightly away from the scene of the struggle at Battle Flats, forming a broad 'S' curve in a staggering, general course toward the recognised battle site. Burton Fields Road does, in fact, meet Battle Flats Way; yet it is not Battle Flats Way but rather Burton Fields Road that actually skirts the true location of the final phase of the battle, with but a single line of homes in the way.

Some investigators who have not personally visited the site – at and near the end of Whiterose Drive – will not fully understand these geographical features and some seem to have assumed that 'Battle Flats' is on low-lying, perfectly flat ground, such as a mud flat or salt flat along a river or estuary. This is where the monument square was constructed and can be misleading as the combat on 25 September 1066 occurred in phases – the opening clash, the race across the river and up the slope, the encirclement and the final victory for one side and an absolute, crushing defeat for the other. However, Battle Flats is in reality a gently arcing 'flat' upon a low and broad-shouldered ridge. In fact, the single line of houses indicated above is at the high point of the local terrain and it is likely that the Viking shield wall was originally deployed there and then curving back and around into a ring on the adjacent farmland now to be found to the east-south-east.

The Vikings and their Anglo-Saxon allies and mercenaries had taken advantage of the terrain in trying to establish a defensive ring on and above the slopes near or at the crest of the ridge, but were outflanked, surrounded, then destroyed by encirclement and a gradual closing of the ring by the Anglo-Saxons, at first some, even many, on horseback, with the bulk of the English army then completing the process on foot. The Vikings, King Harald Hardrada and Tostig Godwinsson and his rebels and mercenaries had no good options as they were forced to fight to the death, despite the fact that King Harold of the Anglo-Saxons had called upon his treacherous brother, twice, to throw himself on his mercy and surrender.

Of course, I photographed all of the terrain features in the area, then headed back down North Main Street to the central square of town, appropriately named 'The Square', just a couple of dozen yards from the little plaza with its commemorative plaque about the battle being 'in this neighbourhood'. I made inquiries of the shop owners there and one very helpful and cooperative gentleman (the proprietor of a specialty liquor dealership – where I was able to obtain a bottle of single-malt Scotch for my stepfather) drew a map and gave me detailed verbal instructions directing me up and along some side streets to the crest of the gently sloping ridge – at the aforementioned Battle Flats.

Within a few minutes I encountered yet another small park – at the end of Whiterose Drive, which also possesses its own commemorative plaque informing readers that the open meadow beyond the park's boundary hedge was Battle Flats. Taking photos, I surveyed the topography, noting that, yes, indeed, King Harold's mounted Anglo-Saxon force would have swept up the gentle slope from the left, enveloping the defending Viking force to its left, centre and right, being contested from a distance all along the way by a retreating and gradually diminishing Viking force as the Scandinavian warriors pelted their English attackers with stones, arrows and spears. I believe the park and plaque at the end of Whiterose Drive are accurate in describing the site of the battle as being located there and along and behind the final row of houses on Burton Fields Road and the immediately adjacent areas.

After that and one more visit to Stamford Bridge later during my stay in England, I investigated the site of the current bridge and on either side upriver and downriver, taking photos of the waterway and its banks as far as I could without violating the privacy of inhabitants who had clearly posted signs against trespassing. It was my observations and photographs during those visits that convinced me of the overall accuracy of the accounts of the battle at Stamford Bridge as relayed to us by Snorri Sturluson. While the exact location of the old bridge is uncertain, I, like many others, believe it would have been where the river is shallowest, just upriver from the current bridge. Moreover, bridge sites, like roadways, seldom change without very good reasons. I now elaborate a bit further.

The earliest human inhabitants of any area on earth will utilise game trails for their travels into new territories for two valid reasons. First, if you're hunting game, well, it is only logical to follow game trails. Second, the animals know from generations of experience the best routes to cross any terrain in search of water, food or just a convenient pathway overland and the best places to cross rivers. Once a human trackway along the old animal path is established, there are few to no incentives to change a well-established route. Exceptions might be floods, landslides or property owners closing off access or government intervention to preserve, for example, the king's proprietary game animals, as was so often the case in medieval Europe, even on 'public' lands.

The same situation applies to bridges, which are usually built across rivers at, adjacent to or nearby, fords and especially at muddy fords such as are common in Europe in general and England in particular. (Whereas, in the American West, for example, where I live, many fords are on ledges of solid rock or at sandy, rocky or pebble-strewn river crossings.) Once built, bridges are rebuilt and/or replaced at the same location or just to one side of the old bridge. A telltale sign that a bridge is located just to one side of an old bridge or ford is if the roads leading up to the bridge make a 'last-minute' curve or sudden jog to one side or another as they meet the newer bridge's approaches. Such a situation exists at Stamford Bridge, with the A166 – Stamford Bridge West, which becomes 'The Square', then North Main Street. As the A166 approaches the River Derwent, on both banks it veers over in a curve on the Stamford Bridge West side of the river and in a double- or 'S'- curve on the Main Street/Square side of the channel. It is evident that the old river crossing and the former bridge(s) there, cut through the location of the current mini-mall housing the Co-Operative food market and on the far side of the river where the present-day sluice meets the waterway, behind the Battle Flats Veterinary Clinic. This evidence tells me that it is very likely that the battle memorial plaques are both correct: that the battle was fought 'in this neighbourhood', beginning near the memorial site on North Main Street, then progressing uphill to 'Battle Flats' where it reached its bloody finish.

As for my own further conclusions: I likewise remained confident that the eyewitness and 'historical accounts' of the battle at Fulford as described in the *Heimskringla* were also to be for the most part believed for the fight at Stamford Bridge, due to my walking through all parts of the physical site to verify the particulars myself. However, I was still assailed by many doubts concerning the precise location of all or even most of the events at the town of Battle, some 6.5 miles inland from Hastings. I would return to Battle four more times to complete my observations and take more photographs during my travels through the whole area of not just Battle Abbey and adjoining streets but the entire town and the countryside surrounding the supposed battle site. But all of that will come later. For now, let us return to the 'historical records', such as they are, concerning the decisive clash-of-arms at Stamford Bridge.

The *Heimskringla* and *Anglo-Saxon Chronicle* Reports on the Battle at Stamford Bridge

Before we briefly diverted from Snorri Sturluson's coverage of the battle, we were told that the English were approaching, evidently on horseback and very rapidly. In the *Heimskringla*, at the start of #91, titled 'Of Earl Toste's Counsel', the text's translation states: 'Then said King Harald, "Let us now fall upon some good sensible counsel; for it is not to be concealed that this is an [*sic*] hostile army and the king himself without doubt is here".' Tostig's reply is given: 'Then said the earl, "The first counsel is to turn about as fast as we can to our ships to get our men and our weapons and then we will make a defence according to our ability; or otherwise let our ships defend us, for there these horsemen have no power over us."'[30] We are reminded here that the Vikings had left their chain-mail armour and heavier weapons such as battleaxes behind; and we are also told again that the Norwegians were facing mounted Anglo-Saxons. So, I'll pause to analyse why and how the English would have deployed their mounted warriors, whether intended as dragoons or cavalry, that unusually warm autumn day.

King Harold II was very aware of the seriousness of the situation. While he had been on the south coast of Sussex, anticipating the Norman invasion by Duke William, he had subsequently been distracted by his renegade brother's activities and depredations ranging from the Isle of Wight to Sandwich, then Lindsey, as reported in *The Anglo-Saxon Chronicle*:

> . . . came in Earl Tosty from beyond [the] sea into the Isle of Wight, with as large a fleet as he could get; and he was there supplied with money and provisions. Thence he proceeded and committed outrages everywhere by the sea-coast where he could land, until he came to Sandwich. When it was told King Harold, who was in London, that his brother Tosty was come to Sandwich, he gathered so large a force, naval and military, as no king before collected in this land.[31]

Following that, the *Chronicle* reports,

> '. . . When Tosty understood that King Harold was on the way to Sandwich, he departed thence and took some of the boatmen with him, willing and unwilling and went north into the Humber with sixty skips [ships, then spelled 'scips' – an obvious minor mistranslation]; whence he plundered in Lindsey and there slew many good men. When the Earls Edwin and Morkar understood that, they came hither and drove him from the land. And the boatmen forsook him. Then he went to Scotland with twelve smacks [ships].[32]

But, as if that troublemaking had not been enough, Tostig later returned, accompanying the 300 Viking ships of King Harald Sigurdsson's armada.

Harold II knew he had to put down the Scandinavian invasion quickly, then return to the south coast to intercept the expected landing by Duke William and the Normans. So, he would have wanted to surprise, shock, overwhelm and obliterate the Viking army as rapidly as possible; and the best way to do so would be by rushing the Norwegians at Stamford Bridge with the equivalent of a massive cavalry charge – whether or not his mounted force was really equipped for such an attack, for, when the horse-borne warriors dashed forward and engaged the Vikings, the Anglo-Saxon infantry – who were likely accompanying the men 'on horseback' by travelling in wagons pulled by oxen or riding other horses and ponies, donkeys, even the few mules to be occasionally found in England – would then follow as closely as possible. That is exactly what I hypothesise happened at Stamford Bridge: the Englishmen on horseback would have charged across the old ford on both sides of the bridge while the infantry dismounted from their mounts, draft animals and wagons and some assaulted the bridge itself, while others splashed across the ford.

All the while, King Harald Sigurdsson was far from idly awaiting the attack, as the *Heimskringla*, #91 informs us: 'Then King Harald said, ". . . Put three of our best horses under three of our briskest lads and let them ride with all speed to tell our people [with the fleet, at Riccall] to come quickly to our relief. The Englishmen shall have a hard fray of it before we give ourselves up for lost."'[33] He would, of course, have sent an advance party – soon to become a blocking force – to try to hold the ford for as long as possible while he ordered the majority of the Vikings into their battle deployment of a ring-shaped shield wall atop Battle Flats.

As noted before, the *Heimskringla*, #92 next reports:

Then King Harald arranged his army and made the line of battle long, but not deep. He bent both wings of it back, so that they met together; and formed a wide ring equally thick all round, shield to shield, both in the front and rear ranks. The king himself and his retinue were within the circle; and there was the banner and a body of chosen men. Earl Toste [*sic*], with his retinue, was at another place and had a different banner.[34]

This disposition makes sense, all the more so if the mounted Anglo-Saxons were sweeping past the Viking advance party's flanks and were about to close with King Harald Hardrada's main force on the ridgetop at Battle Flats.

Battle Flats is just about 2,200ft – almost half a mile – upslope from the River Derwent, near to but not exactly at the ford, giving the Norwegians just barely enough time to set-up their circular shield wall, the horses, archers, their king and the English former earl Tostig and their entourages within.

While all of this had been going on, in my estimation, a heroic drama was being played out on the bridge itself. According to *The Anglo-Saxon Chronicle*:

But there was one of the Norwegians who withstood the English folk, so that they could not pass over the bridge, nor complete the victory. An Englishman aimed at him with a javelin, but it availed nothing. Then came another under the bridge, who pierced him terribly inwards under the coat of mail. And Harold, King of the English, then came over the bridge, followed by his [dismounted?] army; and there they made a great slaughter, both of the Norwegians and of the Flemings [who had, presumably, accompanied Tostig from his stop in Belgium].[35]

Here Sturluson says that King Harold was leading the dismounted part of his army, while the cavalry – in my estimation – forged ahead toward Battle Flats. Next came the greater part of the battle.

The *Heimskringla* continues:

> The army was arranged in this way, because the king knew that horsemen were accustomed to ride forwards with great vigour, but to turn back immediately. Now the king ordered that his own and the earl's attendants should ride forwards where it was most required. 'And our bowmen', said he, 'shall be near to us; and they who stand in the first rank shall set the spear-shaft on the ground and the spear-point against the horseman's breast, if he rides at them; and those who stand in the second rank shall set the spear-point against the horse's breast'.[36]

It is here that I'd like to pause to briefly comment on the contention of Bruce E. Gelsinger, who asserts, in a journal article[37] that Snorri Sturluson in his accounts confused two battles far apart in times and places – Jaffa, Palestine, in 1192; and Stamford Bridge, England, 1066. The self-explanatory title is 'The Battle of Stamford Bridge and the Battle of Jaffa – a Case of Confused Identity'. Without going further into what are, to me, many distracting and ultimately peripheral details, I believe that if anyone looks a bit more closely at the battle in the Middle East, the differences between these struggles far outweigh the similarities – in fact, the fight at Jaffa is so vaguely and often unclearly described as to make it differ little, if at all, from almost any combat incident anywhere and at any (medieval) time – other than to observe that King Harald Sigurdsson would, of course, be familiar with anti-cavalry tactics due to the fact that, according to the evidence introduced earlier herein and elsewhere, the Scandinavians as well as the Anglo-Saxons had themselves evidently been engaged in both mounted and counter-cavalry warfare for centuries past. What comes next is an example of Sturluson being more kind to the (English) enemy of his own people – the Vikings – than we usually encounter in historical accounts, whether 'objective' or not:

In the *Heimskringla*, #93, 'Of Harald Godwinson [Harold Godwinsson]':

> King Harald Godwinson had come with an immense army, both of cavalry and infantry. Now King Harald Sigurdsson rode around his [own – Viking] array, to see how every part was drawn up.

He was upon a black horse and the horse stumbled under him, so that the king fell off. He got up in haste and said, A fall is lucky for a traveller'.

The English king Harald (Harold) said to the Northmen [sic – either this should read 'English' or it indicates that at least some, but more likely many, Danes – his Huscarls, personal and palace guards – were accompanying the Anglo-Saxons] who were with him, 'Do ye know the stout man who fell from his horse, with the blue kirtle [tunic or coat] and the beautiful helmet?'

'That is the king himself', said they.

The English king said, 'A great man and of stately appearance is he; but I think his luck has left him.'[38]

The next controversial passage from the *Heimskringla* (#94, 'Of The Troop of The Nobility') continues: 'Twenty horsemen rode forward from the Thing-men's [Thegn-mens' roughly the same as thegns, lesser vassals such as sokemen or freemen, with the added office of being jurors or grand jurors in officiating at court hearings, who also had even lesser vassals as armed auxiliaries] troops against the Northmen's array; and all of them and likewise their horses, were clothed in armour.'[39] This statement will likely be dismissed by some people as inaccurate because, as far as we can discern today, with the Anglo-Saxons generally believed to have not employed cavalry often, if not at all, it would be doubtful that their horses would be 'armoured'. However, there is an illustration of a 'Celtic horse helmet Bronze Age protective headgear for a horse', exhibited in the National Museum of Scotland.[40] The website 'The Vintage News' informs us: 'The enigmatic Torrs pony-cap from Scotland appears to be a bronze chanfron [horse helmet] from about the 2nd century BC, perhaps later fitted with the bronze horns found with it.'[41] Okay, so what does this have to do with the possibly erroneous report of armoured horses in Sturluson's account of the fight at Stamford Bridge? If there were helmets to fit horses in Scotland, 107.5 miles from York and if they were in use 1,200 years before the Stamford Bridge battle, it is not unreasonable to suspect horse armour (in the form of chain-mail headgear and breastplates or partial coats, at least) also being present then and there. The same website informs us that 'Surviving period examples of barding [horse armour] are rare; however, complete sets are on display at the Philadelphia Museum of Art, Wallace Collection in London, the Royal Armouries in Leeds and the Metropolitan Museum of Art in New York'.[42] Even complete sets of chain mail intended for

61

human wearers are seldom found today as they were repeatedly repaired and reused due to the fact that they were so expensive and difficult to manufacture to begin with. So, we are forced to conclude that Sturluson's accounts are probably not as 'unreliable' overall as they may seem at first.

With regard to the above remarks and the occasional references to the Anglo-Saxon use of 'cavalry', readers must keep in mind that I am not suggesting the use of heavy cavalry, requiring the use of high cantles or saddlebacks and stirrups, giving armoured warriors a stout seating and footing to engage in horse-borne charges with heavy lances or spears to virtually run through the ranks of opposing infantry or even masses of enemy cavalry – heavy or light. What I envision is 'light cavalry', a sort of *ad hoc* formation drawn from warriors who are more accustomed to fighting as dragoons or mounted infantry who dismount to engage in combat. This improvised 'light cavalry' would instead, as shown in the quotations above, have resorted to charging forward, suddenly halting, hurling spears, stones or stones tied to sticks or battleaxes or shooting arrows, then whirling around and galloping off to get out of range for the purpose of replenishing spear-loads and re-nocking arrows onto bows for the next 'charge'. Or, in a pursuit mode against, for example, fleeing infantry, the riders would bear down on their victims, impaling them from behind with their spears or slashing and chopping at them with swords and battleaxes.

We will continue with what the *Heimskringla* has to say:

One of the horsemen said, 'Is Earl Toste in this army?'

The earl answered, 'It is not to be denied that ye will find him here'.

The horseman says, 'Thy brother, King Harald (Harold II), sends thee salutation, with the message that thou shalt have the whole of Northumberland; and rather than thou shouldst not submit to him, he will give thee the third part of his kingdom to rule over along with himself'.

The earl replies, 'This is something different from the enmity and scorn he offered last winter; and if this had been offered then it would have saved many a man's life who now is dead and it would have been better for the kingdom of England. But if I accept of this offer, what will he give King Harald Sigurdsson for his trouble?'

The horseman replied, 'He has also spoken of this; and will give him seven feet of English ground or as much more as he may be taller than other men'.

'Then', said the earl, 'go now and tell King Harald [Harold] to get ready for battle; for never shall the Northmen say with truth that Earl Toste left King Harald Sigurdsson to join his enemy's troops, when he came to fight west here in England. We shall rather all take the resolution to die with honour or to gain England by a victory'.

Then the horseman rode back.

King Harald Sigurdsson said to the earl, 'Who was the man who spoke so well?'

The earl replied, 'That was King Harald Godwinson [Harold Godwinsson]'.

'Then', said King Harald Sigurdsson, 'That was by far too long concealed from me; for they had come so near to our army, that this Harald [Harold] should never have carried back the tidings of our men's slaughter'.

Then said the earl, 'It was certainly imprudent for such chiefs and it may be as you say; but I saw he was going to offer me peace and a great dominion and that, on the other hand, I would be his murderer if I betrayed him; and I would rather he should be my murderer than I his, if one of two be to die'.

King Harald Sigurdsson observed to his men, 'That was but a little man, yet he sat firmly in his stirrups'. [Did Harold II use stirrups or was Sturluson speculating without sure knowledge or was the use of this word a mere poetic device?]

It is said that Harald made these verses at this time:—

'Advance! advance!
No helmets glance (not aiming or turning aside or away –
    proceeding with determination),
But blue swords play
In our array.
Advance! advance!
No mail-coats glance (not aiming or turning aside or away –
    proceeding with determination),
But hearts are here
That ne'er knew fear'.

His coat of mail was called Emma; and it was so long that it reached almost to the middle of his leg and so strong that no weapon ever pierced it. Then said King Harald Sigurdsson, 'These verses are but ill composed; I must try to make better;' and he composed the following:—

'In battle storm we seek no lee,
With skulking head and bending knee,
Behind the hollow shield [not committed to the fight].
With eye and hand we fend the head;
Courage and skill stand in the stead
Of panzer [armour], helm and shield,
In hild's [one of the Valkyries – should've been capitalised] bloody field'.
    Thereupon Thiodolf sang:—

'And should our king in battle fall,—
A fate that God may give to all,—
His sons will vengeance take;
And never shone the sun upon
Two nobler eaglet(s) [birds of Jove, which carried the lightning bolts]; in his run,
And them we'll never forsake'.[43]
[In these verses, while we find the reference to the singular of the Christian God, there are also echoes of the pagan mythology and pantheon – Valkyries and Jove – Jupiter.]

In this section of the *Heimskringla* is found the fact that not only is Tostig cast in a positive light but also in the former earl's words a suggestion that King Harold had not been so accommodating or pleasant in the previous winter's negotiations. We also see that King Harald Hardrada was ruthless enough to be willing to violate an informal truce and to comment, '. . . for they had come so near to our army, that this Harald [Harold] should never have carried back the tidings of our men's slaughter'. In other words, had Harald Sigurdsson known who the opposing war leader was when he rode forward to negotiate, he, Harold Godwinsson, would never have made it back to his own battle lines alive. Then, the Norwegian king compliments the King of England by commenting that, though he considered him to be 'a little man' (the Norwegian king himself often being described as a 'giant') his opponent 'sat firmly in his stirrups', for having the personal fortitude to take a great personal risk in riding ahead of his army to negotiate yet one more time with his estranged brother. The next complimentary component of Sturluson's report is the illumination of the fact that Tostig did not alert

Harald Hardrada of Harold Godwinsson's presence, because, 'I would be his murderer if I betrayed him; and I would rather he should be my murderer than I his, if one of two be to die.' However, the relationship, such as it could be described, between the two kings was far from merciful, for the King of England offered the King of Norway merely enough English soil for his burial site.

I think it is time to divert again from the historical account for long enough to comment more on the terrain in the areas of the fighting on that day of 25 September 1066 as I found it to be into this very modern era.

The 'Lay of the Land' and the Progress of the Fighting at the Battle of Stamford Bridge

As mentioned earlier, my visits to the town of Stamford Bridge gave me enough in the way of insights into how the battle was likely fought to encourage me to accept Snorri Sturluson's account in the *Heimskringla*.

Sturluson reported that the Norwegians and their allies were yet on the move when they spotted the arriving Anglo-Saxons. Had the Vikings been at the shores of the River Derwent, as some other writers state, this would not have been likely due to the presence of trees on the river's banks and the fact that the land on the opposite side of the river also rises to gentle bluffs, which would have blocked the advancing English from view. Therefore, the Norwegians had themselves to have been approaching on the ridgetop at Battle Flats to be able to observe the Anglo-Saxons and their dust clouds.

King Harold II, upon seeing the Vikings on the opposite heights, would have sent his mounted men ahead to charge across the ford and prevent the Norwegians from benefitting by opposing a river crossing – always a difficult task for an attacker when faced with an enemy arrayed on the far bank.

While not explicitly stated, King Hardrada again must have sent an advance party to try to hold the bridge and ford while the Vikings set up their ring-shaped shield wall. This would have been done where they had been halted, with the advantage of defending on high ground, with at least a portion of their shield wall at the crest of the heights; but, due to the relatively small size of their army and the extent of the flat land atop the ridge, about one-half of their shield wall would have been on almost the same level as that of the Anglo-Saxon attackers once the English army surrounded the Viking invaders and invested their position all around. Meanwhile, the Anglo-Saxons on horseback would

65

have stormed across the ford, cut down the few Vikings on the river bank, charged upslope and begun encircling and harrying the Norwegians, their allies and the mercenaries evidently hired in Flanders.

With the geography agreeing with Sturluson's account, I now return with even more confidence in that skald's saga.

The 'Historical Record' of the Battle at Stamford Bridge

We have finally reached the all-important point when and where the main battle kicked off, with the *Heimskringla*, #95, 'Of the Beginning of the Battle', which reads:

> Now the battle began. The Englishmen made a hot assault upon the Northmen, who sustained it bravely. It was no easy matter for the English to ride against the Northmen on account of their spears; therefore they rode in a circle around them. And the fight at first was but loose and light, as long as the Northmen kept their order of battle; for although the English rode hard against the Northmen, they gave way again immediately, as they could do nothing against them. Now when the Northmen thought they perceived that the enemy were making but weak assaults, they set after them and would drive them into flight; but when they had broken their shield-rampart the Englishmen rode up from all sides and threw arrows and spears on them . . . [44]

I'll pause here to remark that this reflects some accounts of what would happen later at Battle, near Hastings, two weeks and five days hence. In that I do not believe in coincidences, this may be a distortion or the result of confused reports. Conversely, while the Normans would later be described as attacking along a front, uphill, it is stated here that the Anglo-Saxons 'rode in a circle around them', so this may be a case more of similarity rather than one that is identical.

The *Heimskringla*, #95 continues with:

> Now when King Harald Sigurdsson saw this, he went into the fray where the greatest crash of weapons was and there was a sharp conflict, in which many people fell on both sides. King Harald then was in a rage and ran out in front of the array and hewed down with both hands; so that neither helmet nor armour could withstand him and all who were nearest gave way before him. It

was then very near with the English that they had taken to flight. So says Arnor, the earl's [or the Norwegian king's?] skald:

'Where battle-storm was ringing,
Where arrow-cloud was singing,
Harald stood there,
Of armour bare,
His deadly sword still swinging.
The foeman feel its bite;
His Norsemen rush to fight,
Danger to share,
With Harald there,
Where steel on steel was ringing'.[45]

Next came, not surprisingly in view of the above passages, in the *Heimskringla*, #96, 'The Fall Of King Harald': 'King Harald Sigurdsson was hit by an arrow in the windpipe and that was his death-wound.'[46] This echoes but also does not duplicate the supposed, by some, fate of Harold Godwinsson at the Battle of Hastings, nearly three weeks later, as he is imagined to have been pierced by an arrow through his eye. We'll address that possibility later.

The *Heimskringla*, #96 elaborates:

He fell and all who had advanced with him, except those who retired with the banner. There was afterwards the warmest conflict and Earl Toste had taken charge of the king's banner. They began on both sides to form their array again and for a long time there was a pause in fighting. Then Thiodolf sang these verses:

'The army stands in hushed dismay;
Stilled is the clamour of the fray.
Harald is dead and with him goes
The spirit to withstand our foes.
A bloody scat the folk must pay
For their king's folly on this day.
He fell; and now, without disguise,
We say this business was not wise'.

But before the battle began again Harald Godwinson [Harold Godwinsson] offered his brother, Earl Toste, peace and also quarter to the Northmen who were still alive; but the Northmen called out, all of them together, that they would rather fall, one across the other, than accept of quarter from the Englishmen . . . [47]

This indicates that, despite the triumph of Christianity in the northlands, the tradition of a glorious warrior's death – possibly with illusions of entering Valhalla – was still very much alive on this final day of the Viking era of raiding, pillaging and conquest. We now resume Sturluson's account:

Then each side set up a war-shout and the battle began again. So says Arnor, the earl's [or king's?] skald:

'The king, whose name would ill-doers scare,
The gold-tipped arrow would not spare.
Unhelmed, unpanzered, without shield,
He fell among us in the field.
The gallant men who saw him fall
Would take no quarter; one and all
Resolved to die with their loved king,
Around his corpse in a corpse-ring'.[48]

Then, a bit late, the Viking rescue mission arrived, as told in the *Heimskringla*, #97: 'Skirmish Of Orre'.

Eystein (Östen) Orre came up at this moment from the ships with the men who followed him and all were clad in armour. Then Eystein got King Harald's banner Land-ravager; and now was, for the third time, one of the sharpest of conflicts, in which many Englishmen fell and they were near to taking flight. This conflict is called Orre's storm. Eystein and his men had hastened so fast from the ships that they were quite exhausted and scarcely fit to fight before they came into the battle; but afterwards they became so furious, that they did not guard themselves with their shields as long as they could stand upright . . .[49]

Readers will recall that it is the shield arm that tires more quickly than the sword arm in such combat. Also, evidently the Vikings had few to no mounts remaining as they had been used by at least the leaders of the main body of troops, and the 'rescue force' had most likely run all or almost all, of the way (12.42 miles[50]) 'as the raven flies', from the Viking ships at Riccall to the battle site.

Sturluson goes on:

At last they threw off their coats of ringmail and then the Englishmen could easily lay their blows at them; and many fell from weariness and died without a wound. Thus almost all the chief men fell among the Norway people. This happened towards evening; and then it went, as one might expect, that all had not the same fate, for many fled and were lucky enough to escape in various ways; and darkness fell before the slaughter was altogether ended . . .[51]

There is some corroboration, but not much due to the lack of details, in the accounts of the fight at Stamford Bridge from *The Anglo-Saxon Chronicle*.

What *The Anglo-Saxon Chronicle* Had to Say About the Battle at Stamford Bridge

The English version of events added missing details and confirmed the *Heimskringla's* reports, to a lesser or larger degree, depending on the scepticism of the reader. While the Norse accounts of Sturluson were written 154 years after the fact, those in *The Anglo-Saxon Chronicle* were sometimes written down within days, weeks or months of the events cited; but it could also take up to 15 years for some of the information therein to be compiled and included in the text of some versions. So, while 'contemporary', the *Chronicle's* reports could also suffer from being removed in time and place, but, of course, to a much lesser degree than the *Heimskringla*.

To avoid repetition of events already covered, we'll start twenty lines down in the longest entry for 1066 from the version at the Ingram translation – a collation of all nine versions: 'Then (prior to the invasion by King Harald Hardrada and Earl Tostig, but in anticipation of the assault by Duke William) came King Harold to Sandwich, where he awaited his fleet; for it was long ere it could be collected: but when it was assembled, he went into the Isle of Wight and there lay all the summer and the autumn. There was also a land-force every where by the sea, though it availed nought in the end . . .'[52] I believe this comment refers not just to the guarding of the English south coast but also to the failed resistance by an Anglo-Saxon force at 'Hellornes', (Holderness) following Harald Hardrada's destruction of Scarborough.[53] The final remark also likely speaks to the later inability of the English fleet to intercept the Norman invasion force at sea, that October.

By then, time had run out for the forces along the Sussex coast as supplies dwindled and the Fyrd had to be released due to the expiration of its term of service and, for some, to bring in and/or process the fall harvest. 'It was now the nativity of St Mary, when the provisioning of the men began; and no man could keep them there any longer. They therefore had leave to go home: and the king rode up [to London] . . .'[54] Next is the mention of the first of the disasters to befall the English forces that year: '. . . and the ships were driven to London; but many perished ere they came thither'.[55] So, evidently, the fleet was partially destroyed by storms.

The Anglo-Saxon Chronicle then reports on the arrival of the Vikings: 'When the [surviving] ships were come home [to London], then came Harald, King of Norway, north into the Tine, unawares, with a very great sea-force—no small one; that might be, with three hundred ships or more; and Earl Tosty came to him with all those that he had got; just as they had before said: and they both then went up with all the fleet along the Ouse toward York . . .'[56] This adds some details to and confirms Sturluson's accounts and we'll continue: 'When it was told King Harold in the south, after he had come from the ships, that Harald, King of Norway and Earl Tosty were come up near York, then went he northward by day and night, as soon as he could collect his army. But, ere King Harold could come thither, the Earls Edwin and Morkar had gathered from their earldoms as great a force as they could get and fought with the enemy.'[57] Still in confirmation mode, the *Chronicle* once more validates the *Heimskringla* and, again, we go back to the English record: 'They made a great slaughter too; but there was a good number of the English people slain and drowned and put to flight: and the Northmen had possession of the field of battle . . .'[58] This is the second major loss of military power experienced by the Anglo-Saxons during the campaign against the Norwegians – at Fulford and after losing part of their fleet to storms and also in suffering a defeat by land forces near Holderness.

The *Chronicle*'s reports go on:

It was then told Harold, king of the English, that this had thus happened. And this fight was on the eve of St Matthew the apostle, which was Wednesday. Then after the fight went Harold [*sic* – this should read 'Harald'], King of Norway and Earl Tosty into York with as many followers as they thought fit; and having procured hostages and provisions from the city, they proceeded to their ships and proclaimed full friendship, on condition that all would go southward with them and gain this land. In the midst of this came Harold, king of the English, with all his army, on the Sunday, to Tadcaster; where he collected his fleet. Thence he proceeded on Monday throughout York. But Harald, King of Norway and Earl Tosty, with their forces, were gone from their ships beyond York to Stanfordbridge; for that it was given them to understand, that hostages would be brought to them there from all the shire. Thither came Harold, king of the English, unawares against them beyond the bridge; and they closed together there and continued long in the day fighting very severely . . .[59]

This, too, confirms that the Anglo-Saxons surprised the Norwegians, 'beyond the bridge'.

The *Chronicle* then reports: 'There was slain Harald the Fair-hair'd, King of Norway and Earl Tosty and a multitude of people with them, both of Normans [*sic* – this obviously means 'Northmen' instead] and English; and the Normans [Northmen] that were left fled from the English, who slew them hotly behind; until some came to their ships, some were drowned, some burned to death and thus variously destroyed; so that there was little left: and the English gained possession of the field . . .'[60] All is in agreement with the *Heimskringla*, which could be taken as another confirmation of the truth of the Icelandic account or as an indication that Sturluson and/or his sources were taking at least some of their own information from *The Anglo-Saxon Chronicle*.

The next passage seems out of sequence with the above, but I think it should be prefaced, at least in our minds, with 'Beforehand' or 'Meanwhile':

But there was one of the Norwegians who withstood the English folk, so that they could not pass over the bridge, nor complete the victory. An Englishman aimed at him with a javelin, but it availed nothing. Then came another under the bridge, who pierced him terribly inwards under the coat of mail. And Harold, king of the English, then came over the bridge, followed by his army; and there they made a great slaughter, both of the Norwegians and of the Flemings . . .[61]

While the above entries in *The Anglo-Saxon Chronicle* are also confirmatory regarding the accounts in Sturluson's saga, at least in my not-very-sceptical view, they omit the many references in the *Heimskringla* to the Anglo-Saxons being on horseback with even a part of their army.

71

These could have been omissions or, to the writer(s) of the *Chronicle*, they could be unimportant details; and it is the omission of details throughout that often plagues the *Chronicle*'s entries, as well as those in many other ancient and medieval works. However, I believe I've stated my argument regarding the English fighting on horseback in this case adequately earlier, so no further advocacy is needed about that now.

The Consequences of the Battle at Stamford Bridge

The Anglo-Saxon Chronicle then skips ahead to deal with the aftermath of the battle, which had been the third episode in the multiple calamities inflicted on English arms up until the ninth month of 1066. This is reported in both the *Chronicle* and the *Heimskringla*. The English account says there were slain 'a multitude of people with them, both of Normans [Northmen] and English'.[62] The Sturluson version says '. . . and now was, for the third time, one of the sharpest of conflicts, in which many Englishmen fell . . .'[63] The cumulative effects of losing so many fighting men, including those who manned the ships lost at sea, would prove a decisive detriment in the upcoming battle with the Normans, just 19 days later, near Hastings.

The *Chronicle* then adds more details to the sparing report in the *Heimskringla*, which says, in the final sentence of #97: 'Olaf Haraldson had not gone on land with the others and when he heard of his father's fall he made ready to sail away with the men who remained.'[64]

The *Chronicle* elaborates:

> But Harold let the king's [the Scottish king, Malcom III] son, Edmund, go home to Norway [*sic* – this should be 'Scotland'], with all the ships. He also gave quarter to Olave, the Norwegian king's son and to their bishop and to the earl of the Orkneys and to all those that were left in the ships; who then went up to our king and took oaths that they would ever maintain faith and friendship unto this land. Whereupon the King let them go home with twenty-four ships. These two general battles were fought within five nights . . .[65]

So, here we see that of the northern invasion force of about 300 Norwegian ships, plus an unknown number belonging to the force sailing with the former earl Tostig, just about two dozen were enough to carry all that remained of the surviving Viking and allied warriors and the nobles and their retainers, attendants and personal body guards and the ships' sailors, away from England. If we assume that the original fleet carried

72

some 7,000 to 10,000 people – we'll reckon on the higher number – and if we divide that number by 300, we find an average of about 33 people aboard each craft. If it only took 24 ships to carry the survivors away, the total number of remaining invaders would have been just under 800 (792). The attacking Viking army, which reportedly amounted to about one-half of the able-bodied fighting men in Norway[‡] for that portion who were Norwegian warriors, meant that country retained barely enough military force to act as a home guard after the Battle of Stamford Bridge. The annihilation of the Norwegian army and the losses imposed on their Viking allies from Denmark and outlying islands spelled the end of the Viking Age of raiding, pillaging and conquests. Henceforth, Viking seafarers would become explorers, harvesters of oceanic resources such as walrus ivory, and merchants, traders and mercenaries ranging as far as Constantinople. From 1066 onward, Europeans would owe a generally unacknowledged debt of gratitude to the Anglo-Saxon King Harold II and the Anglo-Saxon men-at-arms, for guaranteeing their safety from any further depredations by Scandinavia's Viking plunderers.

King Harold II and the Anglo-Saxons Must Face the Southern Invasion

The *Heimskringla*, #99, 'Of William The Bastard', continues:

> When the Earl of Rouen, William the Bastard [soon to be known as 'The Conqueror'], heard of his relation, King Edward's, death and also that Harald Godwinson [*sic*] was chosen, crowned and consecrated king of England, it appeared to him that he had a better right to the kingdom of England than Harald, by reason of the relationship between him and King Edward. He thought, also, that he had grounds for avenging the affront that Harald had put upon him with respect to his daughter. From all these grounds William gathered together a great army in Normandy and had many men and sufficient transport-shipping.[66]

This passage seems reasonable enough and is supported by 'Master Wace',[67] but, there follows an entirely fanciful account in the *Heimskringla*,

---

[‡] 'King Harald sent a message-token through all Norway and ordered out a levy of one-half of all the men in Norway able to carry arms', *Heimskringla*, #82.

which damages its overall credibility, but which may be the product of some Viking jealousy as it is certainly not supported by any evidence or historical records: 'The day that he [Duke William] rode out of the castle to his ships and had mounted his horse, his wife came to him and wanted to speak with him; but when he saw her he struck at her with his heel and set his spurs so deep into her breast that she fell down dead; and the earl rode on to his ships and went with his ships over to England'.[68] In fact, his wife, Matilda, whom he married in 1053, outlived William. Sturluson continues: 'His brother, Archbishop Otto [Odo], was with him; and when the earl [Duke William] came to England he began to plunder and take possession of the land as he came along. Earl [Duke] William was stouter and stronger than other men; a great horseman and warrior, but somewhat stern; and a very sensible man, but not considered a man to be relied on.'[69] The very unfavourable view of Duke William in the Norse sagas is contrasted with his introduction in *The Anglo-Saxon Chronicle*, which continues with the next sentence after the passage quoted above, as follows: 'Meantime Earl [Duke] William came up from Normandy into Pevensey on the eve of St Michael's mass; and soon after his landing was effected, they constructed a castle at the port of Hastings.'[70] This is very mild and sketchy treatment for a character of such historical import, but, since it was also recorded post-Conquest, perhaps the Anglo-Saxon scribe was pulling his punches with an eye toward possible retribution from the new, Norman rulers of England, for not adhering to the new rulers' party line.

Before turning to my investigations of and theories about the third, and most important, of the three battle of 1066, it is time to take a look at what others have said in their interpretations of the evidence – written 'historical records' – such as they are, in artistic representations and the physical facts of the geography and terrain. Initially, we will present a relatively brief overview of some competing ideas regarding the actual location of the Battle of Hastings before continuing on with the presentation of the facts, as I found, interpreted and re-interpreted them. After that, we will resume where we have left off here, with usually brief and incidental revisitings of the concepts of other observers and investigators of the decisive battle on the Hastings peninsula, on Saturday, 14 October 1066. Later, I will summarise some of the observations of these other writers that, in my view, actually reinforce, rather than disprove, my conjectures and conclusions.

Chapter 6

The Battle of Hastings – What Others Have Had to Say About its Actual Location

While I was unaware of it at the time, in part due to the fact that I wished to not be influenced by the theories of others, I was initially ignorant of the existence of three important, competing books on the subject of the location of the Battle of Hastings. Then, I was alerted to that fact by John Grehan, of Pen and Sword Books, who is also a co-author of one of those works and who graciously extended to me the benefit of his wisdom and his kind advice in assisting me in rendering this book into its final, more publishable form. The three books in question are: *The Battle of Hastings at Sedlescombe* by Jonathan Starkey and Michael Starkey; *Secrets of the Norman Invasion* by Nick Austin; and *The Battle of Hastings, 1066: The Uncomfortable Truth – Revealing the True Location of England's Most Famous Battle* by John Grehan and Martin Mace.

I will begin by critiquing the contents of these books in order to set the stage for introducing my own, conflicting theory regarding the site of the Battle of Hastings. I will then present my case, while including material relating to my interesting and enjoyable quest in the English countryside and among the very hospitable English people. As I seek to establish a firm basis for my own views, I will – perhaps ironically, perhaps not – rely on some of the contents of these other books where they, in my opinion, bolster the assertions I am making herein regarding the actual, factual location of the Battle of Hastings.

Of these books, I found the volume by the Starkey brothers to be the least convincing, followed by the second – by Nick Austin; then, while closest to mine with regard the site of the battle, I found the last – by

Messrs Grehan and Mace – to be the most acceptable, other than my own, of course. So, I think it is best to begin with *The Battle of Hastings at Sedlescombe* by Jonathan and Michael Starkey.

A major reason I found the Starkeys' book less than convincing is that in order to prove their case that the 'Hastings' battle was actually the 'Sedlescombe' battle, they therefore had to move not only the site of the battle itself but also of the events leading up to it – the landing place of the Normans, their pre-battle manoeuvring and encampments, the approach of King Harold and the Anglo-Saxons and, finally, the 'true' battlefield's location. To achieve their ends, the Starkeys first had to cast doubt on the early accounts by several of the medieval sources and to then claim that the Norman fleet did not put their army ashore at Pevensey and then Hastings, but, instead, the debarkation site was in the then deep estuary of the River Brede – at Winchelsea, to be precise, which is some 17.58 miles east-north-east of Pevensey and 7.56 miles from Hastings, 'as the raven flies', but, of course, is a bit farther along the overall gently curving coastline along that part of south-south-eastern England.

To try to 'prove' their theory, the Starkeys attempt also to contradict almost all of the early accounts regarding the fact that Duke William – soon to become William the Conqueror – set up a subsequent base at the site of the present-day city of Hastings – at Hastings Castle, to be exact. They take this effort by trying to show that when all of the early writers and reporters on the Norman invasion wrote 'Hastings', they instead meant 'Hastings port'; and the Starkeys then proceed to further assert that 'Hastings port' was not at today's Hastings but was somewhere else – in the Brede Estuary. It is time to get to some specifics.

On pages 40 to 45, as elsewhere throughout their book, the Starkeys resort to too many ambiguities regarding clearly establishing if Hastings was recorded in historical accounts as being a region, peninsula or port site. The authors leap to too many unfounded conclusions regarding supposed uncertainties in those medieval reports – some of which are forced upon the old writings by the Starkey brothers' own interpretations and re-interpretations with absent or scanty supporting or corroborating evidence.

The authors also take the stand that the Battle of Hastings was reported as being 9 miles from Hastings (presumably the current city and castle when that is convenient to their argument), when most other sources and observers place the fighting about 6 or 6.5 miles from those fixed locations. This brings to the fore another question regarding the distance from the port and castle to the site of the fighting. The straight-line distance, as the raven flies, from Hastings to Battle is 5.76 statute miles or 5.01 nautical miles or 9.28km.[1] The trek, mostly along the A2100 (the ancient ridgeway) route, is longer – about 6.3 miles via Battle Road / the B2159 and the A2100.[2] Therefore, it seems that if, as most people, including this writer, believe, the Normans advanced from the generally accepted site of Hastings port / Hastings Castle – at or near where they stand today – Duke William's army would have almost exactly matched the distance in their march as reported by various medieval sources.

However, the ridgetop route from Hastings Castle to Battle starts out along the Old London Road, until it meets the current B2093, which is also known as 'The Ridge' and, later, as 'The Ridge Way'; so, the route-of-march that would adhere to the highest point of the local terrain would have gone this way, via the Saint Helen's area and then along the B2093 until Baldslow, where one could branch off toward London by way of the A21 or proceed to Battle Hill along the A2100. This diverging ridgeway route is about 22,000ft from the castle to the junction of the A21 and the A2100; whereas the more direct, but lower in altitude, avenue would be along today's A21 near the castle to the branching-off of the A2100, about 12,000ft. The 'extra' 10,000ft represent about another two miles. It is this bit of a roundabout but tactically advantageous route that I believe Duke William would have had his army follow in order to be on the high ground should they have encountered King Harold's army while on the march. This reckoning of the distances from Hastings to Battle Abbey and other locations does not disprove the findings of the early and many later observers; it merely cautions us as to an over-reliance on measuring times and distances based on more modern, preferred routes of travel in opposition to the more likely, to me, desire by the Duke of Normandy to have his army on the high ground whenever possible, including his erecting the fort on Hastings heights and encamping his army, which I believe was at the road / pathway junctions at and near Baldslow and Beauport Park.

On page 46, among other places in the book, the writers take issue with spelling idiosyncrasies and particularities in many of the original source texts as they parse words in an effort to deny the mass of contemporary or near-contemporary reports that the Norman fleet made landfall at Pevensey. They also try to shift the actual historic site of the Norman landing to the Brede Estuary, at a conjectured harbour entrance there postulated as having been near or at the present-day Winchelsea Beach – some 17.5 miles (15.28 nautical miles, 28.3km) east-north-east, in a straight line, from Pevensey to Winchelsea proper.[3] This, obviously, is quite a stretch. However, in the end, the Starkeys cannot disprove the continuing existence of the Roman fort at Pevensey, which the Normans were reported to have further fortified with a prefabricated wooden 'castle' they quickly assembled from a portable 'kit'.

Also here, as on other pages in their book, the Starkeys err in guessing that so many early accounts were drastically wrong as they insist on very precise place-name spellings and overly elaborate descriptions. In this, the writers conveniently overlook the fact that spelling conventions varied considerably even just within the Anglo-Saxon, Latin and/or Old French languages – and even more so with regard to one another; and descriptions in the old texts were often to usually to almost always sketchy at best, with just one or two remarks, clues and/or specifics mentioned in order to save precious writing materials. One only has to look at the Bayeux Tapestry, as I have, in Bayeux, Normandy, to see that plainly embroidered on it is the word 'Pevensey', rendered as 'P-E-V-E-N-S-E-Y', to indicate the true Norman landing site.

The Starkeys resort far too often to conjecture based on suppositions, assumptions, interpretations or, worse still, re-interpretations based on few to no objective facts – blurring the boundaries between what actually exists with their preconceived notions and almost religious devotion to an overall theory that has a tenuous and unstable foundation. In all of this, contrary and actual, factual evidence is too often discounted or outright ignored. For example, they contend that Pevensey was not a port location due to the lack of roads at the site, yet the map they cite, which appears on page 12 of their own book, shows an ancient road leading right up to the old Roman fort located there.

On page 55, in the item listed as '#3', that paragraph attempts to shift attention to four possible alternate sites for Hastings port; but the vicinity of Hastings port was not thoroughly or properly discounted or disproven earlier or later in the book. Then, on pages 56 and 57 the authors try to further shift the location even farther – to Winchelsea, based on supposed ship levies on coastal or port towns that were imposed in the year 1227 – 161 years after the Conquest; but they do not acknowledge that ship levies on towns and regions were made on the basis of wealth and population, not seacoast locations – ship levies were made even on cities and areas deep inland.

With regard to the lattermost above, the ship levies on Winchelsea were first tabulated and listed by the Starkeys as a combined total with regard to Hastings port, then separately; they can't be both. On page 58, the first paragraph says that 1227 is 140 years after 1066; it is, in fact, 161 years later. This is but one small example of too many oversights and errors in the book that are in opposition to actual facts. Again in

1. This is Duke William's impressive fortress in Falaise, Normandy. The author has benefitted from an unplanned weight-loss regimen after just five weeks, out of eight, of hikes at historical sites in England, from the south-east coast to Hadrian's Wall. A very accommodating family of German tourists, using the author's camera, took the photo.

2. Where the Viking fleet beached at Riccall, looking south-west. The Vikings would have begun beaching their 325 ships here, then farther along the east shore of the River Ouse as far as today's 'Landing Lane', where the Norwegian King Harald Hardrada, and King Harold Godwinsson's brother, the former Earl Tostig, are thought to have come ashore.

3. Fulford Marsh along the River Ouse. This flooded area is not as deep as it seems, particularly at low tide. The Norse *Heimskringla* ('Chronicle of the Kings of Norway') tells us that the Vikings flanked and outflanked the Anglo-Saxons at the ford and along Germany Beck by wading across here, then bursting out from the woods ahead and to the right.

4. The Viking side at Fulford. Looking west along the glacial moraine on the south or 'Viking' side of Germany Beck. The beck (small stream) is on the right. Straight ahead in the distance (past the clump of trees in mid-frame), the ford, and just beyond and to the right, the woods from which the Vikings erupted, outflanking the Anglo-Saxons. This caused the Anglo-Saxons who would have been in the shield wall in the foreground to turn and flee to save themselves.

5. Shallows at Stamford Bridge ford. Looking upstream from where the bridge likely stood in 1066, scores of yards east-north-east of today's more modern bridge. It is here that the Anglo-Saxons swarmed across, some on foot, others on horseback.

6. The old and crumbling castle at Pevensey, built upon the ruins of an ancient Roman fort, is where Duke William and his nobles and knights spent their first night in England. It is roomy enough inside the walls to also shelter the horses, while the bulk of the army would have camped all around, where the ships were beached.

7. This huge old tree in St Mary's Tract was likely broken in half by the occasional powerful storms to strike southern England. Tropical storms have made landfall in south-east England in 2004, 2006, 2008 and 2021.

8. The author stands at about the spot where, as tradition has it, Duke William stood as he directed the battle. Battle Abbey is visible on the ridgetop in the background. Unfortunately for many historians, and English Heritage, the battle actually took place off-camera – to the right, with only the final phase, where the Norman knights drowned in the 'Malfosse', taking place about where the author stands.

9. The leaves, pollen, dust, and twigs floating atop the flooded areas along the lower reaches of the trail around the traditionally-accepted battlefield make them seem to be solid ground, until one approaches very closely, and crouches down to observe the 'forest floor', as the author did when taking this photograph.

10. This is the gate on Powdermill Lane, looking toward where the author stood on the historically reckoned battle site. However, as the author shows in the text, the battle was actually fought to the rear of where this photo was taken.

11. The author not only found an ancient (hoar), twisted, struggling apple tree near where King Harold fell, in St Mary's Tract, he harvested about a dozen apples and shared them with his flatmates at the University of Sussex. (They were tangy and a bit sweet – not as sour as anticipated.)

12. The 'scenic meadows' break up the woods on both sides of the valley now holding the Southeastern Railway line. It is believed by some, including the author, that 'Scenic Meadow', or 'Scean Leagh' (Anglo-Saxon for 'scenic meadow') was corrupted to form what the Normans called 'Senlac', a name now assigned to 'Battle Hill.'

13. This was but one of many huge old trees the author encountered in St Mary's Tract, near to the A2100 and continuing near the Southeastern Railway line, where the Anglo-Saxon shield wall held the 'fosse,' or fortified 'ditch' until late in the battle, when the Normans at last broke through and won the day.

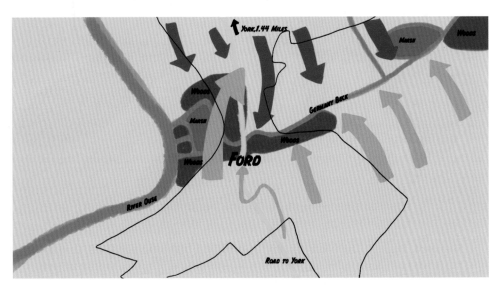

MAP 1

Fulford: The armies meet at Germany Beck. The Vikings seem to be checked. The Anglo-Saxons press the attack at the ford, where the Vikings briefly turn back while their main thrust – along the River Ouse, across the marsh and into the woods on their left – breaks through and bursts from the woods. Not shown: the Anglo-Saxon army is surprised, outflanked, routed, and hastily retreats to the relative safety of the walls of York. The outline shows the municipal limits of today's Fulford.

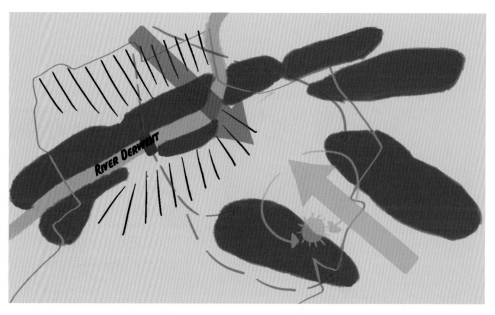

RIVER DERWENT

MAP 2

Stamford Bridge: The Viking army approaches from the south-east on the heights when they see the Anglo-Saxons rapidly advancing from the north-west on the high ground across the River Derwent.

Seeing that he is being attacked by a large force, the king of the Vikings sends an advance guard to block the bridge while the Viking army and its allies form a hedgehog defence on the heights, at what is now known as Battle Flats.

King Harold sends his mounted men in a dash across the ford just upstream from the bridge, along with the main body of infantry, while he accompanies a mounted column as they attack the bridge. There, after a brief struggle, King Harold and the second mounted group complete the encirclement of the Vikings.

Not shown: The Anglo-Saxons and Vikings engage in a bitter, drawn-out fight, reducing and eliminating the Viking army, killing Earl Tostig and King Harald Hardrada of Norway. Then, too late, a Viking relief force arrives, only to be defeated in turn. As dusk falls, the Anglo-Saxons pursue the few surviving Vikings all the way back to their ships, beached at Riccall.

The outline shows the town limits of modern Stamford Bridge.

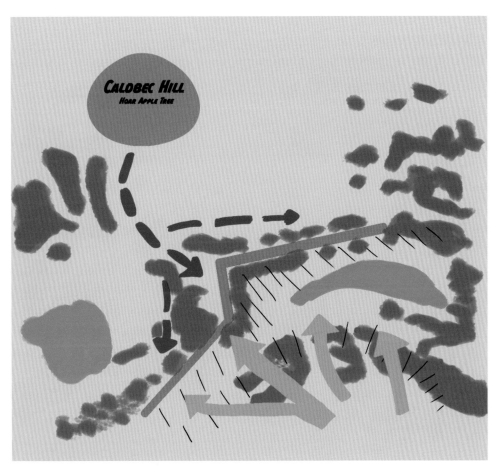

MAP 3

Hastings, Phase One: Each side being aware of the presence of the enemy, advances – the Normans from the south-east along the Hastings-to-London ridgetop road; the Anglo-Saxons from the north-west at their rallying point near 'the hoar apple tree' on Caldbec Hill.

The Anglo-Saxon 'shield wall' blocks the road as the Normans fan out, discovering that their flanking movements are blocked by marshes to the east, and a ravine to the west, which the Anglo-Saxons have 'fortified' with sharpened stakes driven into the ground along the top of the slope on the northern edge of the narrow valley there.

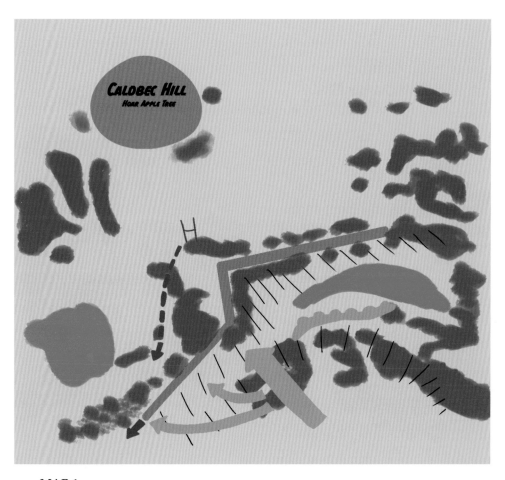

MAP 4

Hastings, Phase Two: The Norman right flank remains checked behind marshes while the Norman main body is also stalled by a stout Anglo-Saxon defence on the ridgeway; but the Norman heavy infantry and cavalry press the attack on the left, across the 'fosse' or fortified 'ditch' (narrow, steep-sided valley or ravine). Seeing the threat, King Harold shifts from his initial command position on the high point just south of what is now the Marley Lane traffic circle, and advances into the present-day St Mary's tract. As he does so, he sends reinforcements – likely including many of his personal guards, his Huscarls – to fortify and extend the Anglo-Saxon battle lines toward the south-west.

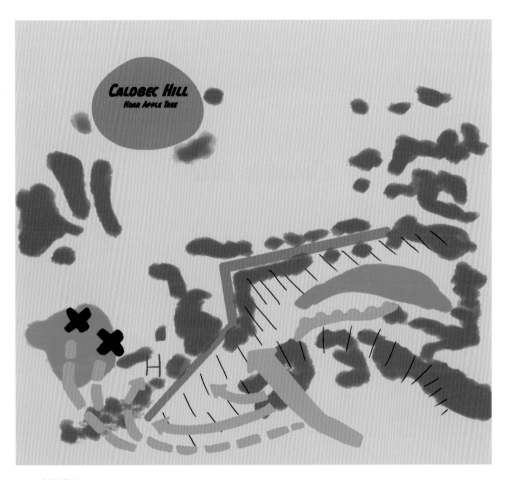

MAP 5

Hastings, Phase Three: The Norman heavy infantry and cavalry – after an all-day fight of repeated attacks – finally break through. Some of the cavalry swings wide, coming to grief in the flooded terrain at the southern edge of what has been the historically-accepted battlefield site below Battle Abbey. Meanwhile, Duke William and other knights close in and kill King Harold. Not shown: As evening falls, the Anglo-Saxons try to mount a last stand, likely at the present day St Mary's Church, across from Battle Abbey, as the scattered survivors flee, many of whom are pursued and killed by Norman cavalry.

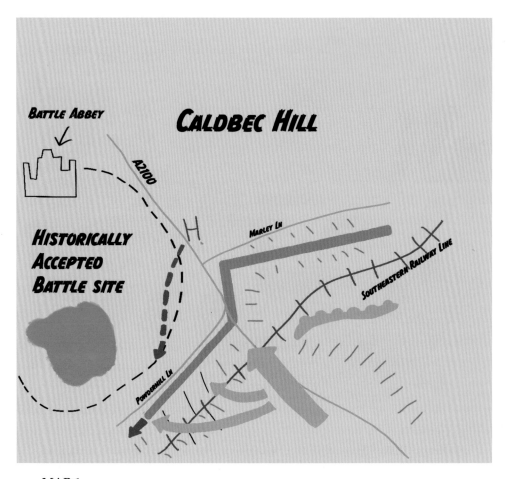

MAP 6

Hastings Today: The deployments of the armies are shown in relation to a few modern features of the town of Battle.

the same paragraph the text completely contradicts prior statements regarding the location of the supposed Norman landing place and port by citing the *inadequacy* of Winchelsea as a port!

Page 59 then goes on to reverse the claims made just one page earlier by stating that Hastings, which the authors sometimes deny was in fact a medieval port at all, had a capacity of 15 ships and that the Winchelsea 'port' had a projected ability to handle 115 ships!

The few examples above barely go beyond the surface in demonstrating that all through the book the authors resort to speculative and vague terminology to cast doubt on traditionally accepted views that others regard as fact, using terms such as, 'perhaps', 'might', 'could have', 'sounds like', 'suggests', 'implies', to be almost immediately followed by an imperative declaration that an alternative view put forward in their own theories therefore '*must* be', etc. But, meanwhile, they have not adequately refuted the contentions of other observers who have written on the subject of the Battle of Hastings for up to about 950 years. Such avowals merely assume the existence of 'facts' that were not introduced as evidence or are not adequately supported by the same. For example, on page 69 the authors cannot prove but only presume that the Romans had cut a breach in the spit that blocked entry to the then – some 600 years earlier – closed (to sea traffic) Brede Estuary, but, if the Romans had *not* done so and had the spit reasserted itself in the intervening centuries, then Winchelsea indeed could not have been the port of Hastings or even any sort of port at all.

On page 70, with regard to the existence, development and history of Rye, there is again far too much speculation without any proof of anything offered and with numerous sentences starting with 'Perhaps'. It is all far too excessively speculative to support any viable assertions regarding the existence of a port there in 1066 or soon after or not . . .

The authors concede, on page 76, in their attempt to move the medieval reports of the Norman landing at Pevensey to opposite Winchelsea, that in the first edition of their book they thought Duke William's fighters had first come ashore instead at Rye. However, in either case, the Pevensey landing-site was never adequately disproved. The vast majority, if not all, reports dating from medieval times state that the Norman force came ashore at Pevensey, not in the Brede Estuary.

On page 80, in the first paragraph the writers declare: 'None of the candidate landing sites has the surviving remains of a fort'. However, there *is* a ruined Roman fort – at Pevensey! I visited and walked within this ancient fortification myself and I estimate that it could have easily sheltered up to several hundred men and their horses – enough to provide cover for Duke William, his allied barons and their immediate entourages of knights, sergeants, servants and retainers. The ruined portion of the walls near the entrance would have been the place to erect the prefabricated wooden fort, providing adequate protection while forces inside were being mustered to repel, for example, a surprise assault and while the bulk of the Norman army that was encamped outside the fortifications and aboard ships, held off any attackers.

Despite a medieval report that an Anglo-Saxon knight witnessed the Norman landings from the foot of a sea cliff, the Starkeys deny that any such cliffs exist when they do, in fact – at Hastings. While Hastings Castle is 10.45 miles from Pevensey, a Norman fleet of from 700 and up to 3,000 ships going ashore would have been plainly visible from even below the heights at Hastings.

On page 11, in the last sentence the writers contend that the Anglo-Saxons could have approached the Hastings Peninsula area via many different routes, including the most direct, driest – along the ancient road cited at a website that, ironically, posits that the Battle of Hastings was actually fought at or near Netherfield.[4] The pertinent passage from that website: 'An 1878 map [not cited*] shows a road with a milestone present in Ashes Wood, which read '55 miles to London' and 3 miles to Ashburnham. We know that the coastline was much closer to the Netherfield area in 1066 and that the estuary came very close to Ashburnham. This road would thus seem to have been the quickest route north from Ashburnham . . .'[5] Such a road would have led to the ridgeway along the current A271, which merges into the North Trade Road, leading directly to the Anglo-Saxon rallying point at Caldbec Hill and then to what is to me the true site of the Battle of Hastings, just off the historically accepted location on the grounds of Battle Abbey.

Regarding that last sentence on page 11 of the Starkey brothers' book: 'Alternatively, there was probably a route around the river on ancient ridgeways via Netherfield.' So, here, again, the Starkeys admit that an alternate route existed; and, moreover, they also concede on this page that there were many alternatives to reach the Hastings Peninsula, to which I add: this (aforementioned) ridgeway route led to London; Duke William could have planned to divert from the Hastings peninsula ridgeway onto the old Roman road toward Rother, then east toward Canterbury and Dover – until he learned the Anglo-Saxons

---

* However, by inspecting a topological map of southern England, it is possible to trace the likely routes and ridgeway roads in use since pre-medieval times.

were massing on Caldbec Hill. He probably would have changed his plans, in part, because of his potential adversaries possibly threatening Normandy and, therefore, his need to conquer England quickly, so he would have chosen to fight at Battle Hill rather than to march farther east at that time.

In the first paragraph of page 13 of their book, the Starkey brothers cite the first two maps therein, showing the many ridgeways existing on and around the Hastings Peninsula in 1066, including the ridgetop route from Hastings to Battle Hill. Note that while his army was probably arriving from different directions, King Harold could have himself instead taken a route less convenient for a large armed force, such as via the proposed ferry crossing over the Rother, whether or not he attended a pre-battle council at Appledore. However, both King Harold and his army would have preferred the ridgetop route, not the Rother way, due to the sogginess of the ground, then and now.

However, prior to all of this, in contradiction to all of the subsequent wordage devoted to trying to refute the facts of the Norman fleet putting in to Pevensey Bay (it was a deep estuary and lagoon in 1066), on page 18, in the second paragraph, the authors concede, illogically if you ask me, that, 'In retrospect, we now think it really does not matter where the Normans landed . . .' In reality, this *does* matter *very much*, both with regard to the arguments of the Starkeys and also the theories put forth by Nick Austin, as we will see shortly, for, again, the Starkeys' entire case rests on the Normans landing in, then setting up their base in the Brede Estuary. Without a Norman landing in the Brede Estuary and a subsequent encampment there, Duke William's army would not have found itself advancing toward the supposed Anglo-Saxon approach from across the Rother River and there would not have been a 'Battle of Hastings at Sedlescombe'. In short, the Starkeys simply do not realistically and therefore convincingly make their case.

Other than the unsupported assertions by the Starkeys, there are no reliable reports, particularly in the early source materials, for the Normans to have landed in the Brede Estuary. Pevensey had a sheltered bay, an isolated and at least partly intact Roman fort and was an excellent rallying point as it was easy place to spot and navigate or march toward or from, as Duke William had them do the following day.

With regard to pages 22 and 23 of their book, the Starkeys do *not* refute the Pevensey and Hastings landings. In fact, they perhaps unintentionally support those landfalls because Hastings was and is at the foot of cliffs, mentioned earlier. Also, there was, and is, a cleft in the

81

ridge that extends out to sea and below water there. We will revisit this fact shortly.

The isolated initial landing site at the old Roman fort in the Pevensey Estuary was ideal for marshalling the entire invasion force prior to sailing across and riding around Pevensey Bay to Hastings. Just as the Anglo-Canadian landings at Gold, Sword and Juno Beaches in Normandy in 1944 were only the initial landing sites, with the rallying points and objectives being ashore and inland – at Ouistreham and Caen, and Bayeux, St Lô and St Mère-Église for the Americans advancing from Omaha and Utah Beaches. (The author had the pleasure of staying in Caen while visiting Bayeux, Falaise and Omaha Beach while researching this book; battle damage from that fighting was still visible in the area, as of 2016.)

With regard to pages 24 and 25 of the Starkeys' work, their declarations on these pages ignore the presence of the Roman fort, the limited routes of access for potential attackers and the ease of re-embarkation for points east once the entire invasion force had rallied there, as, again, was done the next day in 1066.

The Starkeys claim that Duke William did not know that the Anglo-Saxon garrison at Pevensey had been called away, as they say on page 20; but he had excellent intelligence sources and probably would have been well informed. Overall, Duke William can be observed to be an astute and capable military commander; he would have been apprised of the lack of defensive troops ashore even before initially embarking on his invasion from Normandy.

On page 25 the Starkeys' arguments against a landing at either the Bourne Estuary or Priory Valley end up favouring an opening landing at Pevensey. Moreover, the objections regarding winds and possible navigation errors also argue in favour of a Pevensey landing site. Additionally, a seabed survey[6] of the coast off Hastings and below Hastings Castle shows cloven rock ledges extending out to sea that could have – given the rise in sea level and/or lowered coastline over the past 950+ years – formed protected inlets in 1066. Furthermore, with regard to possible rough seas and high winds, asserted by the Starkeys, the same seabed report states that the portion of coast at and just eastward of Hastings (for but a couple of miles) is not a high-impact tidal, surf and, presumably, wind zone: 'This is a low energy area, characterised by the lack of bedforms and wave and tide data. Tidal stream data offshore of Hastings indicates that the peak spring flow is classified as weak (< 1 knot) and the shoreline is moderately exposed.'[7] The maps on pages 29 to 33 of this report give added substance to the report's text – that Hastings as a port site was *not* frequently endangered by high winds and rough seas.[8]

However, not all of the Starkeys' observations lack merit. On pages 18 and 19 of their book they reach what I judge to be valid conclusions in connection with the tactical considerations and techniques of the Normans, but these, paradoxically, could be applied just as well to the generally accepted and oft-reported (in original sources) landing site at Pevensey and the following Norman base at the location of the current town and castle at Hastings.

In view of the fact that the Starkeys did not make what was to me a convincing argument against an initial Norman landing at Pevensey and move to Hastings the next day, and in that they did not clearly establish on a firm basis their contention that Duke William's army landed in the Brede Estuary, with a following set of circumstances that would have led to a battle at Sedlescombe, I think it is best to move on now and analyse some of the contentions of Mr Nick Austin in his book *Secrets of the Norman Invasion*, in which he attempts to place the Hastings battle nearer to the officially recognised site of the Battle of Hastings, specifically at the village of Crowhurst.

Already, in the introduction to his book, Mr Austin states his desire to preserve certain tracts of real estate in his adopted hometown of Crowhurst, which is the primary motivating factor in creating and putting forward his theory. What stems from this noble aspiration is an attempt to fit 'historical facts' into a preconceived design and to mould said 'historical facts' – such as they are – to implement this programme. As we have seen, the Starkey brothers' belief is that the Normans landed in the Brede Estuary, east-north-east of Hastings. Nick Austin takes the supposed landing site in almost the opposite direction – to the west-north-west of Hastings, but not so far away – just a couple of miles – at the present-day Bulverhythe.

In attempting to shift the places of the initial Norman landing and their follow-on move to Hastings the succeeding day to different locales, Mr Austin commits the same errors as the Starkey brothers. As of page 27, the author's exacting and particularistic parsing of language, reports, referred-to details in the early texts and the Bayeux Tapestry, with regard to their being slightly or even significantly vague or only partially accurate demand a manner and persistence of correctness imposed on later and more modern accounts that did not exist in olden times. This overly challenging requirement of the ancient sources does not reckon with the medieval style of recording impressions or trends or general themes, which were necessary in those days to preserve scarce writing materials and trim already lengthy labour times. For example, the Bayeux Tapestry's scenes may include relatively minor distortions for many reasons, including the need to indicate events happening in rapid succession and not as a continuous narrative flow, a snapshot or series of freeze-frame images, which only came about centuries later with the introduction of cameras and motion-picture films.

To satisfy his need to move the Norman landing and then fortified campsite to the eastern shore of the substantial Pevensey Bay, to Bulverhythe and Wilting respectively, Austin must condemn the early sources to numerous errors of fact that may only vary with regard to interpretation and more modern re-interpretation. Again, this problem reflects those found in the book by the Starkeys. Yet, in point of fact, Austin admits to the likelihood of such over-expectation with regard to the medieval works with his observation, on page 30 of his book. In the first paragraph of that page, Austin concedes that '. . . the rhetoric was sufficiently flowery to allow artistic interpretation to prevail'.

The text of Austin's book, on pages 107 to 110, details discrepancies on maps that are not really relevant – on page 109 Austin asserts that a waterway to enable the Norman use of Bulverhythe 'could have been open'. But this is pure speculation. It is just as easy to state that a waterway could *not* have been open. So, his 'evidence' that Bulverhythe was the Normans' supply and reinforcement port is lacking in that key aspect.

In his book, Austin relies on his theorising that the Norman army sallied forth from the Wilting area, encountering the Anglo-Saxons at Crowhurst, not at Battle Hill. In so doing, Austin ignores the most likely route of advance from the historically accepted Norman encampment at or near Hastings, which I speculate was in the Baldslow–Beauport Park area for the main army, with Duke William and his nobles ensconced at the wooden Hastings 'castle'. Despite lengthy, convoluted, repetitive efforts to try to show that Hastings port was at Bulverhythe, it is not definite that Hastings port was not instead located at the current town of Hastings, below Hastings Castle, and has been washed away and/or been covered by rising sea levels and/or land subsidence since 1066. Even so, there is no real proof that the Normans did *not* journey forth along the Hastings-to-Battle-Hill ridgeway. Austin does assert that the ridgeway route did not exist prior to the 1800s (page 207, paragraph one), but the map on page 236 of his book clearly shows that in 1066 there was a ridgeway road direct from Hastings to beyond Battle, but with a choke point in the terrain near Battle Abbey. This ridgetop road is shown on numerous older maps of the area, which demonstrates that it was there prior to 1840, when it was expanded and improved – not initially constructed, as Austin claims – to serve as a coach road.

I contend that the fighting was centred around the choke point at the ravine where the Southeastern Railway now runs. This is in accordance with the early account that the battle occurred in 'a narrow place'. On page 155 of their book, the Starkeys quote from John of Worcester: 'The English were drawn up in a narrow place.'[9] Such a location would not apply to their conjectured battlefield at Sedlescombe. Likewise, as evidenced by the photos on pages 276 and 277 of Nick Austin's book, John of Worcester's account definitely rules out Austin's imagined fighting location at the wide-open 'battlefield' at Crowhurst; and this statement also casts doubt on the proposed open terrain of Caldbec Hill as the true battlefield, as Messrs Grehan and Mace theorise. However, this is an accurate description which would apply to an ancient trackway through the woods, along the ridgetop and especially so where it would cross the small canyon where the Southeastern Railway is now located. Further, in their book, Mr Grehan and Mr Mace also refer, on page 89, in paragraph two, to this statement concerning the Battle of Hastings happening at '. . . a narrow place', which, again, definitely does not describe Caldbec Hill, which is also wide-open and not that narrow even along its south-western flank where it meets the 'neck' of Hastings Ridge. I believe that this narrow place was where the ridgeway crossed the narrow and steep-sided valley, where, instead of a bridge, more of a 'bridgeway' or two-ended ramp would have been created by the construction of one or more arched stone or brickwork culverts, which would then be topped by an earthen 'causeway'. Such stone-arched culverts and earthen causeways were known and built in England since Roman times, if not before.

Austin makes the declaration that the Normans would have marched through Crowhurst on the way from their presumed camp at Wilting on page 239 and elsewhere in his book. However, it is more logical, even if he had originally moved from Wilting, for Duke William to have led his army upslope and then along the ridge, on the high (and dry) ground and had taken a road to his extreme right, to Beauport Park and then along the ridge crest. There would therefore not have been an encounter and battle at Crowhurst. So, again, as with the Starkeys' book, in order for Austin's theory to hold up, there must be conclusive proof, in the face of the medieval reports, that the Normans did *not* land at Pevensey; did *not* move to the site of today's Hastings and Hastings Castle; and also did *not* utilise the safest, most secure, most direct route-of-march from Hastings inland, along the ridgetop road. In all of these respects, such evidence is absent.

In attempting to refute the report by William of Jumièges regarding the fact that the Norman erected a wooden fort at the site of Pevensey castle, on pages 17 and 18 Mr Austin errs in stating, categorically, that since there was already a fort there, an additional structure would not have been needed. However, some of the old Roman fort's walls had fallen in, near the entrance, so a wooden fortification there would have completed the defences for up to several hundred men, plus their horses, within the old Roman fort's 10-acre walled grounds.

Frequently, Mr Austin also relies on imperatives to declare as fact what may only be tenuous, unproven claims. For example, on page 19 of his book, in the second paragraph he states that *we must assume* that the Norman invaders were on foot. To this we must reply that, no, *we must not assume* that the Normans – not all of them – were on foot. The Bayeux Tapestry illustrates horses being unloaded from the ships of the invasion fleet, which shows us that they were present to serve as mounts from the very first day.

On page 20, regarding point #3, Austin claims that Duke William's army would have been forced to cling to the coastline as they sailed east for fear of becoming lost; but this is not true. The Normans need not have hugged the coast because Duke William had experienced sailors, ships' captains and pilots in his fleet, some of whom had familiarity with travelling to English waters and even making landfall at Hastings in the past. What we must not do is to forget that the Normans, being 'Northmen', were descended by just a few score years from being Vikings and that their sailing skills had hardly lapsed since then as they remained active coastal raiders against English shores for decades after they had 'settled down' in Normandy.

Mr Austin tries to sell us the notion that the Normans would automatically have marched through Crowhurst after leaving their presumed – by Mr Austin – camp at Wilting. However, instead, as shown by the map on page 10 of his book, which clearly shows that once the Normans reached Telham Hill, it is only a short distance to Telham hamlet and drier, easier footing along the ridgeway. This route of advance would have been much preferable as it is not only drier, but it would also have provided Duke William's men with the advantage of being on high ground in the event they encountered an Anglo-Saxon army while on the march.

As with the Starkey brothers, Mr Austin fails to adequately account for the fact that for almost 1,000 years the decisive battle of 1066 has not been known as either the 'Battle of Sedlescombe' or the 'Battle of Crowhurst', but is well known even overseas beyond England as the 'Battle of Hastings'.

Moving on to *The Battle of Hastings, 1066: The Uncomfortable Truth – Revealing the True Location of England's Most Famous Battle* by John Grehan and Martin Mace, of the three books I am citing that present alternate theories regarding the actual site of the Hastings battle, I found this to be by far the best written and most informative and even the most helpful in reinforcing my own ideas about the battle at Battle Hill.

With regard to the 'lay of the land' at the historically-accepted location of the crucial battle of 1066, on pages vii and viii of their introduction Messrs Grehan and Mace observe that the Battle Abbey 'battlefield' slope is too gentle and the ridgetop is too low and cite Caldbec Hill as an ideal defensive position. This is true, up to a point, but King Harold evidently lacked the forces to hold it and Duke William could have sidestepped him, both tactically and strategically, by taking what is now the Marley Lane path eastward. The insufficient manpower to hold Caldbec Hill stems from the fact that what would have been the Anglo-Saxon left flank 'hangs in the air' and is at about level ground at the current Uckham Land/Virgins Lane area. Or, if the Petley Wood or another extension of the ancient Andreadsweald forest reached that far then, allowing King Harold to anchor his flank there, Duke William would have been able to take any one of several tracks east, outflanking the Anglo-Saxon defensive line, forcing King Harold to relocate his army to a new blocking position. While it now seems likely that Duke William was anxious to get to the major combat and shorten his campaign in England, King Harold was not necessarily aware of that at the time, so he could not count on Duke William evading a fight that day by manoeuvring to threaten Dover and Canterbury to the east and London to the north, by marching around and/or away from Caldbec Hill. Moreover, the Caldbec Hill position, like that at Battle Abbey, faces the wrong way – to the south-east and the Normans would have been approaching from the south, along the Hastings ridge, not advancing from the lowlands near the current Marley Lane area and across the marshy ground below the crescent-shape of Caldbec Hill. All Duke William would have required was to send the bulk of his army along the 'isthmus' created by the narrow neck of Hastings ridge where it meets the southern flank of Caldbec Hill while dispatching cavalry formations to both sides to outflank the Anglo-Saxons aligned along that promontory's south-east-facing crest.

The lack of adequate Anglo-Saxon manpower available on 14 October 1066 is corroborated in Grehan's and Mace's book: On pages 36 and 37 they observe that King Harold had too few troops that day. On page 37 they quote from medieval historian William of Malmsbury, who wrote, '[the] English were too few in number'. On pages 37 and 38 the authors note that there had been not enough time to muster the full Fyrd (the Anglo-Saxon armed levies). And, on page 38, they estimate that King Harold had as few as 5,000 men available at daybreak on that Saturday morning. This lattermost number, based on my observations of Caldbec Hill, would have been too few to prevent the Normans from outflanking their defences on each end and enveloping the entire Anglo-Saxon force with waves of cavalry, followed by further masses of infantry to completely crush the defenders in a relatively short time – much quicker than the all-day fight described by the earliest historical sources.

On page 40 of their book, in paragraph one, Mr Grehan and Mr Mace cite *The Anglo-Saxon Chronicle* and 'Florence' (later identified by historians as probably 'John' instead) of Worcester as both sources observed that only a portion of King Harold's army had arrived as of about 9 a.m. on 14 October 1066. This is a primary reason why I contend that he deployed his men forward, at the steep-sided and narrow valley that now contains Southeastern Railway tracks, where he conceivably had enough manpower to hold that position. The other major factor for this deployment is that the small gorge there constitutes a grand 'ditch', which, when a palisade of spears and stakes were driven into the ground at its lip, would have provided a formidable defensive position, provided one had enough men to defend it, the rest of the main line of resistance and its flanks. Evidently, in the end, King Harold did not have quite enough men on hand to be ultimately successful in his defence.

So, how is it that King Harold had too few men to defend the slopes of Caldbec Hill – about 2,500ft from the ridgetop isthmus near Battle Abbey to Uckham Lane / Virgins Lane, almost at Petley Wood – but he had adequate or almost enough, manpower to defend the proposed battle line I theorise was deployed from near the Battle Abbey Farm to just beyond where Marley Lane meets the present-day railway crossing at the Harrier tract – a distance of about 6,500ft? As shown elsewhere, an Anglo-Saxon shield wall on the relatively bare and open inclines of Caldbec Hill would have required a formation at least three and up to five ranks deep all of the way along it, whereas even the 'S'-shaped deployment I propose for a fight at the present Southeastern Railway right-of-way and its environs would have been in its majority set up in thickly wooded land, where a continuous shield wall would be impractical and the Anglo-Saxons would have been defending in short stretches of shield wall of about two or three ranks in depth, except at the ridgeway, where up to five ranks of men or more would have stood to resist the invaders and, likely more often, in clumps or squads of men in loose formations or even posted as individuals, pairings or triplets of pickets in the thickest parts of the forested tracts that likely existed in that area in 1066. An estimated 5,000 to 7,000 fighters would probably have been not enough to defend Caldbec Hill, but would be sufficient, or almost so as the situation developed that day, if deployed on more thickly-wooded land.

In all, Grehan and Mace take the least degree of difference regarding the variations of potential Hastings battle sites, with the Starkeys being farthest removed from Battle Abbey, followed by Nick Austin – from some three miles away to about two miles, with Caldbec Hill rising above Battle Abbey barely 1,000ft and up to about half a mile away; but I have concluded that the actual site of the struggle was in almost the opposite direction, just off and possibly ebbing slightly onto the Battle Abbey grounds, yet never more than about, again, 1,000ft or up to half a mile distant.

Grehan and Mace's theory differs but little from mine with regard to the movements of the armies, with their concept being that King Harold's troops had rallied at and camped upon, then fought at the same location, on the slopes of Caldbec Hill; whereas I believe that the Anglo-Saxons, whether bivouacked on Caldbec Hill or Battle Abbey ridge, instead rushed forward to confront the Normans and attempt to stop them at the 'choke point', where the Hastings ridgetop road crossed over the narrow, steep-sided and relatively small gorge (or 'ditch', according to the early accounts) in the thick woods there would provide the best position to defend against Norman archers, cavalry charges and infantry assaults. On page 42 of their book, Messrs Grehan and Mace cite the 14 October early-morning reconnaissance of the Norman camp by King Harold himself and his brother Gyrth, when they became aware of the large number of Norman cavalry horses there. In response, it is my assessment that the Anglo-Saxon king had sufficient reason to quickly deploy forward to the ravine that now encloses the Southeastern Railway line as there was yet time to do so.

So, while I will concede that Messrs Grehan and Mace make a generally good argument and also that they could well be correct in theorising that the Battle of Hastings took place on Caldbec Hill and not

Battle Hill, I still believe my case is stronger, as I will attempt to show on my own and with occasional corroborative material quoted from not only Mr Grehan's and Mr Mace's book but also from the works of Mr Austin and Messrs Starkey. I will now return to my narrative to reveal my own findings and conclusions.

Just three days after the overwhelming victory of King Harold and the Anglo-Saxons over King Harald Hardrada and his ally Tostig Godwinsson, William, Duke of Normandy, landed at Pevensey, Sussex, on England's south coast with the intention of enforcing his claim to the throne of the island nation.

Before continuing with the historical record and the author's hypotheses regarding the likely possibilities or even, if accepted, probabilities, of at least some alternatives to the official views on how and even where, the battle at Battle, near Hastings, was actually fought, I'll return to what I saw and experienced on my ensuing trip there.

What the Author Found on His Second Investigation at Battle

On my next visit to Battle I decided to start at the first roundabout nearest to Battle Abbey, where the A2100 meets Marley Lane, and to proceed from there. I had already made a cursory survey of the terrain to the east side of the roundabout, where it plunges down a slope that runs beside Marley Lane. Going down that grassy hillside, I was again surprised by the unexpected sight of yet another beck and some muddy ground, even in early July, under a line of trees that widened toward the south-east into a small woodland. Having just reviewed the night before, again, a broad outline of the course of the battle as it is generally now thought to have occurred in 1066, I wondered if this could be the 'Malfosse' ('evil ditch') where, toward the end of the fight, Norman cavalry had pursued the fleeing Anglo-Saxons until the mounted invaders were surprised to find themselves plunging into a flooded ditch, where many horses and men drowned. Seeing that the remaining meadows, hedgerows and 'shores' ('shores', in English terminology, are wider than hedgerows but narrower than 'woods', which are in turn smaller than 'forests' – readers in the British Isles will please forgive my retention of North American word usage and spellings) ahead were below Caldbec Hill and having already determined that I would go to that hill on another day, I went back up the slope to the roundabout, turned east-south-east and went down Marley Lane.

During this excursion I observed that the land to the north-east, east and south-east of the roundabout slopes at a steeper angle than the ground atop the ridge crest, along the A2100 and is also steeper than on the land at the supposed 'real' battlefield, below Battle Terrace, on the old Battle Abbey grounds. As soon as I started out, I noticed a footpath behind the businesses at the point just south of the intersection of the A2100 and Marley Lane, between the two streets. This walkway led up a very small and slight but somewhat conical rise there, making it the high point of the local terrain, excepting, after a minor dip, the continuing slow upslope to the north, toward St Mary's Church, which is across from Battle Abbey, both of which are on the A2100. Marley Lane arches back, from a south-easterly to become a more east-running ridgetop, even as it falls slowly in elevation until it reaches the Southeastern Railway right-of-way – the lane tracking a gentle 'S'-curve as it does so. Following the A2100 southward to Marley Lane and making a left turn onto Station Approach, I continued east and veered onto another path skirting the north side of the tracks. I doubled back to the Battle train station, noting an unnamed public driveway across from Battle Station to its north that leads to several businesses, residences and other structures that line both sides of it and the adjoining carparks there. These structures are all along a steeper slope below Marley Lane than had been evident from upon Marley Lane itself, on the crest of the ridge; but this gradient had been concealed from my view from up above by houses and trees along and just to the south of Marley Lane. Even at this early point in my observations, it seemed to me that the steep slopes extending back from the short bridge over the Southeastern Railway tracks, at the aforementioned ravine and then arcing back toward Marley Lane and then continuing below the high ground of the crest along Marley Lane itself, would have been an ideal place to situate the Anglo-Saxon shield wall(s) for this, the left flank of King Harold's army.

Proceeding south-westward on Station Approach, I rejoined the A2100 and turned right (north) and now slightly uphill again, to get a better look at the side lanes and little streets that branch off that main avenue; and I then crossed to its west side and surveyed the land to the west of the A2100, where I, along with many others, had previously believed that the Normans had likely diverged to their left from the ridgetop to advance across and upon the Anglo-Saxons' (backwardly placed, I reckoned) supposed left flank (and then rear) on today's Battle Abbey grounds – that fateful day in 1066. (About the names of the streets and roads, etc. While some likely share their ancient names, such as 'London Road' as it was in fact the road to London, many – no, most – others have 'newer' names, some dating back to the early days of the Norman Conquest, but travel routes seldom change and the current avenues of moving around are very likely the same as they were in ancient times, even pre-dating Anglo-Saxon England. They follow prehistoric roads and paths and game trails, no matter what they were called then; and it is more convenient and accurate, to refer to them by their modern names whenever possible, which is just about in every case.)

Continuing uphill, northward along the A2100, I deviated from the main road to go down two side avenues for a better look at the slopes flanking the west side of the ridge, to take pictures and talk to any people I might encounter. (When I announced to one suspicious-seeming woman who was watching me why I was in the back carpark of a commercial structure, taking photographs, that I was investigating the possibility that the Hastings battle had been fought in that area and not on the abbey grounds, she just harrumphed sceptically, shook her head, hopped into her car and drove off.)

I turned back south and encountered the 'other' roundabout, where the A2100 meets Powdermill Lane – the B2095. Both roads there at that time were jammed with Friday-afternoon getaway traffic, so, after a quick look to the south-west, down Powdermill Lane, I continued on, then crossed to the east side of the A2100 with the intention of going down Station Approach and returning to Battle Station for the first of my two train rides that day that would deliver me to the university campus. But, curiosity overcame my vague feelings of fatigue, so I continued on south, remaining on the east side of the A2100, then ventured onto the side streets there, all the way to Starr's Meade and which would have been on the Norman right flank. I took photos of the slopes, many of which are quite steep, and investigated the as yet pristine-seeming fields and remaining bits of forest just beyond the built-up strips along the A2100 and those numerous little lanes there. I also found a public footpath in the area, just off of Starr's Meade, at the foot of Kingsdale Close and took it down to where it ended – at the Harrier tract, then doubled back and returned to the A2100.

Along the way while on these peripheral journeys, I talked to the few people I encountered as I recrossed the main avenue of the A2100 to its west side and took a walking survey of Glengorse housing developments and their environs on what would have been the left flank of the Norman advance along the ridgeway from the original Hastings Castle and ancient port, in 1066.

While in that tract I was challenged by two 'neighbourhood watch' patrol officers (they showed me their identification badges, which they are required to wear on lanyards around their necks), who told me that photographing the homes there was forbidden. I then explained to them that I was going up and down each street and the public alleyway and taking numerous photographs in 'odd' directions – toward the fields and open spaces and not in angles facing the houses – for a writing project. They soon left, evidently quickly tiring of my lengthy explanations regarding my research and theories regarding the battle at Battle. I was then free to continue with my photography. It was getting past mid-afternoon by that point, so I determined once more to beat the rush-hour train and bus traffic and head back to Falmer, leaving a look at the countryside from the crest and/or slopes of Caldbec Hill – next on my agenda – for another day.

Later, while on the trains, it occurred to me that the area around Powdermill Lane might have greater significance than either I or anyone else had suspected, to my knowledge, so far. I had already established in my mind that the Anglo-Saxons could have defended the area from the first roundabout where the A2100 and Marley Lane intersect because the ridge line running from that central spot and, going toward their left flank at any rate, was steep – steeper than the slope below Battle Terrace, on the Battle Abbey grounds. I knew, further, that a far-forward line of defence could, theoretically, have been stood up just as well – I suspected, not having thoroughly investigated the land to the west along Powdermill Lane yet – at the second roundabout, where the A2100 meets that lane, also known as the B2095. It was even conceivable from my surveys of the land there that a defence line could have been set up as far south and south-east as Glengorse to the west and the lanes to the east of the A2100, where there is another series of formidable slopes to make successful Norman flank attacks difficult to achieve. The 'main line of resistance' of the Anglo-Saxons, would, ideally, have been placed farther back, however, roughly from the line of the ridge below Marley Lane and then extending to the second, more southerly roundabout, at Powdermill Lane. I planned to take a closer look when I could at the lay of the land toward the railway line, on the west side of the A2100, near the second, more southerly, roundabout where it meets Powdermill Lane and the adjoining tracts of land there as well. Before continuing with my treks and surveys of the area, I think it is appropriate to return to the historical accounts and their likely accuracy regarding the 'Hastings' battle at Battle.

What *The Anglo-Saxon Chronicle* Tells us About the Preliminaries of the Battle near Hastings

In the most lengthy entry in *The Anglo-Saxon Chronicle* for 1066, the scribes recorded, as noted earlier, that: 'Meantime Earl William came up from Normandy into Pevensey on the eve of St Michael's mass; and soon after his landing was effected, they constructed a castle at the port of Hastings.'[10] So far, all is in accordance with the likely facts. The *Chronicle* then goes on to state, 'This was then told to King Harold; and he gathered a large force [7 he gaderade þa mycelne[†] here] and came to meet him at the estuary of Appledore'.[11] Also, here is where things tend to diverge into unknown territory. At least one writer has said that King Harold went to Devonshire before mustering his army near Hastings. What that writer and others managed to do is confuse the village of Appledore, at the mouth of the Torridge River in the county of Devon, with another town with that name in Kent, just a few miles from Battle Hill. The *Chronicle* then reports: 'William, however, came against him unawares, ere his army was collected; but the king, nevertheless, very hardly encountered him with the men that would support him: and there was a great slaughter made on either side.'[12] In this passage we find, when compared with the previously cited entry an indication that there was a serious, or at least some, division within the Anglo-Saxon ranks. I will elaborate.

Duke William had made landfall on 28 September, having left the Norman port of St Valery on the 27th. Whether this was part of a clever strategy or just fate, as dictated by the winds of the English Channel, no one will ever know for sure. It is possible though, even likely, that William himself circulated rumours of unfavourable winds to keep his troops from becoming too impatient and restless, and to confuse King Harold's spies.[13] However, it is almost certain that Duke William's supporters in England had spies throughout the island and probably even within King Harold's camp. Duke William would definitely have had it confirmed to him, within days, that King Harald Hardrada of Norway and Tostig Godwinsson had effected a landing near York, which had initially occurred on 14 August – more than 10 weeks earlier. Or, he may have had other sources who could have sailed directly from the north – from either northern England or Scandinavia – to

---

† 'Mycelne' also translates, probably more accurately in this context, as 'mighty', not 'large'.

Normandy with the news. So, with the Norwegian fleet stopping off in the Shetlands and Orkneys, then landing on the English coast near Holderness and burning and pillaging before going inland to York, Duke William had ample time to learn of and take advantage of the diversion and to almost immediately embark for England. Possibly knowing of the Viking invasion, Duke William would have, as he did, set sail for the south coast of England at what he would judge to be the opportune moment, realising that his opponent would be hurrying north to defend his kingdom from the Viking invaders. Duke William certainly had intelligence sources in England; and King Harold had the same, even in William's camp. One of these was caught and sent back, evidently unharmed, to King Harold with a defiant message.[14] Duke William's own sources of intelligence included a 'monk of Fécamp', who held lands in Sussex. As for the story of unfavourable winds, R.H.C. Davis and Marjorie Chibnall cite the fact that despite tempestuous winds and rough seas, William the Conqueror had no trouble in making a rapid return when sailing back to Normandy on 6 December 1067.[15] They go on to say that in his shrewdness and care, Duke William delayed in order to complete his preparations and training for the invasion and to confuse King Harold.[16] However, in the text of the *Gesta Guillelmi* William of Poitiers also asserts that it was by prayers and pleadings to Heaven that favourable winds at last became manifest, indicating a divine will that the invasion should succeed.[17] Wace concurs in this:

> They waited long at St Valeri for a fair wind and the barons were greatly wearied. Then they prayed the convent to bring out the shrine of Saint Valeri and set it on a carpet in the plain; and all came praying the holy reliques, that they might be allowed to pass over sea. They offered so much money, that the reliques were buried beneath it; and from that day forth, they had good weather and a fair wind.[18]

Thus would Duke William's invasion seem to have further approval of divine providence, at least in the estimation of those participating in and supporting the endeavour. Moreover, Duke William would have known, also through his pro-Norman sources in England, that King Harold would have by necessity dismissed his massed army on the southern coast of England due to the fact that their term of service would have ended for both his land and sea Fyrds in September.[19] In any case, the timing, as far as it affected the eventual outcome of the campaign, was perfect.

With regard to the foregoing, on page 17 of their book, the Starkeys misquote *The Anglo-Saxon Chronicle*, in their quotation #1 on that page, which has King Harold 'coming against' Duke William at the Rother Estuary. But the text actually says,

> Meantime Earl William came up from Normandy into Pevensey on the eve of St Michael's mass; and soon after his landing was effected, they constructed a castle at the port of Hastings. This was then told to King Harold; and he gathered a large force and came to meet him at the estuary of Appledore. William, however, came against him unawares, ere his army was collected; but the king, nevertheless, very hardly encountered him with the men that would support him . . .[20]

This translation says King Harold 'came to meet' Duke William and was not 'coming against' the Norman duke, who, in turn, it is reported, 'came against him unawares, ere his army was collected . . .' Now 'ere' means 'before', as in 'before in time'. So, Duke William came against Harold before the Anglo-Saxon army was collected. Appledore is mentioned – as, I believe, it should be – as a place where King Harold met with other Anglo-Saxon leaders and warriors, but, again, 'with the men that would support him'. So, once more, this lattermost remark suggests that not all of the Anglo-Saxon army supported King Harold in the upcoming fight (at Battle Hill), which further suggests that the site of the battle was not at or near Appledore but elsewhere. It is also possible that the disagreement was concerning whether or not to oppose the invaders at the blocking position at or near Appledore or if King Harold should be supported by the bulk of the Anglo-Saxon army in massing at Caldbec Hill in preparation for a pre-emptive strike against the Norman base at Hastings.

The parsing of words to which I have resorted above would not be necessary except for the fact that the Starkeys themselves rely on so much parsing of phrases and words in order to try to reshape the original texts reporting on the Battle of Hastings to try to force the evidence into their pre-conceived mould as they attempt to shift the site of the battle from Battle Hill to Sedlescombe. The text of their book then goes on to indicate that the Normans 'came against' where the Anglo-Saxons were gathering by surprise and that King Harold deployed to oppose the invaders, but without specifying exactly where it all took place.

Returning to the pro-Norman 'Monk from Fécamp', William of Poitiers also reported that Duke William sent the monk as an envoy to King Harold's camp. His messages to Harold supposedly included a magnanimous offer by the duke to have either the noble and ecclesiastical authorities of Normandy or of England to decide on the validity of William's claim to the throne – according to the laws and customs of either nation; the choice of which to be King Harold's.[21] However, in this William of Poitiers overlooks the fact that the Anglo-Saxon Witan had already made such a decision, according to Anglo-Saxon law and tradition, in approving Edward the Confessor's evident deathbed choice of Harold as king of England.

William of Poitiers then goes on to assert that Duke William offered to spare the lives of many of the men who would fight on both sides by having King Harold and Duke William decide the issue of who would be king through trial by individual combat.[22] However, in this, were it to be true, Duke William would very likely have faced a serious rebellion from the numerous lords and warriors who had been promised lands and booty for accompanying the duke on his invasion venture. How would he repay them for services *not* rendered if the contest had already been decided by individual combat? Worse still: if his invasion force was so irresistible, why risk the loss of a potential conquest as a result of a man-to-man fight that could easily turn against the Normans through a lucky move on the part of King Harold or a mistake on the part of Duke William? Obviously, a defeat of the Norman duke would not satisfy the lust for land and wealth in the hearts of the invading warriors, who might just decide to not honour the result of the individual combat and resume their harrying of the English countryside unless and until stopped from doing so by the Anglo-Saxon Fyrd and 'regular army' of King Harold's nobles and Huscarls. William of Poitiers tells us this: 'For the furious king (Harold) was hastening his march all the more so because he had heard that the lands near to the Norman camp were being laid waste.'[23] As for King Harold's response to the challenge to individual combat: King Harold II preferred to 'Let God decide' (the outcome of a pitched battle).[24] We are also told that King Harold indeed seemed to be contemplating a pre-emptive strike at Duke William's position: 'He thought that in a night or surprise attack he might defeat them, unawares and, in case they should try to escape, he had laid a naval ambush for them, with an armed fleet of up to 700 ships.'[25] Such a surprise attack could only take place from a location that would threaten the Norman base at Hastings port and castle, not in the Rother Estuary; an ideal place to rendezvous for such a surprise attack would be at Caldbec Hill, with the intention of advancing toward Hastings via Hasting ridge.

Concerning William of Poitiers' report that the Normans had 'laid waste' lands in Sussex and Kent, in his book, Nick Austin cites the relative losses to landholders due to Norman foraging and wasting activities in order to show that their landing site was not at Pevensey and that their camp had to be at or near Wilting. However, many factors are not included that may have been more haphazard and not organised according to his preconceived notions. For example, on page 40 Austin quotes Wace as writing that initially the Normans had meat aplenty. This means they did not need to forage for up to several days after their first landing, leaving Pevensey and the closest estates almost untouched. There is also, to me, the possibility that Duke William did not plunder the Pevensey area because he may have had collaborators at Pevensey and, later other, nearby, unplundered properties. Further, the relatively heavy damage done to estates farther along the shores of Pevensey Bay indicates a more highly-organised approach in that area, with foraging parties on horseback reconnoitring and surveying properties along the shoreline and ships beaching at select locations to load confiscated crops and livestock aboard for a more efficient delivery to the Norman base at Hastings.

In his estimates of Norman landings, and movements and encampments, Austin relies on references to values appraised in the *Domesday Book*. However, those valuations were self-reported by the landholders, almost two decades later. Such self-reporting must, at best, be often suspect. Moreover, foraging is a hit-or-miss project, not always a well-organised, thorough ransacking, with well-known, wealthier tracts targeted while poorer, lesser, smaller, out-of-the way properties are spared, ignored or not found.

In Austin's book, on pages 46 and 47, item #2, he refers to areas 'during the time the army was in residence', but the army had largely if not almost entirely left the land spit where the fort at Pevensey yet stands and, since, as Austin contends, it was largely out of the way, therefore, to me, it was not worth the effort to plunder. Also, the Normans, again, could have concentrated on foraging from and back to Hastings via ships and horseback around Pevensey Bay, ignoring the ridgeway, which was wooded and had few properties to loot; the route around Pevensey Bay from Hastings was much more convenient and productive.

Returning to King Harold's next steps, after his decisive victory over the Vikings, upon learning of the Norman invasion, he promptly marched his now evidently greatly diminished army (according to both Scandinavian and English accounts) back south, sending word to all the lords of England to come to his aid in the expected impending battle in Sussex or Kent. By Friday, 13 October, he and his men were at Caldbec Hill, overlooking the site of the current town of Battle, at least 6.5 miles from Hastings along the now multi-named old road to London, known today as the A2100. More reinforcements no doubt constantly joined his meagre army as the day and night of 13 October 1066 wore on, and more would likely have arrived even as the battle was being fought and decided the following day.

Continuing With the Author's Investigation in the Battle Area: A Third Visit to Battle

Curious about the ridgetop way along the A2100, on my third visit to Battle I took the bus, which follows that road all the way to Battle Abbey and beyond. In that the railway tracks remained diverted to the left or western side, of Hastings Ridge and sometimes plunged below ground into lengthy tunnels, I took the bus for the third visit because I wanted to make sure the terrain was approximately similar all the way from Hastings to Battle and I found out that it is so along the entire road/ bus route. The ridge undulates, with alternating patches of forest and meadows. It is evident that centuries of road and building construction have smoothed out some of the ups and downs along the way. Even before all of the building-up and excavating of the right-of-way, the ridgetop route would likely have been the gentlest and most convenient as it avoids the many hidden becks and small lakes and marshlands that historians and maps confirm were and are on both sides of that ridge to act as impediments to anyone trekking along from Hastings to Battle; all the more so for an army of 7,000 to 10,000 men in medieval footwear and lugging awkward and heavy eleventh-century weapons and gear. The bus ride merely confirmed my anticipation that adhering the ridgetop route was preferable to deviating from it to cut across becks, lakes, marshes, valleys and hilltops to embark on a tiring trek with an army that would be expected to not be too physically worn out upon going into combat on either 14 October or on the following day.

Arriving at Battle, instead of going south again I set out north from the bus stop across from the entrance to Battle Abbey, along the A2100, where the road is known as High Street and, foregoing my intention from before of investigating the area around and outside the Abbey property on that day. I kept on to the north, going past Battle Abbey and on to Mount Street, which runs north and north-east up to the crest of Caldbec Hill.

First, I remained on Mount Street, going along the crescent-shaped crest of Caldbec Hill, surveying the steepness of the slope and its cant downward and south and south-east, to the right of the road as I proceeded north and north-east. (Later, I revisited the crest and took the photos of the windmill converted into a home that is now at the actual peak, from which location King Harold supposedly commanded the marshalling of his forces.) Seeing an opening between homes on the southern side of Mount Street, I went through the alleyway and dormant construction site there to emerge upon the meadow covering the south-east to south-facing slope, approximating the view of King Harold and his Anglo-Saxons, who were gathering there on the morning of 14 October 1066, toward the expected route of approach of Duke William and his Normans. The Caldbec Hill position is indeed formidable, with a wide and long, steep, open, grassy slope that gently arcs inward in a south-east-facing slight concavity. In the distance, on the horizon, is Telham Hill, of which I was unsure of as to exact place and identity at the time I spotted it then but was able to confirm later that day. I continued on for long enough to gauge that Caldbec Hill as a defensive position was inadequate due to the facts that it would be too long for even more than 5,000 and up to 7,000 men to properly defend and all the more so as its extreme, eastern-to-south-eastern 'slope' gently merges into level ground on its north-eastern side, with no woodland, marshland, beck or gorge upon which to anchor the Anglo-Saxon left flank.

Returning to Mount Street and heading back down it to the west-south-west, toward the A2100, I encountered a man doing some work in his side yard and asked him if I could trespass for a moment to take some photos from his backyard. He responded, 'Because you had the courtesy to ask, you can stay as long as you like and do whatever you want back there. Some people just go back without even asking and start taking pictures until I ask them what they think they're doing in my yard.' We chatted about the community of Battle; my point of origin now – the San Francisco Bay Area, which he had visited many years before; the events of 1066 and the likely Norman route of advance; and we also exchanged general pleasantries – before, during, after my photo session with the terrain – and we parted as friendly acquaintances. From his backyard, as with the open land behind the dormant construction site, I could look down upon a beck at the south-eastern-facing base of Caldbec Hill and then another and its accompanying marshy ground beyond – below the Marley Lane/A2100 roundabout. I decided to forego another inspection of the valley below Caldbec Hill and between it and the Marley Lane ridge just then and to instead continue on to the A2100 and walk south along it farther than I had before.

Going past Battle Abbey, the Marley Lane roundabout, then the Powdermill Lane/B2095 roundabout, I continued beyond the Starr's Meade tract of side lanes on the east side of the road and continued, generally to the south-east. At first, the road had sloped downward, reaching a low point at the bridge over the Southeastern Railway line. From there on the land climbs slowly till it reaches the Glengorse neighbourhood, then falls slightly before resuming its upward slant until I found that I was across from Telham Lane, near where the road peaks. Remaining on the east side of the A2100, I found a side lane and went farther east along it toward a secondary crest of the ridge until my way was blocked by a farm gate and a sign warning that it was private property and that I should keep out. However, looking left, to the north, I was pleased to take in a view between the widely spaced trees from that location all the way back to Caldbec Hill, on the northern horizon. As I took photos from there, zooming in and out at various angles, I was struck by the fact that the Norman scouts who had reportedly spotted the Anglo-Saxons assembling along the ridgetop of the distant Caldbec Hill would have been straining their eyes to make out even men on horseback, much more so for those – the assumed vast majority of the Anglo-Saxon warriors – who were on foot. I wondered for a moment how the Normans could have possibly seen the defenders at a time prior to the inventions of binoculars and telescopes until deciding that small gatherings and larger groups of men moving around on that faraway slope would have created plainly evident ebbing and flowing dark blobs of colour against the otherwise pale green meadows of the distant hillside.

After backtracking to the A2100 I continued south and south-east toward Hastings, staying on the east side of the road, going downhill all the way, past the remainder of Telham Hill, but still on the Hastings-to-Battle ridgetop, until I reached the outskirts of Hastings, just before the reunification of that route with the London Road/the A21 near Conquest Hospital, Baldslow and Beauport Park, where the latter road takes its more northerly jog a little to the right on the way back north-north-west toward London.

It had been another long, tiring day, with miles of walking while carrying a backpack full of gear (at the age of 68), so I took the first available bus back to the Hastings train depot and returned to the University of Sussex campus, where I reviewed my findings. I had confirmed the early and later accounts of the layout of the terrain. Based in part on my observations, I remained convinced of the accuracy of the many reports – medieval and more modern – concerning the initial positions of the antagonists – the Anglo-Saxons on Caldbec Hill and the Norman advance scouts on the flank of Telham Hill – at the current Telham Lane, on 14 October 1066. I had personally traversed the most likely and convenient route of the Normans' approach, albeit in the reverse direction. I concluded that if I could do this relatively easily at the age of 68 – while carrying a backpack of accoutrements such as extra socks, two first-aid kits (that included medical items of every kind that could possibly be needed on my ventures to sometimes very secluded areas, but, thankfully, only small adhesive bandages were needed to cover blisters during the entire summer), water, trail mix, camera, rain gear, etc. – then surely the early middle-aged and younger men of Duke William's army would have had no trouble carrying their weapons and equipment on their march forward from Hastings onto the battlefield that day – that is, if they had adhered to the ridgetop route now covered by the A2100; but the key question remained: Where, exactly, did the armies' encounter each other and also where had the Battle of Hastings actually taken place?

In my initial reactions – once I set aside my suspension of disbelief regarding the site of the battle being on and below Battle Terrace, on the Battle Abbey estate – I had thought that maybe the theories I had heard about regarding the roundabout, which I had assumed to be the first roundabout one encounters on the A2100 south of Battle Abbey – at Marley Lane – would be the most likely site of the spot – the high point in the area – from which King Harold had commanded the fight. However, my tour of the supposed battlefield led me to a farm gate that let out onto Powdermill Lane/the B2095, which terminates, counter-intuitively, at the second roundabout to the south of Battle Abbey. So, I thought it even more likely that Harold's 'command position' would have been nearer to there, where Powdermill Lane meets the A2100, just outside the southern boundary of the Battle Abbey parklands. Then, on my subsequent tours, I decided that Marley Lane itself was a likely place for the furthering of the Anglo-Saxon battle line to the east, but wondered how this could be if it conflicted with the Powdermill Lane extension of the battle line to the west.

As my explorations on foot had continued, I thought it possible that the Anglo-Saxons had deployed even farther south, from the Glengorse tract to the west and extending onto the modern-day Starr's Meade housing developments east of the ridgetop road of the A2100. However, my travels along the road there indicated to me that this would be too close to the Norman advance scouts and, presumably, the mass of the Norman army just behind, leaving the Anglo-Saxons too little time to establish their main line of resistance there. This was later confirmed to me by looking at maps of the area – the Glengorse/Starr's Meade position is much closer to Telham Hill/Telham Lane than Caldbec Hill; King Harold would not have risked his army's ambush and annihilation by moving them too far south for them to form their defensive 'shield wall' battle line before they were attacked.

I remained unconvinced that the battle had been fought on the Battle Abbey grounds, except maybe in part – a very small part; but the evident contradictions involved in an Anglo-Saxon battle line at both the Marley Lane and the Powdermill Lane areas seemed to require at least one more visit to Battle to see if I could obtain more clarity before espousing a theory – any theory, whether confirming or contesting the official views of many experts and English Heritage.

As stated before, having since been to Caldbec Hill, I found it doubtful that King Harold ever intended to make his stand there, for several reasons. First, I believe the selection of that hill as a rallying point to muster his army was due to the fact that it was then well-known locally and that the precise placing of his standard there was – as cited or at least implied in *The Anglo-Saxon Chronicle* – below an ancient apple tree familiar to anyone travelling along the road. But Caldbec Hill was not an ideal or even adequate place to defend, given the circumstances of that day. It was too spread-out for Harold's likely very reduced army (by losses sustained at the battle at Fulford – precluding the participation of the northern earls' armies – and the heavy casualties at Stamford Bridge indicated by both Snorri Sturluson and *The Anglo-Saxon Chronicle*, as well as the loss of land-fighting navy men who went down in their ships in the storms off the east coast) to adequately cover. Caldbec Hill has no natural features at either end upon which to anchor a defensive battle line. The hill was too far north to have prevented Duke William from sidestepping the Anglo-Saxons by moving north-east along the current Marley Lane route to the road that runs through Kent Street toward London – the A21. Once there, Duke William could have marched farther east, toward Dover and Canterbury or threatened to move north-west, toward London, forcing King Harold to meet the Norman invaders on ground much less favourable than the Caldbec Hill position, which was, as we have seen, far from ideal to begin with.

Instead, I believe King Harold originally intended to defend farther forward, from the Telham Hill flank/current Telham Lane area on the Hastings-to-London road or even, possibly, to aggressively 'defend' by going over to the attack and marching on Hastings Castle, as he and his brother had done so successfully in his campaign against the Welsh strongholds in 1063.

The Preliminaries to the Battle

William, Duke of Normandy, did what any security-conscious commander would do first upon landing on a hostile shore – make sure he and his army were secure. He had already, no doubt, been appraised of the local terrain and defensive assets by his spies and a few allies among the English. He would have known that the landward side of the shore around Pevensey was bounded by marshes to the west and north-west and by the estuary that was then there to the east, north-east and north. He therefore had the majority of his army come ashore where the coast at that time cut deeply inland, with most of those marshlands to their west, at what is now known as Normans Bay, with, again, the estuary of 1066 just to the east of Pevensey, which itself is at the site of an old Roman fort. The Romans had probably located their fort at that spot due to identical or similar calculations some 800 years previously.

William had his men promptly add a prefabricated, wooden motte-and-bailey fortification within the old Roman walls at Pevensey. 'Then they cast out of the ships the materials and drew them to land, all shaped, framed and pierced to receive the pins which they had brought, cut and ready, in large barrels; so that before evening had well set in, they had finished a fort.'[26]

The next day, William had his army move east, to Hastings – which still had an actual, harboured port then, but which has since also silted up, collapsed into the sea and been submerged by rising sea levels and/or land subsidence – and he ordered them to disassemble the prefabricated fortification at Pevensey and to re-erect it as a 'second' (but actually the same) wooden motte-and-bailey castle on the heights above Hastings to overlook both that port city and the more direct road from there to London – the Old London Road. William next had his invading Normans set about trying to draw King Harold and the Anglo-Saxons into battle by sallying forth from their fortification and encampments to harry, burn and ravage the towns and countryside nearby. These manoeuvres are the subject matter of one panel of the Bayeux Tapestry, which this writer viewed during a research trip to Bayeux, Normandy.

It was during my research back in the San Francisco Bay Area that I noticed something that had not caught my eye or, evidently, the attention of many others, as of that date: In *The Anglo-Saxon Chronicle*

(Manuscript 'D'), the scribes noted that Harold had '. . . gathered a mighty army ['mycelne here'] and came to meet him (Duke William) at the estuary of Appledore' ['7 he gaderade þa mycelne here']²⁷ This curious report in the *Chronicle* was a bit puzzling, at first, until I discovered that Appledore was then 'A village on the edge of Romney Marsh'. Why, I wondered, would King Harold go there? A quick consultation with Google Earth and maps on the Internet revealed that the village of Appledore is now just opposite a coastal marsh a few miles from the town of Rye and lies astride the old road to Dover and Canterbury. However, I also discovered that in 1066 Appledore was on the shore of an estuary that has since silted-up and all but disappeared, except for today's marshland; it would have been on a deep inlet of the coast then.

King Harold knew that Duke William's army had landed at Pevensey and occupied and strengthened the ancient Roman fort there, but had then moved eastward along the coast overland and by ship to Hastings, where the Normans quickly rebuilt their prefabricated castle. It would probably have seemed likely to King Harold II and his counsellors that Duke William intended to march and/or sail farther east and conquer Dover and Canterbury, as Duke William was later to do after defeating the Anglo-Saxons at Battle Hill. If the Anglo-Saxons marshalled at least a part of their army at Appledore it would be in a perfect blocking position to frustrate Duke William's anticipated route of advance along the coast. However, instead, Duke William evidently decided to strike inland, toward today's Robertsbridge (formerly 'Rotherbridge' – a bridge over the Rother River), with London beyond. Such a route of advance, if made along the route of the A21 from Baldslow toward the then Rotherbridge, would have, ironically, taken the Normans along the Starkey brothers' conjectured way to an encounter with the Anglo-Saxons at Sedlescombe. However, the Anglo-Saxons, evidently unbeknownst to the Norman duke at the time, were being deployed by King Harold at Caldbec Hill, just behind Battle Hill, along the ancient ridgeway through the woods on a more westerly avenue to the same objective. So, Duke William moved his forces not toward the Rother, but instead along the ridgeway, anticipating a clash with King Harold's men along the way. In this move, Duke William was taking the medieval equivalent of Germany's 1940 strike through the Ardennes Forest, because that route led the Normans through more thickly wooded and uneven terrain and not along the smoother, less heavily forested, more convenient near-coastal route from Baldslow. This would have been a counter-intuitive move because it would negate one of the Norman army's main strengths – cavalry, which, like today's modern armoured forces, relies on open country and not forests to perform at optimum effectiveness.

King Harold had also perhaps believed that Duke William would want to remain as close to the coastline as possible in order to protect his connections with ships coming from Normandy with reinforcements and supplies, instead of striking boldly inland over less favourable terrain. It is also conceivable that King Harold was considering a repeat of his successful campaign against the Welsh in 1063, when he sent his main force inland with his later-to-be-estranged brother Tostig, while he, Harold, sailed along the shore to conquer the coastal strongholds in Wales. (On page 39 of their book, John Grehan and Martin Mace agree that King Harold may have contemplated an attack on the Normans on 14 October.) Since Appledore was on the estuary that let out onto the sea, there may have been a plan, to be abandoned, that would have sent a force of sea raiders to threaten or possibly seize Duke William's base at Hastings. In his telling of the events of the time, Master Wace reports, in Chapter XV, that '. . . Harold had planned a surprise on William's army and had sent another force round by sea to intercept his retreat'.[28] It is also worth noting that the then main port of Rye had been a Norman stronghold since King Canute's wife, Emma, had awarded it to them, making it a tempting objective for Duke William to seize on his conjectured contemplated march toward Dover and Canterbury. Whatever the case may be, it is possible that King Harold at least held a war council at Appledore prior to his evident discovery – probably uncovered by his spies or sympathisers within or close to the Norman camp – on 12 or 13 October that Duke William would be on the march within the next day or two not along the coast but inland, toward London, from his and his nobles' base at Hastings Castle and his army's campaign bivouac at or near Baldslow and/or Beauport Park.

The next sentence in the *Chronicle*'s Manuscript 'D' reports: 'William, however, came against him unawares, ere his army was collected.'[29] The account continues: '. . . but the king, nevertheless, very hardly encountered him with the men that would support him'.[30] Now this curious remark indicates that not all of the Anglo-Saxon leaders and their men-at-arms were supportive of King Harold or at least of his intended plans. This may be reflective of the fact that Anglo-Saxon England was rife with division, even before the very brief reign of King Harold II; or it may be indicative of a decisive difference of opinion that kept at least part of the Anglo-Saxon forces to the east, to cover the approaches to Dover and Canterbury, while the remainder – likely the greater part of the army – marched as rapidly as possible to its rallying point on Caldbec Hill, on the northern end of the modern-day town of Battle.

But all of this conjecture may be in error due to what was an inaccuracy in the *Chronicle*'s Manuscript 'D' account, for nowhere else in the various texts does it in fact mention an 'estuary'. The text in Old English reads: '7 com him togenes æt þære haran apuldran'. This translates to 'And came him [to] 'escape from or flee' or to be 'near – as in a road' – at the ancient apple tree'.[31] There was no such single word as 'togenes';[32] however, 'genes' is an imperative for 'To preserve; save; escape from; flee' or 'near [of a road] – Ðe ða.) So, we are forced to assume that King Harold instead likely assembled his men near an ancient apple tree and not at an estuary-town named 'Appledore' (Apuldran). The 'Appledore' in Kent, as mentioned, is just about 12 miles ('as the raven flies', but much farther along the meandering roads of East Sussex) from Battle Hill; but to associate this with the Manuscript 'D' text is likely in error as the scribe who wrote this passage was probably working from a second- or third-hand account and the word 'estuary' was, for some unknown reason, inserted by the translators who were, perhaps, familiar with another 'Appledore', a town in Devon, on the Torridge River Estuary; but this site is far from Battle and Hastings and closer to Worcester – the site of origin of *The Anglo-Saxon Chronicle* Manuscript 'D'. I find myself forced to conclude that the relevant passage in Manuscript 'D' refers to an order by King Harold that his rallying forces rendezvous with him at an old apple tree, probably on Caldbec Hill. As will be shown later, the area is friendly to apple trees and at least one ancient one may have been found at the peak of Caldbec Hill, where a modified windmill now stands, as apple trees can even now be found in residents' backyards not too far away.

By 13 October 1066, Duke William and the Normans had accomplished their goal for, to maintain the stability of his regime in response to those who were crying for King Harold to take strong action against the marauding Normans, the English monarch must have felt compelled to come to grips with the invaders as soon as they should appear close enough to his position. He was also likely driven by his predilection to take prompt, pre-emptive action, as he had done in his Welsh campaign in 1063 and in hastening north the month before to defeat the Vikings in a decisive and proactive counter-attack, swiftly dispatching their entire force in a surprise move. This conjectured action is 'confirmed' by the Norman monk Duke William had sent to parlay with King Harold and who reported back to William that 'Harold hopes to be able to catch you unawares. He is reported to have sent five hundred ships to obstruct our passage home.'[33] Again, this contention is probable because such a strategic move echoes King Harold's successful campaigns against the Welsh just three years previous.

This opportunity, King Harold would probably have thought, arose on the next day, on 14 October, when the Norman advance scouts on Telham Hill reported spotting the Anglo-Saxon army marshalling on the open slopes near the crest of Caldbec Hill and, likely, King Harold's own English pickets in turn sighted the invaders. Instead of trying to turn King Harold's left flank by advancing along the other of the two routes to London from Hastings, on what's now the A21 – Kent Street – Duke William directed his troops to close with the defenders by continuing along the ridgetop road presently known as the A2100.

Informed that the Normans were at Telham Hill, I believe that King Harold would have decided to hastily reposition his troops who had been gathering on Caldbec Hill farther forward, on 'Senlac Hill' (or Battle Hill). Why he did so is a matter of puzzlement and some controversy to this day. Having personally visited the terrain five times and extensively reviewed maps and satellite images of the area, and in view of the reports of the battle in *The Anglo-Saxon Chronicle* and other sources, I hope to be able to provide some realistic insights regarding King Harold's decision to deploy his army closer to the Norman advance, instead of just standing fast on the presumably more easily defended Caldbec Hill. Before continuing, it is time to take a closer look at King Harold's army.

Chapter 7

The Composition of the Anglo-Saxon Army – Of Fyrdmen, Hidesmen, Huscarls and Thegns

Who were the members of the Anglo-Saxon 'Fyrd'? For a quick answer, we'll turn to the website 'Spartacus Educational', which states that the Fyrdmen (that is, members of the Great Fyrd, not those in the Select Fyrd) were farmers, tradesmen and other town and village dwellers who were mustered to 'fight for Anglo-Saxon kings in times of danger'. The leaders of the Fyrd were the Thegns, who were equipped with spears and swords, while the mass of average Fyrdmen were generally self-armed with bludgeoning weapons – some made from iron – and axes (such as what a woodsman, farmer or construction worker would use – not the 6ft-long war-axes wielded by the Huscarls). The rural Fyrdmen might carry farm implements such as scythes, sickles, haymaking forks and so forth. Experienced hunters would be armed with their own bows and arrows, while others made often masterful use of slings. Town-dwellers could carry implements such as hammers and homemade maces.[1] The aforementioned website summed up the Anglo-Saxon Fyrd's likely armaments very well and I included some additional observations of my own made as a result of research into weapons wielded across Europe, the Middle East and Asia at the time. As for some supporting evidence, I, among others, witnessed how the Bayeux Tapestry showed that many of the Englishmen were unarmoured and possessed crude weapons, which suggests much of King Harold's force was, in fact, made up in bulk of Fyrdmen, with only a minority of Hidesmen, Thegns and Huscarls. Also, in *The Chronicle of*

109

the Norman Conquest, Master Wace reports: 'The villains* were also called together from the villages, bearing such arms as they found; clubs and great picks, iron forks and (fence) stakes.'[2]

The usual armament carried by a (Select) Fyrdman,† as cited by contemporary sources, included the spear, a shield, a helmet and a mail coat. He would also be expected to have a 'palfrey', which was a riding horse. Oftentimes, if he could afford it, a Select Fyrdman also carried a sword. The website Regis Anglorum emphasises that while a horse is included in the list, it was intended only for mobility, not mounted combat.[3] However, as we have seen earlier, fighting on horseback was not entirely beyond the realm of possibility in Anglo-Saxon England.

Anglo-Saxon archers were apparently thought by their English contemporaries to be not that valuable and only one is shown on the Bayeux Tapestry. Also, being men of less wealth, many of them would not have been able to afford a horse to carry them along with King Harold's mounted and probably wagon-borne army as it hastened to the fight at Battle Hill after the Battle of Stamford Bridge in northern England. The relatively few archers at Battle Hill were likely Fyrdmen from Sussex, Kent and nearby towns and regions.[4]

Without doubt, both sides would have resorted to the use of simple wooden clubs and their more sophisticated descendants, maces. The Bayeux Tapestry shows unarmoured and unhelmeted Anglo-Saxons wielding clubs; however, these illustrations were almost entirely fanciful reconstructions sewn in as part of the restoration process that repaired and altered damaged parts of the Tapestry centuries later. Despite this, there can be no denial that people with rudimentary arms, such as many of the men in the Great Fyrd, would have wielded clubs, some with spikes driven through them. The Bayeux Tapestry displays Norman nobles, including Duke William and his half-brother, Bishop Odo, also carrying maces.

We will now defer to *Anglo-Saxon Military Institutions on the Eve of the Norman Conquest* by C. Warren Hollister to further describe the Anglo-Saxon Fyrd. It is Hollister who divides the Fyrd into the 'Select' Fyrd and

---

* Villains' originally meant 'village dwellers', as it was used here. The more sinister connotation of 'villain' as a criminal only came later, when, in hard times, people of the villages were reputed to resort to all manner of chicanery and thievery in their struggles to survive or get ahead.

† Here we refer to the better-trained and better-armed men of the Select Fyrd, as opposed to the mass of less well-trained and less well-armed men of the Great Fyrd. Other differences between them will be addressed below.

the 'Great' Fyrd. He says that Fyrdmen in the Great Fyrd only defended their immediate neighbourhood from invasion, with the limitation that they had to be close enough to home to return there 'by nightfall', which likely means after a battle that usually occurred in the morning and only lasted an hour or two. The proviso is added that if the men in the Great Fyrd were marched farther away, the king would be obliged to pay them daily wages.[5] As noted before, these Great Fyrdmen would be armed with whatever came to hand in the way of weapons – whether improvised or not – tools, farm implements, even slings and stones.

Before we dismiss the use of more primitive weapons, let us take a look at the English 'byls' or 'bills' and similar devices. From a Web search for 'Medieval Warfare', under the listing of 'Guisarmes' (bills): A 'guisarme' or 'gisarme' is made from hooks, and sometimes blades as well, mounted on a long pole. It was used to unhorse mounted knights and was in general use in Europe between the years 1000 and 1400. As with most pole-arms, bills were usually used by farmers and poorer city dwellers by securing hand tools to poles. Later developments included placing a spike on the back of the blade and/or replacing the flat or hooked blade with a small crescent-shaped axe-head – creating what were known as 'halberds'.[6]

Better-armed men would be assigned to the Select Fyrd, which very likely made up a majority of the Fyrdmen at the Battle of Hastings. These 'Select' Fyrdmen were also sometimes known as Hidesmen, according to what Hollister wrote. With regard to these, as noted above, they would have been better trained and better armed, but there was no required annual training and several years could pass between being called up for deployment in military service demanding the use of their combat skills. Hollister says the 'Select' Fyrd or Hide, included Thegns or, if not available, those known by the title of 'cniht', ('A boy, youth, attendant, servant, KNIGHT: hence the modern knights of a shire are so called because they serve the shire.'[7]) These men were referred to in general and *en masse*, as *'radmannus'*, ('*ráde*; f. I. riding, going on horseback or in a carriage; '*mann* – French from *homo* or *homme* – refers to one who is a mounted minor noble.') Note that the cnihts or radmanni, were an intermediate class between Thegns and peasants and that some of them may have been the equivalent of mounted sergeants.[8]

The aforementioned 'Hidesmen' were the members of the Select Fyrd who were levied for military service on the basis of one each per five 'hides' of land. A hide could be about 40 acres or more and was calculated based on the productivity of the land in rural hides.[9] Hides were also calculated regarding the size, wealth and development of town hides. In addition, the warrior was to receive 20 shillings for his support during the generally forty days to two months of service upon which he could be deployed.[10] Hollister emphasises that Hidesmen were the king's men, not, in this regard, retainers of the earls or lesser lords.[11]

Other minor nobles included in the Select Fyrd were 'Sokemen'. A 'soke' was, in part, the ability to preside over or have jurisdiction over an estate or a part of one. A Sokeman could be an attendant to a greater lord on an estate or could himself be a lesser Thegn who had jurisdictional rights over the lands he owned, leased or administered. For added emphasis, we will add, from Webster's: 'Definition of "*soke*": Noun. English. 1. the right to hold court and dispense justice within a given territory. 2. the territory under the jurisdiction of a court.'[12]

This definition clearly reinforces and emphasises the previous description – a 'Sokeman' would have been a minor magistrate or minister – governmental, not religious – and would therefore automatically also carry a military obligation. Perhaps it was these lesser 'lords' to whom Snorri Sturluson, William of Poitiers and William of Jumièges referred when they wrote of the Anglo-Saxon 'nobles'. (Sturluson also mentioned 'Thingmen', which are a rough Norse approximation to Anglo-Saxon Sokemen.) However, those writers also no doubt included the 'Thegns', whom we will take a look at in a later section.

Huscarls and Mercenaries – How Did They Differ?

Regarding the term 'Huscarl', we will narrow down the variations of the definition to give a more precise interpretation of their office, as opposed to mercenaries. Let's start with 'hus': '*hus* (Middle English) Alternative forms: *hous*. Origin & history. From Old English *hūs*, cognate with Dutch *huis*, Low Saxon (Low German) *Huus*, German *Haus*, Swedish *hus*. Noun. *Hus* – house.'[13] Now let us move on to 'Carl': '*Ceorl* | English peasant. *Ceorl*, also spelled Churl, the free peasant who formed the basis of society in Anglo-Saxon England.'[14]

Now we can move from these individuated definitions to combine them into the form this writer believes is most appropriate. As evidenced by the fact that some Huscarls were also property owners, it is logical that the Old Norse meaning of a 'freeman' is most applicable; and, of course, 'hus' retains its meaning of 'house', as in a royal house or the 'house' of a family of nobility, not just any residence. So, while Huscarls were hired fighting men, they were not mercenaries in the strictest sense but were, rather, a permanently retained staff and not just hired

112

for short times of service, while, on the contrary, mercenaries or 'hired swords' were generally propertyless warriors who were engaged for a few campaigns or even a single one or just one battle.

The historical research, events-staging, movie-prop provider and *de facto* museum creators and curators of a fortified Anglo-Saxon manor house – in southern England – organisation 'Regia Anglorum', in its column, 'Who were the Huscarls?' informs us about how the Huscarls were armed, stating that their combat gear would have been of the highest quality available. In addition to his sword, the Huscarl was required to have a horse to take him to the fight, a chain-mail hauberk, a helmet, shield, spear and, most important of all, his long-handled battleaxe.[15]

The same report tells us that Huscarls were often individually identified, not as a class of people, as being both the 'cynges Huscarl' and 'minister regis' in combination. A pure Huscarl – one who was landless and had not received any form of lordship bestowed upon him – had a strictly military duty; he was known as a 'milites regis' and not also as a 'minister regis'. Thus, a Huscarl was an attendant upon the king or earl, whose specialty was war, but who in some cases – by virtue of his having ascended into the minor nobility through the acquisition of land rights – was not limited to fighting duties alone but also, for example, tax collection. Thus, some, even many, Huscarls also held a lordship-to-vassalage bond, which further strengthened their military obligation. In this case, as in most other medieval societies, the vassals were themselves lesser lords as well. In addition to a cash payment was a reciprocal obligation to be rendered to Huscarls by their lord and master.[16] In other words, unlike practices in many other societies – ancient and modern – obligations and loyalty requirements extended in both directions – loyalty was a two-way street, whereas the emerging Norman and Continental practice was for loyalty to generally run in one direction only, from the lower to the upper strata of society.

With regard to the 'Lithsmen' and 'Buscarls', they were purely mercenary troops who would sometimes be inclined to cast loyalty aside and align themselves with the highest bidder.[17] However, as the Regia Anglorum handbook also points out, Huscarls were not themselves mercenaries, for, despite being paid in coinage, the added requirement to serve as warriors originated from their sometime and even oftentime status as land-holding lesser lords; the payments were add-ons for a more extended military service.[18]

Regarding the fates of the Huscarls, Regia Anglorum says that they probably served as the army's shock troops, with correspondingly high casualties. In Norman England, the Huscarls were no longer to be found. While most of King Harold's Huscarls likely died at Stamford Bridge and Battle Hill, the others, being held in low esteem by their Norman conquerors, would therefore have become exiled soldiers of fortune – mercenaries, ranging across the European continent as far as Byzantine Constantinople. The same fate no doubt befell many, almost all, surviving Anglo-Saxon Thegns.[19]

Next in this regard we will again refer to an early acknowledged expert in the realm of the Anglo-Saxon military. In his book *Anglo-Saxon Military Institutions on the Eve of the Norman Conquest*, C. Warren Hollister asserts that the Huscarls were mercenaries, but then, on the following page, he concedes that they were landholders.[20] But this contradiction merely proves, to me, my assertion that Huscarls were *not* mercenaries in the sense that they were merely hired swords (or battleaxes) but were instead often if not usually vassals or sub-vassals who also functioned as (the king's or an earl's) household troops. This would, by extension, also hold true for those Huscarls who did not own land, at least in the initial phase of their service as part of a privately retained standing army and were not just occasionally and temporarily hired men.

As for the Huscarls' fighting tactics, at the blog page 'The Deadliest Blogger: Military History Page, The historical writing of Barry C. Jacobsen', in an item titled 'Military History Blog of "Deadliest Warriors"', Jacobsen writes that on the battlefield the Huscarls stood in the centre of the army, circling the king and his standard; or they could have been deployed by their leader as 'stiffeners' for the Fyrdmen and Hidesmen all along the shield wall.[21] I believe they were deployed as both the royal or noble guards and as reinforcing troops deployed all along the battle line and perhaps and likely in groups of reserves as well.

With regard to the more recent history of the Huscarls, Jacobsen continues that during King Canute's reign the Huscarls were predominantly Danes, facilitating Canute's remaining in power in otherwise predominantly Anglo-Saxon England; but he adds that after his death Canute's successors had begun recruiting more Anglo-Saxon Huscarls and that by the time Edward the Confessor was restored to the throne many of the royal Huscarls came from the earldoms of England, largely from Wessex, whose earl, Godwin and then his sons – Harold, Tostig, Gyrth and Leofwyn – relied upon them to keep the family in good favour as they struggled against Edward's Normanisation of England, retaining Godwin and then the Godwinssons as the true powers behind the throne.[22]

Elaborating upon the history of the Huscarls, Jacobsen continues that after Godwin died, Harold Godwinsson became the dominant force behind Edward the Confessor, with, again, the largest contingent of Huscarls. Then, in the campaigns against the Welsh interlopers, in 1063, Harold Godwinsson and his Huscarls invaded Wales and defeated Gruffydd ap Llywelyn of Gwynedd, whose followers killed him and sent his head to Harold. Upon his accession to the throne, King Harold II initially enjoyed the support of about 3,000 Huscarls during the struggles of 1066.[23] Jacobsen does not cite his sources, but the information is consistent with that generally found in many works by various authors elsewhere.

Now that we have clearly established who and what the Huscarls were, it is time to take a look at medieval mercenaries; so, I now ask readers to please bear with me while I cite a couple of commentators regarding mercenaries and other soldiers in order to bolster my own case. In his book, *Household Men, Mercenaries and Vikings in Anglo-Saxon England*, author Richard Abels notes that despite the fact that hired warriors played a key role in both the conquest and then loss of England by the Anglo-Saxons, there is little evidence left behind about their existence.[24]

Abels goes on to say that, as an instructor at the US Naval Academy, he asked cadets in class if they enrolled to serve the country or merely for pay. Then he inquired if they would do the same if unpaid. Of course, most agreed they served for patriotic reasons, but insisted that it was necessary to be paid – to support themselves and their families. Moreover, the cadets reacted negatively to the thought of being perceived as entering military service out of a disproportionate desire for monetary gain,[25] thus reinforcing the long-held notion that combat for pay as the primary motivating factor had a pejorative connotation for most people, even with the concession that fighting for free was not practical or even understandable.

Abels then cites Stephen Morillo's definition of the difference between war-fighters who are not embedded in the society for which they fight and those warriors who are integrated into their society and who therefore experience some forms of moral imperative to serve as soldiers.[26] Of course, the latter are also influenced by market forces to choose the fighting professions; and, again naturally, the former are motivated by finding the highest-paying employer for whom to fight, no matter the worth or lack of same in that employer's 'cause'.[27]

Abels then explains that while the Latin term *'mercennarius'* accurately described the commoditisation of combat skills, when translated into Anglo-Saxon terms for hired men – no matter for what type of labour performed – 'cebnert monn', 'esne-man', 'med-wyrhta' and 'hyra' – are also descriptions that applied to non-mercenary troops.[28] Abels also makes these points at Medievalists.net.[29]

Many commentators over the centuries have noted that hired fighting men fought not just for profit but also during times of famines and wars, when they became displaced; or that they fought for pay due to the lack of an inheritance; or that they hired-out as warriors from a competitive spirit; to seek escape from boredom; out of the sheer joy of physical exertion – particularly that required for combat. I will add that men will also fight, as noted above, for glory – real or imagined; for a cause; or, as foolishly romantic as it may seem today, for love of kindred, king and country.

So, overall, I think both the scholarly experts and amateur historians engaged in private research and activities such as participating in historical re-enactments support my view that men serving in regular military functions differ from hired mercenaries in that the former are employed in a more enduring manner in a profession that requires them to remain consistent in their loyalties and actions, and the latter enjoy more flexibility and changeability due to the temporary nature of their employment.

Do I think King Harold II had hired troops – mercenaries – in his army at Battle Hill? Yes. He had lost probably 2,000 to 2,500 Huscarls at Stamford Bridge (out of an estimated 3,000 available altogether).[30] Neither Earl Morcar nor Earl Edwin had hastened south with the remnants of their armies to his aid. Evidently, according to *The Anglo-Saxon Chronicle* – Manuscript 'D' – as we have seen, not all of the available fighting men in the south were willing to go with him to meet Duke William on the Hastings-to-London ridgeway road. (These would have excluded the Huscarls, who were duty-bound to serve with him.) Therefore, he had to muster as many Fyrdmen and Hidesmen as he could to join with his remaining Huscarls as he scoured London, Sussex and Kent for reinforcements, then headed for Battle Hill. He was determined, whether or not he met with other noblemen – evidently lesser lords as no earls are mentioned in *The Anglo-Saxon Chronicle* or elsewhere as having gone with him – also whether or not a meeting occurred at Appledore, if not London. In the meantime, I believe King Harold would have paid out for as many swordsmen-for-hire as he could locate and motivate to join his army – meagre though it was, despite being described in *The Anglo-Saxon Chronicle* as a 'mighty force'.[31] This may have been his principal reasoning for not distributing to the army the booty acquired after the victory at the Battle of Stamford Bridge, which may have also motivated at least some warriors to not fight at Battle Hill.

Who Were the Thegns?

Thegns were divided into Greater Thegns and Lesser Thegns. Greater Thegns were the 'King's Thegns', who worked for and were directly responsible to the king. Men in the category of Lesser Thegns were those who owed their loyalty to the king's vassals – earls and ealdormen. Of course, all of the king's subjects owed their loyalty to the crown; the difference was in who was their direct employer or lord. We have already looked at the Lesser Thegns of the 'cniht' (knight), 'radmannus' (riding man) and 'sokeman' (minor magistrate) varieties. The Greater Thegns were the senior nobles and churchmen, who were, relatively speaking, secure in their positions in the social hierarchy and in their estates. While neither *The Anglo-Saxon Chronicle* nor Snorri Sturluson's sagas tell us who were the Thegns who accompanied King Harold II to the battle near Hastings, Master Wace does provide some hints in a partial list of those he says were there:

Harold had summoned his men, earls, barons and vavassors‡ from the castles and the cities; from the ports, the villages and boroughs... Those of London had come at once and those of Kent, of Herfort [Hereford] and of Essesse [Essex]; those of Surée [Surrey] and Sussesse [Sussex], of St Edmund and Sufoc [Suffolk]; of Norwis [Norwich] and Norfoc [Norfolk]; of Cantorbierre [Canterbury] and Stanfort [Stamford]; Bedefort [Bedford] and Hundetone [Huntingdon]. The men of Northanton [Northampton] also came; and those of Eurowic [Warwick] and Bokinkeham [Buckingham], of Bed [Bedfordshire] and Notinkeham [Nottingham], Lindesie [Lindsey] and Nichole [?]. There came also from the west all who heard the summons; and very many were to be seen coming from Salebiere [Salisbury] and Dorset, from Bat [Bath] and from

---

‡ 'Vavasor in British English or vavassor ('vævə͵sɔ:) or vavasour ('vævə͵sʊə) Noun. In feudal society, the noble or knightly vassal of a baron or great lord who also has vassals himself. Word origin: From Old French vavasour, perhaps contraction of Medieval Latin vassus vassōrum – vassal of vassals . . .' (Collins English Dictionary. Copyright © HarperCollins Publishers https://www. collinsdictionary.com/us/dictionary/english/vavassor.)

Sumerset. Many came too from about Glocestre [Gloucester] and many from Wirecestre [Worcester], from Wincestre [Winchester], Hontesire [Hampshire] and Brichesire [Berkshire]; and many more from other counties that we have not named and cannot indeed recount. All who could bear arms and had learnt the news of the duke's arrival, came to defend the land. But none came from beyond Humbre [Earls Morcar and Edwin], for they had other business upon their hands; the Danes and Tosti having much damaged and weakened them.[32]

Regia Anglorum further informs us: 'By the beginning of the 11th century all the Thegns usually held estates of five hides or more and so by this date they probably constituted the bulk of the Fyrd.'[33] By this we can assume they are referring to the Select Fyrd.

About the Anglo-Saxon 'Shield Wall'

Some, many, even most people, including some who are quite expert in the field of studying and commenting on medieval warfare, have, in my opinion, been overly critical in their remarks about the efficacy of the Anglo-Saxon shield wall. The facts of the battle at Battle Hill demonstrate clearly what a formidable obstacle it proved to be on that day in 1066, when, despite the best efforts of a fighting force composed almost entirely of military professionals, the generally non-professional English fighters managed to withstand attack after attack, from mid-morning until almost sunset, despite repeated assaults by skilled Norman infantry, barrages of arrows, hails of javelins and cavalry charges by trained and experienced noble horsemen to break through. (In my estimation, this main line of the shield wall was thrown across the ridgeway, now the A2100.) C. Warren Hollister tells us that the performance of the warriors in the Anglo-Saxon shield wall at Battle Hill was so impressive as to cause the Normans themselves to imitate and perpetuate the use of the shield wall for some time afterward – up until the year 1141, when Anglo-Norman knights were dismounting to fight on foot in tightly-packed formations in the five major and most important battles of the Anglo-Norman period.[34]

Of equal, if not often greater, importance than the size, organisation or even weaponry of an army can be the role played by the local terrain and vegetation at the site of a battle.

Chapter 8

Where the Forests End and Begin – Today and in 1066

During my five explorations of the countryside in and around Battle, I noticed that the woodlands in the area had evidently been reasserting themselves wherever left alone to do so. I later confirmed this first impression by consulting old maps, comparing those with satellite images and relying on my own recollections and photographs.

At 'Old Maps of East Sussex',[1] I reviewed the map Sheet 320 – Hastings (Outline), publication date: 1895. Even at that late date, the 'Great Woods' extended to the north and north-east of the current A2100 and right up to the road, as it does to this day. It reaches from Blackfriars and to the Starr's Green tract and patches of woods also appear on the south and south-west of the road at Quarry Hill, which is just to the south-east of the Tesco Express (actually, the retail outlet is built on that hill) and other patches of woodland are shown remaining on both sides of the Southeastern Railway line and on toward Powdermill Lane, across there and extending onto the grounds of the traditionally accepted battle site below Battle Abbey. Almost all of these areas are now partially given over to meadowlands, including the site I agree should be identified as the 'Scean Leagh',[2] or 'Scenic Meadow'.* Interestingly, the area below and across the railway tracks

---

* In Anglo-Saxon: 'Scean' or 'sceán-feld' or 'scín-feld': The beautiful, Elysîan field, applied to Tempe – Vale of, a valley in eastern Greece, in Thessaly, between Mount Olympus and Mount Ossa. 'Leagh' or 'leah': A lea, meadow, open space, untilled land (The Bosworth-Toller Anglo-Saxon Dictionary http://bosworth. ff.cuni.cz/). Thus, 'Senlac' may be a corrupted or Latinised, version of the same – Scean Leagh or Scenic Meadow.

from Marley Lane, which I've determined to be the right flank of the Norman army's advance and also the location where the Anglo-Saxon warrior's axe-head was found, is marked on these maps as 'Battle Hill'.

As shown on the map, the Great Woods extend to Starr's Green and patches of woods are shown exactly where they remain today – just to the east and south-east of the Powdermill Lane roundabout and below the Methodist Church and cemetery to the west of the A2100.[3] Other patches of woods survive right up to Powdermill Lane, just as I found them in 2016. In fact, in that area I discovered not only a thick growth of trees, some quite old and massive, but indications that they formerly extended beyond as they abruptly cut off where pavements were put in place at the boundaries. At the 'Battle Extensive Urban Survey report and maps' site, Map 5 indicates that between 1066 and 1149 the current routes of Marley Lane, Powdermill Lane and the present-day A2100 were then used as roads and lanes and were not built up; that the 'regular burgage plots' stopped just short of the Powdermill Lane roundabout's site.[4] Map 6 shows that what it calls 'irregular historic plots along the A2100 route and Powdermill Lane were not added until the period of 1150 to 1349. These plots remained almost unchanged until the sixteenth century, as shown on Map 8.[5]

A quick look at the Google Earth image of the Battle area shows the Great Woods to the east and its aggressive reforestation toward Blackfriars and Battle Hill. Likewise, virtually every patch of undeveloped land in the area, and particularly the site of my proposed placement of the Anglo-Saxons' slightly crimped 'S'-shaped shield wall, has been at least partially reforested, proving that not only are these locations capable of supporting heavy forests, they seem to be rebounding on that very course into the future, barring human intervention and also demonstrating that it is very likely that almost the entire area was covered with thick but sometimes patchy woodlands in 1066.

In his translation of *The Carmen de Hastingae Proelio of Guy, Bishop of Amiens*, Frank Barlow presents a map of the Battle area in the introduction. In the caption within the map box, he notes: 'The Carmen describes the Andreadsweald as ending on Caldbec Hill. Telham Hill was probably also wooded.'[6] This is precisely the area of real estate where, in the centre of this territory, I contend that the Battle of Hastings actually occurred.

What the Woods and Terrain Have to do With the Anglo-Saxon Deployments

With, presumably, a much reduced, less well-trained and inexperienced army than he preferred to have on hand to resist almost the entire Norman professional expeditionary force to England and with an even smaller contingent of mounted men, King Harold would logically have opted to make his stand in the thickly wooded tracts that bordered on and grew upon what's now known as 'Battle Hill'. As cited before, the comment in *The Anglo-Saxon Chronicle* that '. . . but the king, nevertheless, very hardly encountered him [Duke William] with the men that would support him [King Harold]' shows that at least a significant part – significant enough to warrant a mention in the generally sparing reports in the *Chronicle* – of the English army did not support King Harold at Battle Hill; and this would have especially applied to the mounted troops, many of whom would have been nobles. It is evident that not very many of the Anglo-Saxon nobility were present at Battle Hill on 14 October 1066 or else they would have been mentioned in the *Chronicle* and other works. Instead, only King Harold's brothers are reported in the *Chronicle* to have been present. We have already shown, in general terms but not as to specific individuals, which noblemen, whether petty or more major we are not told, were mentioned in another text[7] as having been at the site of the Hastings battle that day. This clearly indicates that King Harold had no other choice than to try to defend against the Normans with very few mounted warriors of his own, which dictated that he set up his defensive line as much as possible on wooded terrain, where the Anglo-Saxon infantry would have an advantage and the Norman cavalry and archers would be at a disadvantage.

About Telham Hill: my vantage point, near the 'Telham Adjacent to Black Horse' bus stop, close to Telham Lane, is at an elevation of 488ft and, while not on the peak of Telham Hill, it is atop the crest of the ridgeline extending east as well as west, across the A2100 and it is reasonable to conclude that Duke William's scouts could see Caldbec Hill from the area, as I could, provided the weather was clear enough, as it must have been for the Normans to spot the Anglo-Saxon army gathering there.

Tony Robinson's excellent television documentary in the television series 'Time Team', in the episode focusing on '1066, The Lost Battlefield', decided that the actual site of the battle at Battle was at the aforementioned Marley Lane roundabout.[8] I believe 'Time Team' is correct, but only in part. Instead, I believe the centre of the actual battle line was positioned farther forward and that it extended just beyond the other nearby roundabout, where Powdermill Lane / the B2095 meets the A2100. To the east of that roundabout, King Harold's shield wall would have been on the slope just below Marley Lane and would probably have reached as far as where that avenue makes its level crossing of the Southeastern Railway tracks, being anchored at the thick woods and marshland that were very probably there prior to being chopped down and drained in more recent times.[†] One bit of physical evidence discovered there – the only one found anywhere near the battle sites, actual or conjectured – was an Anglo-Saxon-style warrior's axe-head uncovered when work crews widened Marley Lane in the early 1950s.

Before continuing, I think it is important to note that a large majority of the battle maps found in various written and electronic media works illustrating the supposed deployments of the Anglo-Saxon and Norman armies are incorrect, distorted or outright fabrications with regard to the actual terrain and logical positions of the armies, whether done intentionally or not. Among the exceptions, along with a very few others, are illustrations and digital displays functioning as maps provided for Tony Robinson's aforementioned television documentary regarding the most likely locations of the armies struggling at Battle Hill. These most often show the ridgeway in the wrong place or at an incorrect angle and usually extend the proposed battle lines in distorted and sometimes even tortuous deployments in order to show how the traditionally accepted battlefield location makes more sense when it does not.

Instead of going up to the Marley Lane roundabout, the Anglo-Saxon battle line would have described a generally broad but at its centre a crimped 'S'-curve, sweeping westward along and just below the then wooded heights downslope from Marley Lane but above Station Approach, then briefly swinging south-south-east[‡] and crossing

---

[†] In the introduction to *The Carmen de Hastingae Proelio of Guy, Bishop of Amiens* (p. lxxviii), on the map produced there, the area in front of and extending to the present-day Marley Lane, at the railway crossing cited above, is shown as a meandering stretch of marshlands that extends back toward the narrow valley where the Southeastern Railway tracks are located now.

[‡] Master Wace wrote, 'King Harold issued orders and made proclamation round, that all should be ranged with their faces toward the enemy; and that no one should move from where he was; so that whoever came might find them ready; and that whatever any one, be he Norman or other, should do, each should do his best to defend his own place. Then he ordered the men of Kent to go where the Normans were likely to make the attack; for they say that the men of Kent

WHERE THE FORESTS END AND BEGIN – TODAY AND IN 1066

the A2100 just to the south and south-east of the Powdermill Lane roundabout and facing the advancing Normans just above – to the north and north-west of – the valley enclosing the present-day Southeastern Railway line. From there, the Anglo-Saxons deployed south-westward along the lip of the narrow valley where the train tracks run, which is the forward slope of the ever-more-slight ridge crest upon which we now find Powdermill Lane/the B2095, possibly all the way to the current Battle Abbey Farm and Powdermill Lake. The very slight ridge here is just barely discernible in the Google Earth image of 4 May 2018, stretching from the north-east at GPS coordinates 50⁰54'34.38' N and 0⁰29'15.57' E and south-west to about 50⁰54'17.57' N and 0⁰28'56.55' E, where it curves back to Battle Abbey Farm and Powdermill Lake. As this ridge fell away, the thick woods near the road – the current A2100 and the St Mary's tract area – would have thinned toward the south-west, too, becoming a series of clumps of trees interspersed with 'scenic meadows' and occasional marshy areas, until the woods began to reassert themselves near the farm and lake.

I do not believe King Harold was able, from his initial vantage point just south of the Marley Lane roundabout, with trees intervening and blocking his view, to take into account the fact that his right flank could be extended and overextended, that far, making that segment of his eventual battle line vulnerable to Norman infantry and cavalry charges as they progressively outmanoeuvred his troops' position in that direction, leading to his ultimate defeat when the main line of resistance was stretched, then penetrated, shredded and overwhelmed late in the day.

In tracing this line of deployment, the Anglo-Saxon battlefront would be along the northern edge of the narrow and steep-sided valley that is now occupied by the Southeastern Railway tracks. This valley or grand 'ditch' would cover only the westernmost or right flank of the Anglo-

---

are entitled to strike first; and that whenever the king goes to battle, the first blow belongs to them. The right of the men of London is to guard the king's body, to place themselves around him and to guard his standard; and they were accordingly placed by the standard, to watch and defend it' (Wace, p. 177. https://www.gutenberg.org/files/41163/41163-h/41163-h.htm). By the remark that the men should be arranged with their faces toward the enemy makes sense if it refers to the fact that where the Anglo-Saxon battle line was 'crimped', just to the left of the centre, where it was fronted to one side of the anticipated Norman advance; so he advised that they should be arrayed toward the Normans, their shields, weapons and eyes directed toward the enemy's advance, not facing toward the marshy stretch below, to the east of the A2100 where the narrow 'ditch' opens out toward the left, western side of the Anglo-Saxon shield wall.

Saxon shield wall. Master Wace tells us that 'The English stood in close ranks, ready and eager for the fight; and they had moreover made a fosse [ditch], which went across the field, guarding one side of their army.'[9] This passage perfectly fits the layout of the terrain and would have covered 'one side of their army', if, as I contend, King Harold had deployed his men on the near side of this 'fosse' or 'ditch', which is about 15 to 30ft deep and about 60 to 80ft wide for most of its length, from the A2100 to the right, but not as far as the Battle Abbey Farm and Powdermill Lake as you face south, toward the route of the Norman advance. This is where the Anglo-Saxon battle line would be at its weakest and most vulnerable to being outflanked and/or overrun; but, I conjecture, neither Duke William nor his fighters became aware of this fact until the battle was fully developed and the Normans during the day increasingly side-stepped to their left to stretch out and eventually break the Anglo-Saxon defences.

After forming up across the all-important ridgeway from Hastings to beyond Battle Hill, the Anglo-Saxon warriors would have 'curved' their deployment, bending the shield wall back to face more east-south-east and eastward, following the steep slopes there until the heights arched again, this time 'inward' as the incline gradually turned to face toward the south once more, in the areas now occupied by Station Approach and Marley Lane. (Again, this 'crimping' of the shield wall would have required the men to stand and face at an oblique angle to front themselves toward the actual Norman advance on and alongside the ridgeway.)

This overly-extended line of deployment would have been about 6,500ft in length, which, depending on how many men King Harold actually had at his disposal that day, would have allowed for a concentrated front up to five ranks deep across the Hastings-to-London ridgeway, but then constantly thinning to a man standing about every foot and a half for a dense formation of about one or two ranks deep on either side – except in the woods, where skirmish 'lines' or groups of men or even individuals would have engaged in more disorganised and even single-combats. Then there would be an even looser arrangement of a man placed every 2 to 4ft in a more open deployment in areas such as thicker woods and rugged terrain, and becoming even more thinned-out at the extreme ends, where skirmishers and pickets, on foot and possibly a few mounted, would have tried to screen and cover the flanks of King Harold's hard-pressed defenders.

As for the shield walls themselves: Wace states: 'The English knew not how to joust, nor bear arms on horseback, but fought with hatchets and bills. A man when he wanted to strike with one of their hatchets, was obliged to hold it with both his hands and could not at the same time, as it seems to me, both cover himself and strike with any freedom.'[10] As to the lattermost point, not having been there, Wace would not have seen the two-handed-axe wielders – the Huscarls – standing, whenever practical, in the second rank and their technique of swinging their war axes to one side, the axe-head at a level below their knees, then circling the fearsome weapons back and then arcing them up behind their shoulders and then overhead and bringing the impossible-to-block giant cleavers down, either to the left or to the right, beyond the front rank, of the shield wall, splitting the heads and shoulders of their enemies. Also, the English Heritage website comments about the axe-wielders' weapons: 'Swung with two hands, the battle-axe was capable of cutting off the head of a man or horse. But it was also light and well-balanced enough to be used with one hand, while the other held a shield.'[11] So, evidently, axe-wielding Huscarls could serve in the front rank of the shield wall just as well. In fact, Hollister also asserts that the Huscarls were to be found in the first rank of the shield wall.[12]

Chapter 9

Who Were the Men Who Fought in the Norman Army?

Independently of each other, Christopher Macdonald Hewitt, of the Department of Geography at the University of Western Ontario, and I each came to find that the construction of Battle Abbey on the precise site of the battle is and always was in some doubt. He and I both consulted the same work – *Lordship and Community: Battle Abbey and its Banlieu, 1066-1538*, by Eleanor Searle – which I obtained and read while studying at the University of Sussex. That book asserts that, despite William the Conqueror's reported insistence that Battle Abbey be built on the actual battlefield, the monks charged with the task objected that the battle location lacked proper water sources, had poor stone reserves to build the abbey and was situated on overly rugged ground.[1] They suggested that the abbey be built on a more suitable site nearby (presumably the location of Battle Abbey where it now stands). William the Conqueror evidently believed the differences of opinions and plans were resolved in his favour when he provided a supply of stone from Normandy, but the monks replied that they had located their own source for good construction stone in the battle area. By the time the abbey was built, in the 1070s, William was already back in Normandy, never to return to England and verify in person that the abbey was actually situated at the precise place of the fighting and King Harold's fall. So, the evidence of the abbey having been built on the exact site of the battle, and where King Harold II died remains in some doubt, as it always has been.* Professor Hewitt and I disagree as to the actual

---

* Moreover, for reasons having to do with Battle Abbey's special status and tax exemptions, the monks at the abbey were proven to be not above forging its

126

location of the battle, which he believes was on Caldbec Hill, while I am convinced by the evidence I have gathered and presented herein that it was largely fought along – just above, really – the narrow and steep-sided valley now occupied by the Southeastern Railway tracks.

The reason why William the Conqueror was allegedly so insistent upon placing the abbey on the exact site of the battle, as well as the precise spot King Harold was killed, is supposedly due to the admonition by Pope Alexander II ordering the Normans to do penance for slaying so many Anglo-Saxons during the Conquest.[2] Placing the abbey where King Harold purportedly was taken down was also likely to further placate the Pope because William the Conqueror was reported to have been one of the four Norman mounted warriors who slew the Anglo-Saxon king – an act of regicide, as will be covered later herein.

How the Opposing Forces Came Together

It is evident that Duke William's advance along the Hastings-to-London ridgeway and King Harold's counter-deployment on Caldbec Hill – possibly in preparation for a planned pre-emptive thrust toward the wooden Norman castle just erected above Hastings – resulted in not a set-piece battle, as is so often presumed, but was, rather, more of an almost chance 'meeting engagement'. In this regard, John Grehan and Martin Mace quote from Frank Stenton, on pages 58 and 59 of their book: '. . . feudal battles were determined more by the event of a simple collision of large masses of men than by their manoeuvres when in the field: the skill of a great feudal captain lay chiefly in his ability to choose his ground so as to give his side the preliminary advantage in the shock of battle'.[3] After Norman scouts spotted the Anglo-Saxons marshalling on Caldbec Hill, King Harold II – likely almost simultaneously learning of the approaching Normans – redeployed his forces as far forward as possible, on Battle Hill. This assertion on my part is bolstered by Bishop Guy in his description of the interruption of Duke William's planned deployment by the sudden appearance of the Anglo-Saxon army. Davis and Chibnall also note that instead of a pitched battle, Duke William usually preferred to gradually wear down his opponents through a

---

charter. This is corroborated by Nick Austin in his book, which asserts that the Battle of Hastings occurred at Crowhurst. In bringing up this point, on page 211, Austin also cites Searle's book.

campaign of attrition by, for example, working from a secure base, as he had done on the Continent.[4]

Guy wrote that Duke William placed his archers and crossbowmen in the first rank, then arrayed his infantry in the second rank, intending to position his cavalry in the third rank; however, the approach of King Harold's men intervened: '. . . for he could see enemy units not far away and the whole forest glittering with spears.'[5] Note also that Guy places the 'glittering spears' within the forest, not on open ground, such as is found on Caldbec Hill and also at the proposed battlefields at Sedlescombe and Crowhurst, as well as the field below Batlle Abbey.

As Duke William was arraying his forces, Bishop Guy describes how the English came to meet him: 'Suddenly, the forest spewed out its cohorts and columns of men stormed out of their hiding-places in the woods.'[6] Here we see that, once more, Guy's sources tell us the area was forested and that 'columns of men', not a line abreast of warriors or a shield wall, emerged from the wooded land. So, we see that they appeared from the woods, but positioned where? Except for the open meadow(s) mentioned previously, even today, the only open spaces onto which the English could array would be across the Hastings-to-London ridgeway and along the lip of the narrow valley where the Southeastern Railway is now found.

The poem next informs us, 'Near the forest was a hill and a valley and land too rough to be tilled'.[7] This passage accurately describes the terrain from the Powdermill Lane roundabout and toward the long and narrow valley 'ahead' (in the direction of the approaching Normans on the ridgeway and the adjacent Quarry Hill) that is now occupied by the Southeastern Railway line, which, according to a map drawn between 1778 and 1783,[8] was and is too steep-sided 'to be tilled', even before the railway line was placed there.

But we are getting ahead of ourselves here and must take a closer look at the Norman army before proceeding with an accounting of the progress of the battle as I envision it to have been.

Who Were the Fighting Men in Duke William's Army and How Were They Armed?

While the Norman cavalry and archers are generally credited with contributing mightily to the victory of Duke William at the Battle of Hastings, making him William the Conqueror, the great, and even decisive, participation by the Norman infantry must not be overlooked. Master Wace tells us: '. . . the men on foot were well equipped, each bearing bow and sword: on their heads were caps and to their feet were bound buskins [open-toed boots]. Some had good hides which they had bound round their bodies; and many were clad in frocks and had quivers and bows hung to their girdles.'[9] However, he fails to mention spears or shields. As to the spear: 'Used by both sides at Hastings, the iron-headed spear was the poorer warriors' weapon. It could be used for thrusting or thrown like a javelin.'[10] Also, from the British Heritage website: 'The basic weapon of the Norman cavalry and infantry was a spear with a leaf-shaped head of iron . . .' The haft was described as being fashioned from wood, often from ash trees. Contemporary illustrations show that infantrymen's spears were heavier and thicker, with cavalrymen hefting lighter weapons, probably to be thrown like javelins. Also, both types evidently had cross-pieces below the heads, to prevent deep penetrations, causing the weapons to become stuck in victims' flesh.[11]

The Norman infantry also benefitted from an improved design of shields. The long, kite-shaped shields, in addition to other types, appear in the Bayeux Tapestry. They protected the entire body, from shoulder to ankle. They were equipped with a strap to sling them around the neck, leaving both hands free while on the march. There were handholds for fighting on foot. The Norman cavalry also carried this type of shield, which, when strapped to the forearm, allowed a rider to have one hand free to grip the reins while the other wielded a spear or sword.[12] Norman knights and infantrymen would also use round shields. They were usually fashioned of wood, with leather coverings. The shields most often had painted-on decorations, devices and coats-of-arms denoting the identity of the knight or his lord.[13]

The nobility was armed with high-quality swords. While some infantrymen could afford swords, they were more crudely crafted than the fine blades wielded by their overlords. The swords of the elites were held in very high esteem and a sacred aura surrounded them so that they were often named and were, of course, handed down from one generation to the next. In addition to well-made blades, the pommels sometimes contained holy relics and/or were inlaid with precious stones, and the blades themselves were also likely to be engraved with religious inscriptions.

The average Norman soldier's sword was about a yard long, tapering to a point and was double-edged, with a hollow or longitudinal bevel or 'fuller' to lighten it for ease of handling without weakening it. There would also have been a simple cross-guard or quillon to protect the warrior's hand. The grip would have been of leather-covered wood, and the steel pommel balanced the weight of the blade, making the sword easier to handle.[14]

The swords of 1066 were meant to be and were used more as slashing weapons rather than the thrusting usage of the older Roman short sword. The Bayeux Tapestry depicts a Norman knight using his sword to chop off the head of a Saxon battleaxe.[15]

While bow-armed warriors were not held in the highest esteem in Anglo-Saxon England, they were a valued adjunct to the Norman army. There were an estimated 1,000 archers in Duke William's invasion force. It is reported that William ordered them to shoot in high, arching volleys over the Anglo-Saxon shield wall, their arrows falling onto the often unprotected faces and shoulders of the defenders. But, even before that, William of Poitiers reported: 'So the Norman foot-soldiers closed to attack the English, killing and maiming many with their missiles [as in arrows, not spear thrusts or sword slashes].'[16]

The Normans also possessed what was then a new and powerful weapon – the crossbow.[17] While none were thought to have been illustrated in the Bayeux Tapestry,† they were in fact a part of the invasion force. Although their rate of fire was much slower than that of conventional bows and their effective range was far less, the bolts they launched travelled with greater velocity and were able to penetrate English shields, hauberks and the Anglo-Saxon bodies being 'protected' by them.[18]

Men utilising bows and crossbows had to be adaptable to battlefield developments, so they needed manoeuvrability and, while usually moving on foot, with but a relatively few mounted on horseback, they were generally unarmoured and clothed in light garments. They were also often barefoot and without heavy leggings. They carried their arrows and bolts in quivers, shown in the Bayeux Tapestry, some affixed to their belts, others emplaced upright alongside them on the ground.[19]

As with their Anglo-Saxon opponents and the household English and Danish Huscarls, the Normans, descended from fellow northmen, also made us of the battleaxe. This weapon was, of course, just as fearsome in the hands of a Norman warrior as those being wielded on the other side of the fight at Battle Hill.[20]

---

† Here, Nick Austin has proven to many people, including this author, that some of the archers appearing in the border illustrations of the Bayeux Tapestry are actually wielding crossbows (*Secrets of the Norman Invasion*, pp. 296–311.)

Professional military men and women, and historians, have over the centuries come to appreciate the value of the 'combined arms' approach to combat, with various types of weapons functioning in different 'domains' giving a usually decisive advantage to the side that better adapts this concept to any particular engagement. Thus, while the Anglo-Saxons at the battle near Hastings had limited access to some mobility, with a few warriors – probably mostly flank guards, skirmishers and pickets – fighting on horseback, they lacked the massive combined force of mobility blended with 'firepower' provided by large numbers of mounted cavalrymen at Battle Hill. Likewise, the few English archers gave the Anglo-Saxons a very inadequate capacity to function in the 'battlefield terrain' of the air. It was the Norman army, with its hundreds and up to a likely thousand archers that allowed them to dominate the 'domain of the sky' at Battle Hill. Even in the ground fight between masses of infantry, while the Anglo-Saxon shield wall was evidently able to frustrate almost all efforts by the Normans to break through, eventually, by the persistent domination of the 'air battle', as conducted by arrow- and bolt-barrages, the Normans at last created openings in the Anglo-Saxon line, which would have been immediately exploited by infantry and cavalry alike.[21]

Then there was the previously cited 'force multiplier' of mobility combined with the striking power provided by cavalry charges that aided the Norman infantry assaults until they were able to at first penetrate, then shred the Anglo-Saxon shield wall along the slight ridge behind the present-day Southeastern Railway line and along Powdermill Lane that granted Duke William an overwhelming victory late in the day on 14 October 1066. In this, King Harold issued a dire warning and made a prophetic pronouncement when he told his men prior to the battle, 'The Normans', said he, 'are good vassals, valiant on foot and on horseback; good knights are they on horseback and well used to battle; all is lost if they once penetrate our ranks.'[22] Such cavalry charges alone would in all likelihood not have been enough in and of themselves to break through.[‡] The initial purpose of the Norman cavalry would have been to ride forward and make harrying strikes with javelins and a few with arrows, then to wheel around and withdraw to rearm and repeat the manoeuvre. However, after the Norman infantry had made one of its feigned retreats, the cavalry would also have then rushed forward to

---

[‡] Davis and Chibnall agree, citing William of Poitiers (*The Gesta Guillelmi by William of Poitiers*, pp. ii, xxxiii, 17, 129.)

isolate and cut to pieces any pursuing Anglo-Saxon infantrymen who had been foolish enough to follow.[23] Then, after the Norman infantry was able to create breaches in the Anglo-Saxon shield wall, the cavalry would quickly infiltrate such gaps, fan out and hit the Anglo-Saxons on their flanks and from behind. These tactics previewed and are confirmed by those of armoured units used on both sides during the Second World War and later – especially in the Middle East. In these charges, their javelins having been expended, the Norman cavalrymen would have made use of their lances and swords, as they did in ultimately slaying King Harold. Otherwise, their lances would have largely been unused due to the uneven ground in the area.[24] Moreover, the Norman mounted warriors of the time likely did not always, generally or even often, use the heavy cavalry tactics of couched lances and instead threw their javelins overhand, as was shown in the Bayeux Tapestry and as mentioned by Hollister.[25] Here, Messrs. Grehan and Mace concur, noting, on page 55, in the top, partial paragraph, of their book[26] that steep slopes impeded the Norman cavalry. I believe this was the case along the 'ditch' of the steep-sided valley fronting the low ridge upon which is now found Powdermill Lane/the B2095.

Who were these Norman cavalrymen? They would have been from the more wealthy classes of noblemen and their sons, nephews and up-and-coming lesser vassals who served their higher-ranked lords as the aforementioned 'vavasours' or the vassals who also had vassals. We know the names of a very few: Eustace, Count of Boulogne; William, son of Richard – Count of Evreux; Geoffrey, son of Rotrou, Count of Mortagne; William fitz Osberne; Ameri, Count of Thouars; Walter Giffard I, of Longueville-sur-Scie; Hugh II, of Montfort-sur-Risle; Ralph II, of Tosny; Hugh, of Grandmesnil; William I of Warenne. Unfortunately for written history, the list as reported by William of Poitiers ends here.[27] There are other, much more extensive lists, but these are later creations – some compiled many centuries after the battle near Hastings. The problem is that the compilers of these subsequent lists often had ulterior motives and included people who had not been at the battle, for reasons of prestige and the reflected 'glory' of having had a relative at the fight on Battle Hill. Therefore, I rely only on one of the earliest sources here – William of Poitiers.

All of the noble mounted warriors, except those who had somehow worked their way out of the lower classes to break into the petty nobility, would have been trained how to ride and fight from an early age. In Normandy, they were organised into squads, known as 'conroys', of five to ten. These mounted warriors – medieval knights – were supported by the community at large who paid for their upkeep and that of their horses. Each conroy fought as a unit, following the orders of the conroy's leader and remained close to his battle standard, known as the 'gonfanon'. It is worth mentioning here that the barons and lesser nobility of Normandy were only just beginning to accept the tradition that their landholdings were, in reality, those of the duke and that they were obligated to not only materially support him in time of war but to also accompany him and to provide a contingent of mounted fighting men as well.[28]

Yet there were other mounted fighters in Duke William's army who were neither titled nobles themselves nor their first sons, who were not entitled to inherit their fathers' noble estates under the custom of primogeniture, which bestowed the entire estate inheritance on the eldest son. While this practice may be less than equitable for younger sons, it kept the holdings of the nobility intact, instead of dividing and diluting them among many heirs. After the later victory of William the Conqueror, this tradition passed over the Channel to the defeated country of England, where it has remained in place for now just a few years short of a millennium. Before 1066, this practice maintained the wealth and power of Norman barons.[29] Thus, many of the adventurers, soldiers of fortune and mercenaries were in fact the younger sons of noblemen who were destined to not be the inheritors of their fathers' estates. Therefore, they would instead serve as paid mercenaries who could be rewarded by either land or coinage or both, thus granting them at least some level of standing as nobility, no matter how minor their land holdings might be.

Norman knights were clad in knee-length chain-mail hauberks that were split, front and back, allowing them to ride comfortably in the saddle. Their saddles had high cantles, helping riders to remain firmly seated upon the horses' backs during fighting, and their mounts were also equipped with stirrups to further stabilise Norman knights as they fought. Norman-style helmets, for both cavalry and infantry, were conical and made of iron, with nose guards. As mentioned before, Norman knights generally relied upon kite-shaped shields. Also as mentioned previously, Norman cavalry was usually equipped with not only swords but also throwing javelins and heavier spears or 'lances' for thrusting attacks.

Typical tactics at the time included a direct charge, whether by a mass of cavalry or in smaller drives of individual conroys. These attacks could be very intimidating for inexperienced and untrained infantry, causing them to break their own line and flee, allowing the Norman knights to slaughter them at will. Even if there were a stout resistance, the sheer weight of skilled fighters on horseback wielding slashing and stabbing weapons, when added to the momentum of charging horses, could simply smash through a line of improperly prepared infantry who did not adopt the defensive stance Snorri Sturluson described for the Viking defenders at Stamford Bridge, with spears set into the ground to form a double 'hedgehog'.

Used just as frequently, if not more so, was another tactic described by Sturluson – that of riding aggressively forward just far enough to cast a javelin or fire an arrow-shot, swinging the mount aside and having the horse abruptly stop short, then making the throw or bow-shot and quickly retiring before the defenders could answer in kind – whether they too were on horseback or were on foot.[30]

Foreigners and Mercenaries in the Norman Army

While Duke William could afford to raise an army of Norman nobles, knights and average men for his expedition, he could not pay for the large numbers of hired fighters – mercenaries – he would need to 'flesh out' his expeditionary force. He was also too 'cash-poor' to attract foreign allies, who would include Bretons, Frenchmen and Flemings and who would also be expecting some form of reward for their service. Despite this lack of excessive wealth left over after the expense of equipping and supplying an overseas expedition, there was also the substantial cost of building the invasion fleet and paying for the support staff of shipbuilders, sailors and construction engineers to prefabricate and then assemble the portable fort he also brought across the English Channel; and providing for a mass of ever-hungry war horses. All of this was an enormous drain on Duke William's and Normandy's, wealth. But the future conqueror solved his 'cash shortfall' problem by promising would-be foreign allies, the younger sons of the landed class who had no prospect of inheriting estates of their own, and the mercenaries who likely included at least a majority of the crossbowmen and other archers, rewards of lands to be confiscated from the defeated Anglo-Saxons.[31]

As an added incentive for those who felt the need for a moral imperative to justify their pursuits of wealth by military means, Duke William was able to provide the implied if not actual endorsement of the Pope, who supplied the expedition with the Papal banner, under which the Norman and allied and hired warriors would fight. In a time when most people, including military men, were devout Christians, the presence of the Papal banner flying above the Norman, allied and hired-on forces would have been heartening to their troops and demoralising for their Anglo-Saxon enemies.[32] The duke had been able to induce the Pope to provide his blessings by emphasising his charges that Harold had broken solemn vows he had made upon holy relics in refusing to wed one of his daughters and in seizing the throne of England. Duke William also further claimed that King Harold's coronation had been consecrated by a bishop (Stigand) who had been excommunicated for being initially elevated by the Anti-Pope. Whether any or all of these charges were valid or not, the Pope had evidently been convinced and Duke William had secured the official backing of the Church.

Prelude Redux: William's Reaction to Harold Becoming King of England

Upon learning of Harold's accession to the kingship, Duke William was incensed, thinking that he had been cheated out of what he believed was rightfully his – to be crowned King Edward's successor. William's case for his claim to the kingship, which, as pointed out by Davis and Chibnall, is repeated in the accounts of William of Jumièges and William of Poitiers, as well as the Bayeux Tapestry, was likely based on a written document,§ such as Duke William's aforementioned appeal for moral support from the Pope. But Davis and Chibnall add that the essential element of William's claim came earlier, before 1053, in *Inventio Sancti Wulfranni*, wherein it was emphasised that Edward the Confessor was related by blood to the Norman dukes.[33] Having therefore determined to go to England and 'set things right', William appealed to the Pope, as mentioned above, citing Harold's prior oath to Duke William and asking for papal support for William's accession to the English throne – whether or not we believe such an oath was made under duress, as is likely.¶ William also claimed that Harold had promised to marry William's daughter and had supposedly broken that vow, too.[34] The

---

§ However, Davis and Chibnall also report that medieval writers did not cite written sources if they had independent accounts (*The Gesta Guillelmi by William of Poitiers*, p. xxviii).

¶ As noted earlier, Davis and Chibnall cite Eadmer, from his *Eadmeri Historia Normanorum in Anglia* (edited by M. Rule, Rolls Series, 1884, p. 7) in stating that Eadmer did not regard Harold's supposed sworn oath as having been given, if at all, of his own free will (ibid, p. 70, Note 30).

Pope agreed to side with Duke William and sent him a Papal banner – a gonfanon – to bear with him on his expedition to conquer England.[35]

Duke William also requested that the King of France support his invasion of England, but, acting on the advice of his counsellors, the French king declined out of concern that the Duke of Normandy was much too powerful already and strengthening him further by supporting his conquest of England would render Normandy stronger than France.[36]

William likewise tried to enlist the aid of the Count of Flanders, who also declined to help – likely for similar concerns, but in addition because when asked what lands in a conquered England would go to Flanders, William sent his messenger to deliver a folded bit of parchment, the inside of which was left blank. So, without the prospect of gain for the Count, he, too, decided not to join in William's quest.[37]

It was during this time that everyone saw the 'long-haired star', which we now know to be Halley's Comet, and many thought it an ill omen, but for whom almost as many people were not sure.[38] This apparition in the sky is also the subject of a panel in the Bayeux Tapestry.

Meanwhile, Duke William was preparing for the invasion of England by assembling a large contingent of 'carpenters and smiths and other workmen'.[39] These were gathered in all the ports of Normandy's extensive coast or at least that part which directly faced England, centred on St Valerie, to construct the invasion fleet.[40] Master Wace reports that they laboured all summer and all autumn – the latter being an exaggeration as the fleet set sail just about one week into autumn – on 27 September. However, the Anglo-Saxon writers, if not the Normans, then regarded the beginning of winter to be on 8 September, as cited by C. Warren Hollister.[41] As for raising an army, in the same sentence as that quoted above, Wace says, '. . . and collecting the forces; and there was no knight in the land, no good Serjeant, archer, nor peasant of stout heart and of age for battle, that the duke did not summon to go with him to England: promising rents to the vavassors and honours to the barons'.[42]

As mentioned, Duke William was able to motivate his troops with promises of rewards, as Wace points out: 'Then the duke called on his good neighbours, the Bretons, Mansels and Angevins and those of Pontif and Boloigne, to come with him in his need. To those who wished he promised lands, if he should conquer England. To many he promised other rewards, good pay and rich gifts. From all sides he summoned soldiers who would serve for hire.'[43]

Before getting into the further details of the 'Battle of Hastings', I think it is best to again reacquaint ourselves with some of the landscape around Battle Hill.

Chapter 10

The Final Trips to Battle

Upon my fourth arrival at Battle Station, I stopped to inspect the maps posted on the railway station's wall facing the platform and northbound track. I had done this on my first visit to Battle, and the maps had seemed to confirm what I had already learned about the area from my earlier studies of maps available on the Internet of the local streets and tracts in the immediate neighbourhoods. However, as I paused to take a closer look this time, I noticed that a public footpath extended west from the A2100, just north of the railway tracks and arced to the west and north-west from there, toward Powdermill Lane – precisely the area I intended to survey in my search for the site of the elusive 'Malfosse' or 'Evil Ditch', which the Normans reported had been where their cavalry had plunged into a beck and marsh, causing numerous deaths through falls and drownings. I was also interested in taking a look at the topography of that area, to see if it was conceivable for the Anglo-Saxon battle line to extend to the west of the A2100 there and if it could have possibly connected with an eastward-extending shield wall near or below Marley Lane, back on the east side of the A2100. So, I set out promptly on the day's excursions.

Arriving at the place specified on the map, at first I was fooled by a driveway with a 'no entry' sign. Then I noticed a footpath alongside, running adjacent to the northern edge of the valley hosting the Southeastern Railway, and I headed generally south-west along it. I noticed that to my left the ravine was deeper at first, then less so, indicating that the terrain had been at or near its peak closer to the A2100 and then sloped away toward the south-west. The path then arced to the west and crossed a fence line with a now-familiar stile consisting of two steps on either side, made from two-by-sixes laid flat and nailed atop posts shorter than the fence by about one-third and two-thirds, allowing one to step up twice, then extend one foot over the topmost line of barbed wire and descend safely on the other side by using the opposite ends of the same flat-laid boards.

As I alighted from the stile, I was greeted by the sight of a small, rolling, pleasant meadow, ringed on one side, to the north-east, north and north-west by a compact but almost impenetrable woodland. To the west was more of a 'shore', with a road beyond – I would later determine this from the occasional traffic noise coming from a few dozen yards away, on what proved to be Powdermill Lane to the far side when I ventured closer there a few minutes hence. Then there was another patch of very thick woods and some undergrowth of shrubs, thistles – and thickets of stinging nettles – to the south-west. Finally, there was a dense hedgerow of trees, shrubs and woodland undergrowth lining the Southeastern Railway vale to the south and south-east.

I crisscrossed the meadow about half a dozen times, enjoying its beauty as I scoured the area below the trees all around in search of anything that could possibly resemble the Malfosse. I climbed over a fence toward the north-west three times, venturing as far as I could into the dense undergrowth of the thickest woodland – to the north-east, north and north-west. In the first two directions there was nothing that could be considered a ditch – flooded or not. To the north-west, there was a stretch of very rugged land running south-west to north-east, roughly paralleling Powdermill Lane, which lay about 50 yards beyond, but the ditches or gullies within it were all dry. I realised it was within reason to suppose that this ditch had been flooded at one time, recognising that any spring that may have fed a possible former beck there in the past could have, in the intervening nearly 1,000 years, run dry or found another course or that the ditch and its imagined beck could yet run with water in the wetter season, which lay at least two months away.

Returning to the meadow, I found yet another fence-crossing stile that was almost invisible due to the thick undergrowth of weeds, shrubs and an encroaching woodland, and also a virtual miniature forest of stinging nettles at the edge of the closely packed trees that bounded the meadow, roughly along the fence line. It was there that I made what many might consider to be a minor, even inconsequential, discovery (in the form of a plant) that would loom larger, at least in my mind, until I examined in more detail one of the maps available showing what was in the area in earlier modern and not necessarily medieval times.

While stumbling around in these woods behind the St Mary's tract, I came across an astonishing sight – a hoary (grey, ancient and twisted) apple tree. Could this be, I wondered, the spot where, according to legend, King Harold fell and died, beneath the hoary apple tree? There, just above eye level, was the unmistakable shape of an apple – a bright green one, at the end of a limb that stretched from the shaded woods and just barely into the sunlight. Following along the limb, then a branch that reached, tortuously it seemed, across the weed-choked soil back below the undergrowth beneath some overhanging trees I could not identify, the branch finally terminated at a sideways-growing trunk, which also sent other branches and limbs, all to one side, toward the margin of sunlight that managed to penetrate past the edges of the forested land there. Further investigation revealed other limbs bearing fruit and I picked several, taking them back to the University of Sussex student residence that evening, where I shared with them some fellow students. (They were tart, juicy – not bad considering the circumstances of their origin.) I realised, of course, that this lone apple tree could not possible be the one referred to in some of the ancient reports of the battle, for that tree, if it existed and grew at that spot, was already old in 1066 and likely far beyond its fruit-bearing years. I thought there could be the slim possibility that this tree descended from trees growing there during the Anglo-Saxon Age and the idea, intriguing and dramatic as it might be, did not cling to my imagination for long because, upon reviewing maps from the 1800s, I found that in the area where the struggling and deformed tree survived an orchard had been planted at that time. However, the fact that self-perpetuating apple trees had grown in the untended soils, unwatered or otherwise cared for, proved that apple trees could easily grow in the area and had for some time, reinforced the possibility that King Harold had probably been able to rally his army or had even fallen and died beneath an old apple tree, whether on Caldbec Hill, Battle Hill or another nearby location in 1066.

Having investigated the woodland and meadowland of the tract generally to the south of Powdermill Lane and west of the A2100 – 'behind' what's known as the St Mary's tract (across from the Senlac Inn and not to be confused with the little side street known as 'St Mary's Villas', on the opposite side of the A2100) – I returned to the A2100 itself and continued south along its west side and then across the bridge over the valley containing the Southeastern Railway.

At the Tesco Express carpark on the slope of Quarry Hill, just across the tracks, I found yet another public footpath; this one extending generally south-by-south-west. Just as I entered the pathway that followed a fence line between a scenic meadow to my right and a hedgerow to my left, I encountered a family of three who informed me that they had just hiked up that path from Crowhurst, a couple of miles south-south-east of Battle. This is the very same footpath mentioned in Nick Austin's book.[1] I found that path to be steep, narrow and confined by small gullies and trees, twisting and, ultimately, farther down, likely to have been oftentimes flooded as local authorities had built wooden bridges and causeways to help hikers navigate the steep-sided, meandering, tumbling beck that was running with water even in July. This narrow path would definitely not have been suitable for the Anglo-Saxon army to travel upon toward a supposed engagement with the Normans, as Austin contends.

Austin also claims that people in the Crowhurst area and surrounding communities just refer to the town as 'hurst', in an effort on his part to equate this with an ancient reference to 'herste', in connection with the site of the Hastings battle as he tries to move its location to his beloved, adopted home town. However, in my conversations with people in the area, including this family, everyone called it by its full name – 'Crowhurst'. Moreover, 'hurst' or 'herste', does not necessarily refer to 'Crowhurst', but, rather, any wooded terrain, especially on a hilltop. (. . . 'hurst' or 'herest': A wood on a hill or a wooded hillock; stems from Anglo-Saxon word, common in southern England. Also: hurst/ hərst/ noun. archaic. a hillock. a sandbank in the sea or a river. a wood or wooded rise).[2]

After a brief chat with the family of good, helpful folks, during which I asked if there were any becks and/or marshy areas farther along the trail, which elicited an affirmative reply, I started down – and I do mean down as the land descended all the way from there – along the public footpath toward the south-south-west and south-west. To the right, at first between the trees, then through gaps among them and occasional still wider openings, the view of the scenic meadows and then the rolling ridges and hills to the west and south-west beyond fading into the blue-green distance was exceptionally beautiful; it was a series of scenic meadows indeed. But, in the nearer view, I recognised the landscape across the valley enclosing the railway line and knew that the meadowlands and woods I had wandered among earlier that day were either just within or just without of my view.

I continued down the path until I found a water-filled ditch and some marshy ground, but it seemed too far away, nearly a half-mile or so from the ridgetop terrain near the Tesco Express, the St Mary's tract and the A2100/Powdermill Lane roundabout. Besides – both according to the official view of many experts and English Heritage, in agreement with some of my own preliminary conclusions – that ditch – or at least this part of it, or the majority of it – evidently where it lay now and its likely past location before the improvements to create Powdermill Lane and control its accompanying marshlands – would have been *behind* the Norman army as it advanced and not at or beyond the Anglo-Saxons, where they are reported to have broken and run when their shield wall finally collapsed, near dusk.

Backtracking up the hill along the footpath, I took some more photos of the 'scenic meadow' and the other meadowlands on the hillside opposite to it – to the west and south-west – as I had coming down the trail, and reconsidered the possibilities about not just the Anglo-Saxon deployment along their shield wall but also those regarding the most likely route of the Norman advance; yet anything more than sketchy conclusions would have to await further inspections of several more locations around Battle so I could either confirm or eliminate any other possibilities before firming-up my theory into its final form.

During that fourth visit to Battle, upon completing my investigations of the area along the A2100 near the Southeastern Railway right-of-way, behind the Tesco Express, the thickly-wooded lot in back of the St Mary's tract and along Powdermill Lane, I discovered that the lay of the land was a little different from what one would expect by merely glancing at a map or even a satellite image. From the railway line to the south along the A2100 the ground begins to slowly climb, then – as I knew from my trek to Telham Hill – it undulates until reaching a peak near Telham Lane, and then it descends all the way past Beauport Park and Baldslow and into Hastings. Behind the Tesco Express, the land maintains roughly the same level, in a broad curvature, from the south and arcing to the south-west, then west and north-west, toward the Battle Abbey grounds across Powdermill Lane. Below that arc, the terrain falls downhill in those same directions away from the St Mary's tract, the 'scenic meadow' and its environs, the Powdermill Lane roundabout and Battle Terrace.

In view of some of my other observations and discoveries in the area, this topographical fact was at first disconcerting to me as it meant that if the Anglo-Saxons had tried to hold Senlac Hill along the A2100 route, from either the Powdermill Lane or the Marley Lane roundabouts, their Norman opponents would have had the advantage of attacking slightly downslope or, at least, at about the same elevation, if they charged the Anglo-Saxon shield wall by following the A2100 route and to their immediate left and beyond. Even though it is a modest descent or at about the same level, the fact that it *is* a descent and/or level ground, would have shifted the tactical circumstances. They would favour the

141

Normans, because the attackers – especially the Norman cavalry – would have had that great aid to close combat with stabbing and bludgeoning weapons – gravity-enhanced momentum – on their side. Why, I was forced to wonder, would King Harold and his Anglo-Saxons have permitted such a likely decisive factor in the battle to swing the odds in favour of the Norman attackers?

However, while investigating the area, I had observed that the low point of the A2100 and the terrain toward the wooded areas I had just explored, was *almost exactly* at the location of the Southeastern Railway right-of-way. In that the railway tracks occupied a relatively steep-sided, narrow valley, it occurred to me that I had inadvertently discovered not only the Malfosse, but also the site of the Anglo-Saxon main line of resistance. By blocking the ridgeway at that point and extending their shield wall to the right into the St Mary's tract, the Anglo-Saxons would have placed their defensive line just behind what could accurately be called a very large 'ditch', which also constituted the 'rough ground' or 'difficult terrain' for Norman cavalrymen and infantry alike. My earlier intuitions and gut feelings had hinted at this being the place where the Battle of Hastings was actually fought, and my explorations of the topography confirmed the idea to me – removing it from a mere possibility to a probability.

I wrapped up the day's investigations with a brief jog down Powdermill Lane/the B2095, which is often to usually very busy with many vehicles, forcing me to sprint against traffic – stepping into the roadside weeds and brush as cars and trucks approached because there is neither pavement nor hard shoulder there – then jog ahead some more. This went on for four or five dozen yards, until I reached the farm gate with the familiar views beyond of Battle Terrace and Battle Abbey, confirming that I had been, in fact, just across the road from the officially recognised site of the Battle of Hastings when I was trekking around and through the woodlands and meadows in back of the St Mary's tract and behind and below the Tesco Express carpark – on both sides of the Southeastern Railway right-of-way. My fifth – and, as it turned out, final – visit to Battle would be a busy one as I yet had many loose ends to tie up before my theories regarding the events of the battle, based on the probable decisions of the commanders as dictated to them by the terrain, had progressed, then reached its not necessarily pre-destined final outcome.

So far, I concluded that, in that the land actually descends to its lowest spot on the A2100 at just about – actually just a few yards to the south of – the railway right-of-way. The Anglo-Saxons would have deployed to the east of the A2100 just beyond that point on the ridge road to its immediate north, between the current railway tracks and the Powdermill Lane roundabout, with a steep slope below covering the left wing of their main line of resistance, running above Station Approach and slightly below Marley Lane, nearing the tracks at or just east of Battle Station and ending at the beck and marsh now beneath the northernmost limits of the Harrier tract. The Anglo-Saxons there would have been deployed just uphill from the slightly more level ground, approximately at the railway embankment and Meadow Bank/Marley Lane. The battle line would likely have been anchored at the woods, lake and beck then just beyond the easternmost curve of today's Harrier Lane, which would have been there in 1066.

On the other side of the A2100, to the Anglo-Saxon right, their deployment could have stretched just to the south of the present woods and along the northern rim of what is the south-western extension of the canyon enclosing the railway line, then arcing back across the scenic meadow, almost crossing Powdermill Lane and ending at the becks, lakes and swamps farther below Battle Terrace, but only at the extreme western, west-south-western, south-western and southern edges of the Battle Abbey grounds, not extending to just below the current Battle Terrace. (Again, 'Battle Terrace' itself is likely a later addition, built up to support the foundation of the abbey wall just behind it.)

King Harold would probably have been near the Powdermill Lane roundabout, at the edge of the woods and the scenic meadow, when he and his Huscarls were overrun by Duke William's mounted warriors sweeping up and across the low ridge-line he was defending, where he was hit, fell and died, possibly but probably not beneath the hoary apple tree. The reasons I suspect this possibility is the case will be covered later in this work.

It seems to me, after having reviewed pages 90 through 102 of C.K. Lawson's book,[3] that there is a tendency by the various sources to reconfirm my own suspicions I felt upon visiting the area and that my original analysis may, at least for the most part, be correct: The Anglo-Saxons likely emerged from the 'thick forest'* on and in 'the hill and valley' and the St Mary's tract and adjacent areas, including those across the Hastings Road/Battle Road, ridgeway near to the Battle train station. It is probable that the majority of the fighting occurred in

---

* Frank Barlow notes in his introduction to *The Carmen de Hastingae Proelio* (p. lxxvi), that 'the English emerged from hiding places in the woods'.

these areas. Further, the 'maze of ditches' and the 'partial wall' where the Anglo-Saxons were said to have made their last stand perhaps lay slightly toward the current supposed battlefield on the Battle Abbey grounds – just south of the Marley Lane roundabout, which forms a slightly conical 'peak' before the Hastings Ridge resumes its descent toward the valley encompassing the Southeastern Railway line or, perhaps, on the crest of Caldbec Hill. (This latter possibility would make sense as more Anglo-Saxons would likely have yet been marshalling on Caldbec Hill to join the number of defenders who had fled the left flank of the original site of the struggle – to the south and south-east.) It is even likely both locations were where the Norman cavalry had pursued the fleeing Anglo-Saxons.

Due to the distances involved from Caldbec Hill and Telham Hill, it seems to me that the Glengorse tract and the Starr's Mead tract are just a little too far forward for the Anglo-Saxons to have made their surprise appearance and quick deployment ahead of the Norman advance. The rough terrain I found in the woods in the vicinity of the railway line is the most rugged ground I encountered in the entire Battle area. Extrapolating from that, it seems probable that the lay of the land before the construction of the railway line, the nearby businesses and housing tracts and improvements and additions to the roads, would have destroyed evidence of other rough ground likely to have been there at the time of the fighting. The facts that 'Battle Hill', along with 'Battle Hill Road' are the traditional names of the hill and old Hastings Road, and that it is a hill situated 'behind' (to the north and north-west of) the 'valley' at the site of the bridge over the railway embankment show me that the juxtapositions of the thick woods, rough terrain, hill and valley all give strong indications, again to me, that this is the place specified for the actual site of the Battle of Hastings, as cited the original sources.

One Last Look: On the Ground at the Battle Area

After debarking from the train for the fifth and final time at Battle Station, I immediately proceeded to the area to the west and north of Battle Abbey, to Park Lane, where I first skirted the north side of the Battle Abbey grounds, taking photos of the woods and small beck near there. Then, I went more north-west, taking the public footpath in that direction, passing a meadow, a soccer field, then another, smaller meadow to the west as I proceeded onto Saxonwood Road and, at North Trade Road, I followed that old main road, also known now as the A271 or London Road, for a short distance, then doubled back and resumed my trek along North Trade Road all the way to Asten Fields, just beyond the Battle Recreation Ground. I then returned along North Trade Road to the A2100, having found several possible candidates for the Malfosse, depending on how far and in which direction the Norman cavalry had pursued the fleeing Anglo-Saxons before falling into that 'evil ditch'. However, in view of the fact, confirmed to me by old maps, that the steep-sided and narrow valley that now holds the Southeastern Railway line was, in fact, not only the site of the Anglo-Saxon defensive position, it was also the Malfosse itself, as so many Norman cavalry and infantry, would have fallen there in that no-man's-land between the armies. The old maps suggested that it had been marshy, at least in part – the lower reaches as one moved away from the high-point, where the A2100/ridgeway crosses it – in earlier times.

Returning to Mount Street, I again went up it and photographed the location of the windmill-become-home where King Harold is reported to have stood as his army assembled around him there on Caldbec Hill, when it was, of course, yet more open ground. I then went back toward the A2100, to the carpark at Senlac Vets and photographed the slope and beck on the south-south-east side of Caldbec Hill. On a hunch, I went down and explored the beck, following it until I found that I was, once again, at the beck and marshy area below the roundabout at the A2100 and Marley Lane. I continued along that beck, which runs just to the north of Marley Lane, until I reached the point where the 'Caldbec' beck and the 'Marley Lane' beck meet, at a small flooded 'lake', which is more of a pond. Backtracking and then going up the hill to the Marley Lane roundabout, I followed Marley Lane and proceeded into the Harrier tract, just across the Southeastern Railway tracks.

This side-trip to the boggy ground below Caldbec Hill, on what would *not* have been the Normans' route of advance, demonstrated clearly to me that Duke William would never have deployed his forces there because, as with the supposed battlefield at Battle Abbey, his troops would have been diverting in going downhill from the 'isthmus' that connects Battle Hill and Caldbec Hill, surrendering the relatively even ground to the enemy. He would not have sent his men down, into boggy ground, only to have them wheel around – to their left this time – and attempt to charge up a relatively long and steep slope. The only viable tactic would have been to continue along the Hastings ridge isthmus with the bulk of his army while sending a large force of mounted knights not to the foot of Caldbec Hill but farther on, past the unanchored left flank of the Anglo-Saxons. While his infantry attacked across the isthmus, then turning half-right to continue up the less steep flank of Caldbec Hill, Duke William would have also sent a smaller force of cavalry ahead and to the left, then wheeling full right, to charge against the exposed Anglo-Saxon right flank while the larger contingent of mounted knights swept in from the other side, caving in both flanks of the Anglo-Saxons. At that point, King Harold's army would have been overwhelmed in but minutes – perhaps an hour or two at the most; and there would not have been an all-day Battle of Hastings, as has been reported to us by numerous medieval sources.

On my first trek down Marley Lane, during my initial visit to the Battle area, I had veered into the Harrier tract and investigated the steep slopes above the tracks to the south of Battle Station, in the area to the west and north-west of the Harrier tract, yet just east of the A2100. I had found that the terrain just to the south of the Southeastern Railway right-of-way consisted of one of the most thickly wooded and steepest slopes in the neighbourhood, making it a logical place for the battle line of skirmishers and then a re-established shield wall of the Anglo-Saxons to extend to the west to the A2100, a point which is far enough to the south of the Marley Lane roundabout to actually enable a possible connection between the Anglo-Saxon deployments on both sides of the A2100. In all of these explorations I confirmed that the Anglo-Saxon battle line or shield wall would not have been one continuous front, but, due to the interruptions of thickly wooded areas, the shield walls would have given way to skirmishers operating in the woods and then been re-established on the next relatively clear ground.

Many people, including experienced researchers, writers, academics, even military veterans – who may not have had any direct experience with even observing group medieval-style combat re-enactments that utilise stabbing, cutting or clubbing weapons – have been unintentionally misled by the term 'shield wall' to mistakenly believe it is always a straight-line formation. The actual 'shield wall' or battle line at Battle Hill was an 'S'-curve, from the lowest reaches of the Battle Abbey grounds, across and along Powdermill Lane and below (south and south-west) of the 'thick woods at the corner' (at the St Mary's tract), then across the A2100 north of the railway embankment and below Marley Lane, but still north of the tracks, then along farther eastward and crossing to the south side of the railway embankment, terminating at the trees and beck or 'river' likely to have been in the Harrier tract. It is also possible the Anglo-Saxon line did not extend that far onto 'low ground' on their left and instead wrapped around the 'Marley rise' and terminated at the next stands of thick woods, just below, once more, the Southeastern Railway embankment, behind the street now known as Coronation Gardens.

In all of the locations viewed that day of my final survey of the Battle area, I had been searching for likely candidates for the 'evil ditch' and continued to do so as I walked along all of the streets and curving lanes in the Harrier tract and some adjoining meadows and woodlands.

I had earlier taken the public footpath from Kingsdale Close, east of the A2100 – noting the steeper and more heavily wooded slopes to my left – to the south-west, south and south-east of Battle Station – all of these located just east of the A2100. I kept on, all the way to the Emmanuel Centre Home of Battle, where I met a woman and her grown-up son walking their dog just outside the centre's carpark, in about the middle of the Harrier tract, and she had informed me that the Harrier tract was constructed atop the site of 'an old river'. In that the tract is wide and rectangular, I deduced that she meant 'lake' instead of 'river' and merely misspoke. She also indicated a small lake just beyond (south of) the Harrier tract and yet another beck that descended from the Starr's Meade area nearer the A2100. After personally investigating these latest revelations regarding the (assumed) lake and beck, I returned to Marley Lane, went north and west along it, re-crossed the Southeastern Railway tracks and returned to the A2100 via Station Approach. It was then time to re-enter the thick woods at the junction of the A2100 and Powdermill Lane and re-orient myself with regard to the landscape of the neighbourhood because it had recently assumed larger importance to me as my investigations of the Battle area reached their conclusion.

After that final excursion into the thick woods at the A2100, it was time to return to the University of Sussex to review again the maps and satellite images of Battle and environs and to compare those with my notes – written and memorised – as I finalised my theoretical analysis of how the terrain in and around Battle would likely have affected the pre-positioning and initial deployments of the opposing armies and the conduct and resolution of the Battle of Hastings. The next step would be to re-read the dozen-and-a-half or so books I had already accumulated – some acquired decades before, others found just that summer at the University of Sussex library and at the Sussex County Library – investigate the many written materials I had purchased at various historical sites administered by English Heritage, review Internet articles, and to obtain and read more recently written works by others after my pending return to the United States, a few days hence . . .

Getting Back to the Progress of the Battle at Battle Hill

Bishop Guy details how the Anglo-Saxons deployed on foot, their nobles and other warriors on horseback dismounting and joining King Harold at the crest of the hill, their banners surrounding his.[4] Again, while the peak of the hill at Battle Hill is at the site of where the abbey now stands, it is far to the rear of the valley where the Southeastern Railway line lies, which is also too far from that optimum position to defend against an armed force advancing along the route of the present A2100. Therefore, again, the hill in question – where King Harold fell – was much more likely at the Powdermill Lane roundabout, which was within shouting distance of the crest of the ridge running along the north-western rim of the valley and with a relatively clear view lengthways – the most probable position to deploy the Anglo-Saxon main line of resistance – just 'ahead of' (south-eastward from) what is now Powdermill Lane. From that position, King Harold and his subsidiary leaders could survey the progress of the battle, shout orders and shift their reserves as needed to meet any Norman breakthroughs. I believe King Harold moved forward to the site of the Powdermill Lane roundabout from his initial vantage point at the peak of the hill just south of the Marley Lane roundabout; then, later, when the crisis arose to his right, I postulate that he moved, along with his standard again, into what is now the St Mary's tract and near to where I found the 'hoary apple tree'.

As the battle commences, Guy informs us that 'The infantry go ahead to join battle with arrows. Against [crossbow] quarrels shields are not secure. Helmeted soldiers rush to crash shields against shields.'[5] He continues: '. . . fearing neither the enemy nor the spears that threaten death, so the English phalanx fights on unafraid.'[6] This, to me, would be at the ridgeway and along the ravine to the right and, to a lesser degree, along the slopes to the left.

Guy then describes how a single Norman knight asked Duke William for the honour of making the first kill in the battle, which would have preceded what he wrote before. The duke agreed and the knight rode ahead and taunted the English while twirling and tossing his sword like a juggler, enticing a lone Anglo-Saxon to accept the challenge and 'dash forward', only to be pierced by the Norman's lance and then beheaded.[7] According to Wace, the same Norman knight, identified as 'Taillefer' (French, German – means: 'Works in Iron'), then kills a second Englishman, before being surrounded and presumably killed by the Anglo-Saxons.[8] Blood having been spilled, the Normans unleashed a barrage of arrows and crossbow bolts, followed up by an infantry charge. Bishop Guy accurately depicts the Anglo-Saxon ranks, writing, 'The serried mass of the English stands rooted to the ground', with the word 'serried' (as in a row of people or things standing close together – 'serried ranks of soldiers' or, as it is now so popularly known, a shield wall). In fact, the shield wall was so solidly composed of men compacted together that the bishop then reports: 'They meet javelin with javelin, sword with sword. Bodies bereft of life are unable to fall. Nor do the dead make space for the living, for every corpse, although lifeless, stands as though unharmed and keeps its place.'[9] William of Poitiers corroborates this description of the thickness of the Anglo-Saxon ranks.[10] The attackers would not have been able to penetrate 'the dense forest of the English had not invention reinforced their strength'.[11] So, the Anglo-Saxon defenders were so packed together that those seriously wounded or killed could not fall to the ground, which weakened the shield wall as they could not be replaced in the battle line by living warriors. Here, Guy obviously uses 'dense forest' as a metaphor regarding the bodies of the Englishmen. The use of the word 'invention' is clarified in the next paragraph as the bishop continues: 'The French, skilled in stratagems, skilled in the arts of war, cunningly pretend to flee as though they had been defeated.'[12] The use of the word 'French' here is either misleading or mistaken, for, consulting the original text as presented by Barlow[13] it indeed does say 'Franci'. The problem is that Bishop Guy had placed the French forces in the duke's army in the right wing (while also possibly merely mislabelling their position as being on the left, as Barlow explains in his notes to the text). So, if it were the French and not the Normans, whom Guy placed in the centre of William's deployment, then this part of the fight would have been on the Norman right and Anglo-Saxon left, which, according to my estimations, means that this clever trick was used on the area below Marley Lane (where an Anglo-Saxon battleaxe was found in the 1950s). Indeed, the Latin text presented by Barlow[14] does indicate that the French were 'Set leuam' (On the left), while the Bretons are described as 'dextrum peciere Britanni' or 'Bretons right plot'. So, even though Bishop Guy is the earliest of the scribes to recount the fight at Battle Hill, all of the others who reported on the struggle there, up until and including Barlow, give the opposite deployments as far as the French and Bretons and the left and the right are concerned. While I defer to the likelihood of the earliest reporters, other than Bishop Guy, having been more accurate and also acknowledging the superior scholarship of distinguished experts such as Frank Barlow, the idea that it was the French, not the Bretons, who had deployed to the Norman left, not to their right, does have some reinforcing evidence contained within this same epic poem, which I will get to momentarily after addressing the question of whether or not the ducal army engaged in a feigned retreat or was merely routed, albeit temporarily, to be followed by the subsequent course of the battle, up until the time of King Harold's death.

In support of Guy's account is the report of the employment of the ruse of a false retreat, which is echoed in remarks by Master Wace with regard to Duke William's fight on the Continent with the French:

> Those in the besiegers' [Norman] fort soon heard of the great preparations waiting at Saint-Albin to provision and relieve Arches. Then they selected their strongest and best fighting men and privily formed an ambuscade in the direction of Saint-Albin. Having done this, they sent out another party with orders to charge the [French] king's force and then to turn back, making as if they would flee. But when they had passed the spot where the ambuscade lay, they turned quickly round on those who were pursuing and fiercely attacked the French; those also who were lying in ambuscade riding forth and joining in the assault . . .
> The Frenchmen were thus grievously taken in; and being separated from the rest of their army, the Normans charged them boldly and took and killed many . . . [15]

So, while my initial reaction to the parts of the story of the struggle at Battle Hill was scepticism regarding supposed Norman mock retreats, my doubts were overcome upon reading of them in both Guy's and Wace's accounts, as well as in William of Poitiers' book[16] even though there is the danger that the later works may be overly derivative of the initial report.

I propose that the incident of the juggling knight, Taillefer, occurred on the ridgeway and so with the tightly packed array of Anglo-Saxons in their dense shield wall there. However, the episodes of the feigned retreats would have required more open formations and therefore less restricted ground, so it seems logical the Norman assaults and retreats – whether feigned or real – to be closely pursued by incautious Fyrdmen, who were subsequently overwhelmed and killed by Norman knights charging from 'ambuscade', would have taken place along the Southeastern Railway ravine and the 'scenic meadows' in and near (south-west of) the St Mary's tract.

Bishop Guy then tells us that the English, though stout fighters, were, in his opinion, not very sophisticated: 'The rustic folk rejoice, thinking that they have conquered and pursue them with naked swords. With the removal of the able bodied, corpses fall and the once thick wood is thinned.'[17] This report by Guy is echoed by Wace, which passage was previously quoted above. Also, as noted before, William of Poitiers concurs in the Norman use of the 'feigned retreat' tactic.[18]

In addition to his remark about the Anglo-Saxon warriors being 'rustics', we find that Guy further comments that they pursued the Normans with 'naked swords'. While this may only mean that they had drawn their swords from their sheaths and were not using their spears, it could also refer to the possibility that in their haste to run-down the fleeing enemy, some, many or most of the Anglo-Saxons (probably the less experienced – rather than the Huscarls and the Thegns, Hidesmen and lesser noblemen – men of the Select Fyrd, who would possibly have been armed with swords instead of clubs, farm implements and tools) had also cast aside their shields to be able to better chase after their supposedly routed foes. Bishop Guy continues to relate the progress of the battle: 'When the left wing [of the ducal army] sees that the field of battle is being cleared and the right wing that a breach has been opened up, both wings give free rein and strive to be the first to destroy the dispersed enemy in scattered encounters, while those who simulated flight turn upon their pursuers and, holding them in check, force them to flee from death.'[19] This is the point when, for the original pursuers, the situation changed not only drastically but fatally for those, if any, who had foolishly tossed their shields aside to be better able to chase the retreating Normans. Also in support of the now widely accepted view that the Normans had engaged in feigned retreats at Battle Hill is William of Poitiers.[20]

Bishop Guy then reports that, 'A large part of these perished there, but some, packed even closer than before, fight on . . . Most, however, of those who survived the fighting fought on even more keenly and counted their losses as nothing. The English, superior in numbers, beat back the foe and forcibly compel them to flee. Thus a flight that started with a sham became one dictated by the enemy's strength.

The Normans turn tail; their shields protect their backs.'[21] So we see that in this passage Bishop Guy admits that the Anglo-Saxon fighters were stoic in their courage and turned the tide of the battle once more, although he ascribes this turnaround as being due to the English being 'superior in numbers', which may have been true or is merely an excuse thrown in by a pro-Norman source in order to depict their own troops in a more favourable and heroic light. A touch of realism is added if we consider the possibility that, as a survival technique, the fleeing Normans slung their shields across their backs, as was done on the march, but in order in this instance to prevent being pummelled, slashed or stabbed from behind as they fled, whether in earnest or as mere play-acting.

However, prior to this reliance upon the ruse of a feigned retreat, it is evident and likely that during the approximately seven- to eight-hour battle the situation would have fluctuated back and forth, as Wace tells it: 'Loud and far resounded the bray of the horns; and the shocks of the lances; the mighty strokes of clubs and the quick clashing of swords. One while the Englishmen rushed on, another while they fell back; one while the men from over sea charged onwards and again at other times retreated.'[22] He observes later how 'Again some press forwards; others yield and thus in various ways the struggle proceeds'.[23]

Bishop Guy then goes on to describe the heroics of Duke William, which are most likely true, if not in their entirety then at least for the most part as they accurately describe what war leaders must often do to restore order and morale among beaten troops whose only desire is to escape from an ordeal of combat that has gone against them. Guy wrote,

When the duke saw that his people were beaten and in retreat, he rode up; and, signalling with his hand, he rebukes and strikes them and restrains and checks them with his lance. In his anger he himself removes his helmet from his head. To the Normans he showed a furious face; to the French he made entreaties. 'Where are you off to?' he cried. '. . . how could you, when you had been the victors, allow yourself to appear the vanquished? It is not from men but from sheep that you run. Your fear is mistaken. What you are doing is the most shameful disgrace. Behind you lies the sea. To return by sea is hard when both wind and the weather are against you. Hard it is to return home, hard and long the way. There's no escape road for you here. If you want merely to live you must strive to conquer'.[24]

Rallying his troops, William inspires them by his heroic efforts and leads them by being the first to resume the attack, as Guy tells us: 'At the sight of the duke the enemy trembles and falls away, like soft wax flowing from the face of the fire.'[25] Duke William then goes on a killing spree, including the hacking to death of King Harold's brother, Gyrth, who first kills William's horse with a hurled javelin. Then, the dismounted William signals to a knight 'from Maine' to come to his aid, but the knight shies away. So the duke seizes the nose guard on the knight's helmet, dragging him from his horse, which William mounts as his own. Yet another Anglo-Saxon hurls a javelin and, again, Duke William is unhorsed when his mount falls to the piercing. Count Eustace of Boulogne comes to his aid, giving the duke his own horse, while a loyal knight in turn awards his mount to the count.[26] William of Poitiers agrees, stating that Duke William had *three* horses killed under him at the battle.[27]

Next Bishop Guy informs us that, 'When France [the French, not the Bretons] was almost mistress of the field of battle and was already seeking the spoils of war, the duke caught sight of the king [Harold II] on the top of the hill fiercely cutting down those who were attacking him. He [William] called up Eustace and, leaving there the French to continue the fight, brought enormous relief to those under attack.'[28] So, within sight of King Harold fighting on the hilltop, Guy mentions only the French, not the Bretons. Following his call to the French Count Eustace, William also enlists the aid of Hugh of Ponthieu (Normandy) and Gilfard, from Longueville (Normandy). It was these three – one Frenchman and two other Normans – who accompanied Duke William in their charge toward the Anglo-Saxon king.[29] Again, if all of the historical accounts are even remotely accurate, either the French were deployed on the Norman left or the key phase of the battle was on the Norman right – in and between today's Harrier Tract and Marley Lane. In either case, the battle was *not* fought at the generally accepted site of the battle – on the grounds of Battle Abbey – but, according to my estimations, across and within the narrow valley now hosting the construction of the tracks of the Southeastern Railway, to the south-west of the A2100 or, even more remote from Battle Abbey and the presumed battlefield, to the north and north-east of the A2100 as it approaches and climbs Battle Hill in the Marley Lane area. Nowhere does Guy in these passages mention the Bretons, who were evidently not participating in this key sector of the battle.

However, with regard to the above, due to terrain factors, it is unlikely that this phase of the battle was fought in the Harrier Tract and Marley

Lane areas because, if Master Wace's account is even remotely correct, the lay of the land is all wrong there, for, as Wace reports: 'Meanwhile the Normans appeared, advancing over the ridge of a rising ground; and the first division of their troops moved onwards along the hill and across a valley.'[30] These actions, if accurate, would describe a Norman advance along the Hastings-to-London ridgeway – the A2100 – and over the crest of the hill to the south-west of that road, near the current location of the Tesco Express, known locally as 'Quarry Hill'. In the second part of this movement, the Norman 'first division' – either of infantry or both infantry and cavalry – would be moving farther to the south and south-west, over the lower reaches of the slight ridge near what is now the Southeastern Railway right-of-way and across the shallow but steep-sided valley where that line runs. Further, Wace states: 'The youths and common herd of the camp, whose business was not to join in the battle, but to take care of the harness and stores, moved off towards a rising ground. The priests and the clerks also ascended a hill, there to offer up prayers to God and watch the event of the battle.'[31] These moves would not have been possible if the battle were in fact fought on the present Battle Abbey grounds, but these men could have gone to the higher ground behind the Norman advance – south of the A2100 and south-west of the Tesco Express, where the land is about 268ft above sea level and overlooking my proposed sites of the battle by about 20 to 40ft. These moves could, theoretically, have been made to the east of the A2100 to overlook the Harrier Tract and Marley Lane areas, but views of the fighting would have been blocked by the then thick growth of trees we conjecture was there in 1066, as, indeed, the area there is more thickly wooded than surrounding terrain to this day.

In a previously-cited section Bishop Guy provides a graphic account of the killing of the Anglo-Saxon king by these four knights, including Duke William:

> The first of the four, piercing the king's shield and chest with his lance, drenched the ground with a gushing stream of blood. The second with his sword cut off his head below the protection of his helm. The third liquefied his entrails with his spear. And the fourth cut off his thigh and carried it some distance away. The earth held the body they had in these ways destroyed.[32]

Note that nowhere in Bishop Guy's report do we find any mention of an arrow piercing the Anglo-Saxon king's eye.

Chapter 11

The Bayeux Tapestry, and the End of the Battle of Hastings

The earliest known depictions of the Bayeux Tapestry include some colour illustrations of the first 10m (32.8ft) – the initial one-seventh – of its length. This discovery was made by Claude Gros de Boze, then curator or garde of the Cabinet des médailles et antiques in Paris. The illustrations had previously been in the care of the ex-intendant of Normandy, Nicolas-Joseph Foucault. Foucault had lived in Bayeux from 1688 until 1704. Who actually created the drawings is unclear.[1]

Professor Christopher Norton, emeritus professor of History of Art at the University of York in the Centre for Medieval Studies, has concluded that the Tapestry in its entirety was explicitly crafted to be hung in Bayeux Cathedral as it existed in the late eleventh century. The professor specified that it would have fitted well had it been hung on the north, west and south walkways of the nave; he further states that such a display would align the artwork's scenes with the gallery bays to provide dramatic impact. He agreed that the final panel, depicting William's coronation as King of England, is missing and goes further to estimate that it was 3m (9.8ft) in width. He also noted that the Tapestry's design was planned to gratify a Norman viewership. Norton decided that all of these factors pointed to its intended unveiling at the dedication of the Bayeux Cathedral in 1077, an event to be attended by King William, his wife Mathilda, their sons and the presumed presenter of the Tapestry, Bishop Odo himself.

In 1729, the Benedictine monk and scholar Bernard de Montfaucon brought the existence of the Tapestry to public awareness in the first volume of *Les Monumens de la Monarchie Françoise*, which exhibited romanticised engravings showing approximately the initial 30ft of

155

its length. The engravings were copied from a sketch discovered in the effects of Foucault in 1724 (Foucault had passed away in 1721). When the sketch was discovered, it was not known what it depicted. Montfaucon's research uncovered the truth: it was '. . . a strip of tapestry preserved in Bayeux Cathedral and which is exhibited on certain days of the year'.[2] Montfaucon sent Antoine Benoît, who was described as 'one of the most skilled draughts men of this time',[3] to Bayeux to craft faithful reproductions of the entirety of the Tapestry. From Benoît's copies, engravings were made, which were described as illustrating the Tapestry's 'coarse and most barbarous style'. The resulting artwork was published in Montfaucon's second volume, in 1730.[4]

In 1729, French historian Antoine Lancelot learned of the Foucault sketches. In 1733 he published a paper on the Tapestry. Accompanying the paper was a set of engravings based on the Benoît illustrations of the entire Tapestry. Benoît used dashed lines where he thought parts of the embroidery were missing.[5]

In 1767 Andrew Coltée Ducarel republished the Montfaucon engravings in a work that included descriptions of the Tapestry's scenes that had been previously put forward by one Smart Lethieullier. The author of the report on this, at 'The Viking Age Compendium' website, believes these engravings should be attributed to a 1733 version Lancelot published, citing British historian Dr Carola Hicks.[6]

The London Archaeological Society assigned Charles Stothard to make a colour copy of the entire Tapestry. This was published between 1819 and 1823 in the Society's *Vetusta Monumenta*. Stothard indicated on the drawings what he believed were missing portions of the Tapestry with stitch holes. Stothard also evidently took – that is, stole – two pieces of the Tapestry. These were substituted by reconstructions; one was returned. After this replacement, photos of the Tapestry were taken by a Mr E. Dosseter.[7] In 1838, Victor Sansonetti made engravings of the Tapestry that indicate some parts as being missing with blank sections, whereas Stothard had made reconstructions in those areas.[8]

It is at this point where the Tapestry begins to suffer from some alterations in its representations. These were to be transposed to the actual Tapestry itself in the 1842 'repairs' and 'restorations' of it. These changes were made by the then custodian of the Tapestry – Ed Lambert – when it was 'relined and repaired', according to the suggested reconstructions and sketches of Stothard. This is when the Bayeux Tapestry becomes suspect as a completely accurate account of what happened at the Battle of Hastings. A specific objection is the notion that King Harold was mortally wounded when a Norman arrow struck him in the eye.

Was King Harold Wounded by an Arrow in the Eye?

Before analysing the supposed evidence of King Harold having been felled, or at least injured, by a Norman arrow to the eye, I'd like to point to an in-depth analysis by Professor Christopher Dennis, of Cardiff University. His paper was published by The Historical Association in September 2009.[9]

Professor Dennis begins by noting that several authorities now question the validity of the 'arrow-in-the-eye' story. He cites historians Sir Frank Stenton and David Douglas as sceptics and Henry Loyn and Frank Barlow as entirely rejecting the idea of King Harold II being hit in the eye by an arrow. The controversy stems from the fact that neither William of Jumièges, who wrote of the Conquest in the late 1060s, nor William of Poitiers, who reported on the campaign in the early 1070s, mentioned that King Harold had been injured by an arrow in his eye. In fact, neither writer paid much attention to the Anglo-Saxon king's death in the combat at Battle Hill. Even these earliest of all chroniclers differ on when during the fight Harold II lost his life: William of Jumièges says it was late in the battle and William of Poitiers contends that he went down early in the struggle – during the initial attack. The editor of and commentator on modern renditions and studies of William of Jumièges' work, Elisabeth van Houts, relying on the original Latin, agrees that he mentioned that King Harold had been 'pierced' by wounds, causing his death, which leads some to conclude that the 'piercing' was by an arrow shot; but Barlow differs, contending that the use of 'pierced' was merely a literary cliché of the time. Van Houts also believes that William of Jumièges is correct and that King Harold was killed early in the fight.

Christopher Dennis also reports that King Harold II's biographer, Ian Walker, thinks that the king's death was probably, according to Professor Dennis, 'so distasteful or ignominious' as to have been suppressed in the official accounts, at least initially. Dennis goes on to suggest that William of Poitiers and William of Jumièges 'had deliberately avoided' the details of King Harold's death, likely due to pressure from the Norman court during William the Conqueror's lifetime. Dennis reports that it was not until the early twelfth century that the 'arrow-in-the-eye' story was being put forward and not in the earliest account, written by

Bishop Guy of Amiens. In this telling of the battle, Bishop Guy, writing in 1067 in his poem 'Song of the Battle of Hastings', does not mention Harold II being hit in the eye by an arrow. Rather, Duke William himself is said to have gathered together several Norman knights who then charged King Harold's standard and pierced and hacked him to death. But it was soon realised that such an incident would bring William's accession to the English throne into question and the 'piercing and hacking' event was suppressed and, later – much later – the 'arrow-in-the-eye' myth was concocted as a supposed happening in a prelude to King Harold II's death.

In his investigation of the 'arrow-in-the-eye' story, Professor Dennis agrees that the social, political and ecclesiastical situation after the Battle of Hastings was not as secure or stable for William the Conqueror as is often popularly imagined. This is because, in part, William was under a cloud of suspicion regarding his personal role in the death of a king – King Harold II of England – who had been officially anointed by the Catholic Church. It would not do for someone, even a duke or another king, to have been part of the killing of an officially recognised monarch – all the more so if the man in question subsequently replaced the fallen head of state. Just after the fighting at Battle Hill, the bishop of Amiens – Bishop Guy – penned a poem to celebrate the victory by William the Conqueror and the Normans. In that version, written in early 1067, William is also described as having assembled a group of Norman knights to charge King Harold's position on Battle Hill and is said to have participated in the 'piercing and hacking' to death of the Anglo-Saxon monarch. Consequently, the 'official record', such as it was, at first fell silent regarding the details of the death of King Harold II. Then, in 1170, 'Master Wace' published his account of the Battle of Hastings in his larger volume covering the history of the Normans. In creating his work, Wace carefully researched the oral traditions yet to be found in Normandy, which, while likely preserving much good information about the battle, were related to him up to about a century later. It should also be borne in mind that Wace's intention was to further the then official line, already established, that William the Conqueror was the just and rightful King of England, recognised by the Catholic Church,.

In his telling of the events of 1066, Wace does report on the death of King Harold as being the result of a cavalry charge, but he also reintroduces the notion that the king had earlier been injured in the eye by an arrow, but not nearly as severely as imagined by other observers – contemporary and modern – and, moreover, in another section of his epic romantic poem, Wace reports that the arrow was said to have struck Harold 'above his right eye' – that is, to have hit him in the forehead; but also that the wound was not serious because the English king is described as having pulled the arrow out and thrown it away – unlikely if it had penetrated his eye socket.

Even though I remain doubtful regarding the 'arrow-in-the-eye' concept, in all honesty I must repeat here exactly, according to the translator and chronicler, what Wace wrote:

> And now the Normans had pressed on so far, that at last they reached the standard. There Harold had remained, defending himself to the utmost; but he was sorely wounded in his eye by the arrow and suffered grievous pain from the blow. An armed man came in the throng of the battle and struck him on the ventaille of his helmet and beat him to the ground; and as he sought to recover himself, a knight beat him down again, striking him on the thick of his thigh, down to the bone.[10]

However, again quoting from the same work, in the introduction Edgar Taylor observes: 'Wace's account, published at a Norman court and under the patronage of the conqueror's family, may be expected to represent the leading facts in light favourable to Norman pretensions; but on the whole, the impression left on a perusal of his report will probably be, that it is fair and creditable to the author's general judgment and fidelity as an historian.'[11] In other words, while Taylor accepts the overall historical value of Wace's account, he also realises that the versions of events depicted may have been tilted in favour of the story being told as the Norman court preferred at the time.

Later in his chronicle Wace also states: 'Gurth [Gyrth – Harold's brother] saw the English falling around and that there was no remedy. He saw his race hastening to ruin, and despaired of any aid; he would have fled, but could not, for the throng continually increased. And the duke [William] pushed on till he reached him and struck him with great force. Whether he died of that blow I know not, but it was said that he fell under it and rose no more.'[12]

Wace concludes this part of the action with, 'The standard was beaten down, the golden gonfanon was taken and Harold and the best of his friends were slain; but there was so much eagerness and throng of so many around, seeking to kill him, that I know not who it was that slew him.'[13] So, again, Harold, along with his brother and 'his friends', is described as being overwhelmed by the Norman 'throng'. I believe this part of the account to have great validity and, while not discounting entirely that the English king had been injured, above or in his eye, it is evident, even in this account stating there had been an eye wound, that King Harold II was described in the first of the passages above as still being on his feet, 'defending himself to the utmost', whence a Norman 'armed man' came forward and 'beat him to the ground', then, 'as he sought to recover himself, a knight beat him down again'.[14]

My instinctive, intuitive response is that King Harold's efforts at self-defence and recovery from blows, would not have been possible or even probable, if he had sustained a serious injury to his eye. I can report from my personal experiences that even a relatively gentle jab to one's eye while rough-housing, sports, exercise, martial arts, etc., will leave one incapable of doing much else other than to hold the injured orb and suffer in incapacity and confusion, whether one remains silent or is vocal about it. However, I then consulted with ophthalmologist and eye surgeon Dr James Michael Jumper, who was a military doctor with a great deal of experience treating eye injuries as a result of combat and terrorist attacks, including many patients who suffered eye injuries in the terror bombings in Dar es Salaam, Tanzania and Nairobi, Kenya, in 1998.

Dr Jumper told me of a case where a man suffered an arrow-shot to the eye that missed the orb, went entirely through his brain and exited from the back of his neck, with no serious short-term or long-term effects because it hit no major arteries or essential sections of the penetrated tissues. He related other cases and said that it is possible to sustain serious eye injuries and to keep functioning at a normal or near-normal pace of activity until treated, even if treatment was delayed. He opined that it is pretty much a matter of luck, the influence of adrenaline in a battlefield situation and the outlook and determination of the individual in deciding just how serious an eye injury could be as far as continued physical activity is concerned. Dr Jumper also remarked that there are many more eye injuries in combat, at an increasing rate, since medieval times, in part due to the fact that in those days many warriors' helmets included eye protection (nose and cheek guards), which modern combat gear does not; but the most important factor is that improvised explosive devices and land mines are now fashioned in such a way as to send more projectiles toward victims' faces.

Before continuing, I think it is appropriate to relay exactly what others reported regarding the 'arrow-in-the-eye' story, again according to Professor Dennis. The Norman bowmen sent barrages of arrows against the Anglo-Saxons, but the defenders covered themselves well with their shields.[15] Then, the Normans shot their arrows in high, arcing trajectories, causing them to fall upon the sometimes unprotected heads and shoulders of the men in the shield wall, 'and all feared to open their eyes or leave their faces unguarded'.[16] It was then, according to Dennis' report on the accounts of William of Jumièges, Orderic Vitalis and Robert of Torigni: The key passage says that such an upward-shot, then plunging arrow 'struck Harold above his right eye'.[17] The near-contemporary but then succeeding account goes on to say that King Harold was in great pain, pulled the arrow out, broke it and tossed it aside, then leaned upon his shield. The version also states that, despite the fact that the arrow supposedly struck King Harold's forehead, it somehow put out his eye.[18]

However, there is a problem with Dennis's original sources' assertions. If the arrow were on a plunging trajectory, as it would have been if fired up and then arced downward, it would not have been able to strike King Harold in either the forehead or the eye as his helmet, mentioned in the final death scene, would have prevented such an occurrence. Instead, at most, it would have struck his cheekbone or below. So, while at first chroniclers seem to confirm the 'arrow-in-the-eye' version of the story of King Harold's demise, they instead present a case for the lucky arrow shot to have injured the Anglo-Saxon king's face below his eye, not in it or above, on his forehead, which, as pointed out above, would not have been possible as the king's helmet would have prevented such a wound. Moreover, King Harold would presumably have also been trying to block any arrows with his shield, which was mentioned in the reports. In their translation of *The Gesta Guillelmi*, R.H.C. Davis and Marjorie Chibnall note that the earliest written source to assign King Harold's death (or severe injury) to an arrow in or near his eye was found in a later description written by Amatus of Montecassino, which is only available in a French translation.[19]

We will now turn to what Professor Dennis has to say about the supposed depiction of King Harold II being in struck in the eye, as presented in the now restored and altered Bayeux Tapestry. In his paper,[20] Professor Dennis suggests that the 'arrow-in-the-eye' story predominates primarily because it is, evidently, visually presented to us in the Bayeux Tapestry. However, the earliest representations of the Tapestry, before it was restored, do *not* show an arrow piercing King Harold II's eye, as was explained earlier herein. Professor Dennis tells us that the figure supposedly pulling an arrow from his face or eye is almost entirely a recreation, with the original, damaged and unrestored depiction likely to include only the head and shoulders, with the remainder of this warrior having been the construction of those restoring the Tapestry in 1842, said restoration being based on the erroneous illustrations of Stothard, as mentioned previously, which were published between 1819 and 1823.

Professor Dennis also points to the 1733 engravings by Antoine Lancelot, which demonstrate that, 'Both clearly show that, in its albeit damaged condition in the early eighteenth century, the "arrow in the eye" figure was holding something longer than an arrow; in fact, he appears to be brandishing a spear, in imitation of the figure to the left of the standard-bearer'.[21] Finally, with regard to Dennis' comments regarding the illustration in the Tapestry, he notes that this same depicted warrior appears in an awkward form. Frank Barlow noticed that the 'arrow' itself does not appear to enter the figure's head. His hand, shown gripping something – a line of dashes to indicate missing Tapestry content – is also placed awkwardly and, taking a more careful view, the shape of his hand is identical to the hand of the warrior to the left of the standard-bearer, who is holding a spear. Also, the 'arrow's' alignment is not consistent with a downward trajectory, as if it had fallen from overhead.[22] These remarks echo mine, which I made upon observing the Bayeux Tapestry reproductions and the original on display at Bayeux, prior to encountering Professor Dennis' paper.

With regard to the captioning in the death scene of King Harold, Professor Dennis adds that there is a strong argument, made by C.K. Lawson, that the inscription on the Tapestry scene depicting King Harold II's death, '*Hic Harold rex interfectus est*' was not in its original form and may have instead actually read, '*Hic Harold rex in terra iactus est*' ('Here King Harold has been thrown to the ground'), which would indicate the falling individual, not the one shown to be holding something originally indicated as a dashed line.[23] He concludes with the observation that there is so much in doubt about this scene, as depicted after the restoration, that the notion that the Bayeux Tapestry 'proves' the theory that King Harold II was injured by an arrow strike to the eye is not supported by the facts.[24] In this, too, obviously, I am in complete agreement, as was shown before.

Why the Anglo-Saxons Began to Give Way and What Happened Next

I doubt that King Harold at first intended to deploy his men along such an extended front, but was instead compelled to do so when Duke William saw the opportunity to try to outflank to the Norman left of the Anglo-Saxons' stubborn defence of the Hastings-London ridgeway and the area just to the south, in the present-day St Mary's tract, by thrusting across the series of scenic meadows even farther to the south and south-west.

During the fight, King Harold II would have been obliged to rush to the endangered sector himself on the right-hand side of his main line of resistance, bringing his battle standard with him and to send for reinforcements – thinning his shield walls and skirmishers along his left-hand side – opposite the Flemings and other Norman allies such as the French contingent – if we accept that view of the battle or instead facing the Bretons if we believe Bishop Guy's earliest report regarding the fight on Battle Hill.

It would be during the series of assaults by Duke William's Norman and Breton (or French?) infantry, supported by archers[*] and augmented with periodic cavalry charges, that the Anglo-Saxon line would have been driven back, only to reassert itself through numerous counter-attacks to regain lost ground in order to remain deployed along the slight ridgecrest, which was nevertheless fronted by the grand 'ditch' of the valley now containing the tracks of the Southeastern Railway. This series of counter assaults would have been necessary because the Anglo-Saxon line would have had no depth – there was little to back it up as the ridge they were defending (running along and near the current Powdermill Lane) fell away behind them. There was no cover except for a patch of woods near the centre of the lower reaches of the historically accepted battlefield and the marshy ground, ponds and small lakes that were almost certainly there then and have been dammed and contained in more recent times, where they remain to this day. Eventually, Duke William's and the Normans' and Bretons' (or French) persistence would pay off and the victory would come after great sacrifices on both sides. I do not believe the battle was won when King Harold fell victim to a fortunate – which would have been unfortunate for him – arrow shot to the eye, but, rather, that he simply ran out of enough men to adequately defend his position in the time remaining that day; that the Norman and Breton, or possibly French, infantry broke through in several places; and that the Norman and French mounted noblemen staged their medieval version of an armoured thrust along and to just

---

[*]   Wace mentions two groups of Norman archers: 'The archers of *Val de Roil* and those of *Bretoil*, put out the eyes of many an Englishman with their arrows' (Wace, p. 227).

behind the ridge King Harold and his men were defending; and that it was their persistence of effort and fighting capabilities that eventually won the day for the Normans, their allies and Duke William, making him 'William the Conqueror'.

When the Norman infantry, archers and mounted knights ultimately began to break through along their left flank, below the St Mary's tract and possibly extending all the way to Powdermill Lake, they also commenced breaking up the Anglo-Saxons' shield wall into clumps of defenders and rolling up their line toward the Norman centre and right, allowing the cavalry to break out and rush toward the right-rear of the English all along the slight ridge to their north-east. However, except for some outlying clusters of cavalrymen sweeping farther out to the south-west, I believe most of the mounted warriors rode closer to the 'centre' of this right flank of the Anglo-Saxon positions, nearer to the small lake that now fills-in the southernmost reaches of the 'battlefield' as it has traditionally been held to be, at the foot of the heights extending up to Battle Abbey. It was then, I believe, that some of the mounted Normans fell into the or yet another (in addition to the 'ditch' of the narrow and steep-sided Southeastern Railway valley) 'Malfosse' or 'evil ditch', on the site of the currently accepted battlefield in the as yet marshy ground near where Duke William is traditionally thought to have stood to command the fight, which would not have been true except, perhaps but not likely, in the final stages of the fighting. Instead, I believe he was positioned across the low point now occupied by the railway line, south of the Tesco Express carpark – opposite the English army's right flank around and just below (south of) the St Mary's tract – on Quarry Hill.

When his infantry forces broke through, Duke William, accompanied by other mounted knights, likely rode across the low ground, presenting a prime target for the remaining Anglo-Saxon spearmen, archers, slingers and rock throwers still holding their portions of the battle line on the slight ridge there. I believe this is when Duke William's horse was first shot from under him, probably by javelins or arrows, and when Bishop Odo rallied the troops as William raised his visor to show he was all right, according to the Bayeux Tapestry and also William of Poitiers.[25]

William of Poitiers takes Duke William's actions two steps further, having him single-handedly riding toward the enemy and exhorting his own Norman and allied Breton (or French) troops to renew the attack.[26] After this brief delay, the Norman cavalry, estimated to be at least 1,000 in number,[†] made breakthroughs at several points along the remaining Anglo-Saxon battle lines.[27] Next, I conjecture that the Norman mounted knights encircled King Harold and his Huscarls' now relatively isolated position, in the St Mary's tract, just south of where the Battle Methodist Church now stands; Harold was killed; the battle was won; the Norman and allied forces gradually collapsed the entire Anglo-Saxon line; and the rout and pursuit began as dusk fell.[28]

However, prior to the battle's denouement, there was yet a final effort by the Anglo-Saxons to resist the Norman advance. This is the point where some writers refer to the 'Malfosse' – the 'evil ditch' where Norman cavalrymen supposedly fell and drowned. If such a feature existed, it likely would have been either the 'marshy' terrain at the base of the now generally accepted battlefield below where Battle Abbey now exists; the 'ditch' was probably, toward each end, partly filled with water at the time, at the end of the first third of autumn, when occasional rains fall across Northwestern Europe; or, again, as I believe, this was but a reference to the main 'ditch' where the battle had been fought all that day. In William of Poitiers' account he made no mention of a 'Malfosse' or drowning knights – only the fact that the English made a last stand near a ruined rampart and a maze of ditches, and that Count Eustace was wounded and withdrew as Duke William charged forward then to vanquish the remnants of the Anglo-Saxon army.[29] Such a maze of ditches could have existed in the somewhat chaotic terrain at the same location, at the foot of the ridge upon which Battle Abbey was later built; or, more likely, the 'ruined rampart' and 'maze of ditches' could have been near the crest of Battle Hill, opposite where Battle Abbey now stands, at the present-day St Mary's Church and graveyard. I believe the Anglo-Saxons' last stand was either at the (secondary) high-point of the ridge, just south of the Marley Lane roundabout or even at Caldbec Hill.

In the proposed deployment described earlier, the Anglo-Saxons would have had the advantage of being on higher ground west and north-west of the current railway line and east and north-east of the Hastings-London ridgeway; but, on the other side of the A2100 and along the road itself, both sides would have been on almost even ground, as

---

† '... Then those who kept close guard by him [William] and rode where he rode, being about a thousand armed men, came and rushed with closed ranks upon the English; and with the weight of their good horses and the blows the knights gave, broke the press of the enemy and scattered the crowd before them, the good duke leading them on in front' (Wace, p. 251).

far as their respective elevations were concerned; or on the extreme left flank of the Normans, they would have had a height advantage of 10 to 20ft or more on their side of the narrow valley not yet occupied by the railway tracks. Why King Harold would deploy his shield wall there would be incomprehensible were it not for one key fact: the presence of the thick forests along and on either side of the road that would have been there in 1066 and which are reasserting themselves today. Again, it was at this choke point that the Anglo-Saxons had the best chance of blocking Duke William and his Normans with their superior numbers, mounted warriors and archers. Other than that, the relatively deep valley – almost a gorge – now occupied by the Southeastern Railway line, would have made up for the differences in height on either side, making the valley a more than acceptable enhancement to the defence as it was not only about 15 to 30ft deep but also steep-sided, forcing the Norman cavalry, if not the infantry as well, to make an oblique charge – first downhill, then uphill – assaulting the Anglo-Saxon position atop the far lip of the ravine at an angle, thus increasing their vulnerability to the spears, arrows and other projectiles hurled at them by their English enemies.

King Harold would have been compelled to take up this position because, as has been shown in the quote from *The Anglo-Saxon Chronicle* (Manuscript 'D'), the part of the Anglo-Saxon army that Harold was able to muster – small to begin with, even though the *Chronicle* described it as a large (actually 'mighty') army, was further diminished by those warriors and their leaders who chose to remain at the previous presumed marshalling site at Appledore, if that was, in fact, a true account of what had gone before Harold's move to Caldbec Hill. In any event, it is evident from investigating the countryside in and around the current town of Battle that King Harold certainly would have lacked sufficient manpower that day to defend Caldbec Hill and that his smaller army would have been easily outflanked at that position. Moreover, the terrain around Caldbec Hill is more open and less wooded, which would place the Anglo-Saxon forces at an even greater disadvantage, for the following reasons.

Harold Godwinsson was an experienced and successful war leader who had campaigned with the Norman army himself in Normandy and Brittany. He realised that he could not face Duke William's forces on open ground, particularly with a smaller army, due to the fact that the Norman army enjoyed greater advantages there. Norman cavalry would have readily overrun the mass of less experienced Anglo-Saxon infantry if they were placed in the open – shield wall and hedgehog of spears notwithstanding – as they were proven to do in the last stages of the fight at Battle (Senlac) Hill anyway. Norman archers would have used their bows and arrows to an even greater effect on open ground than they did in the actual battle in the closer, wooded – heavily or not – terrain. These factors would have been magnified by the added circumstance that much, probably most, of King Harold's army would have been relatively inexperienced and unarmoured members of the Great Fyrd. They would have been much more likely to yield and then succumb to both volleys of arrows and cavalry charges than the better-armed and better-trained Hidesmen and lesser Thegns in the Select Fyrd, the mercenaries and the professional Huscarls. So, King Harold was faced with no other choice than to try to resist the Normans on the ridgetop road through the woods, where his shield wall could block that route while his skirmishers of spearmen, slingers, archers and axe-wielding warriors would be at their best performance, particularly so if the Anglo-Saxons were, in fact, outnumbered by the bulk of the Norman army that had travelled up the Hastings-to-London ridgeway that morning and had not advanced east, whether by sea or overland, toward Rye, Appledore, Dover and Canterbury.

Not only would the Anglo-Saxon sword-armed shield wall have been deployed up to five ranks deep across the narrow, tree-confined road, there would be spearmen, archers, slingers and axe-wielding skirmishers in the second through fifth ranks and defending the thick woods on either side. The smaller Anglo-Saxon army would have acted as a 'cork in the bottleneck', able to frustrate the Normans all day, as they did, until near nightfall, when the decisive breakthrough was made by first Duke William's infantry, then the Norman cavalry, driving the Anglo-Saxons back on their right flank, which ran along the low ridge adjacent to what is now Powdermill Lane/the B2095, resulting in the death of King Harold and his Huscarls and any reserves he had mustered close to the 'hoary apple tree' – if it grew there at the time – where, presumably he was pierced and cut down.

How the Theories of Others Have Reinforced My Own Views and Conclusions

In connection with local terrain features and historical records, all of the competing volumes regarding the actual site of the Battle of Hastings battle put forth descriptions of the lay of the land and the fighting that not only did not, in my opinion, refute my conjectures, they inadvertently reinforced them. In many if not most cases, these descriptions apply equally as well, if not better, to the locations and books I had investigated. The geographic features could also refer to Telham Hill, Baldslow, Beauport Park, the narrow Southeastern Railway valley, the Tesco Express carpark on Quarry Hill, Marley Lane, the St Mary's tract and many other places. These references to descriptions of the landscapes involving and surrounding the site of the Battle of Hastings are too numerous to elucidate in great detail, although I have addressed many if not most of them elsewhere herein in my own narrative; but I list and briefly summarise some of them now for readers to have in their awareness should they decide to investigate the other books cited.

In the Starkey brothers' book, such descriptions begin on page 18 – that the Battle of Hastings was fought at a forested and a narrow place. Page 148: There was a fosse, which had three openings; and the terrain indicates their explanations will fit on the Hastings Peninsula as well or better – the 'three openings' likely referring to the ridgeway and the relatively 'open' flanks where the narrow valley or 'ditch' falls away. Page 149: The fosse was a natural feature and the Norman camp was visible to King Harold and his brother Gyrth while they scouted from a hilltop, which could be almost anywhere, but would apply if the reconnaissance occurred on the easternmost portion of Telham Hill (ridge), looking toward Beauport Park and Baldslow, where I believe the bulk of the Norman army had encamped. Page 153: The proposed Norman campsites are more appropriate for my alternate locations at Beauport Park, Baldslow and Hastings Castle. Page 155: The Anglo-Saxons were admonished by King Harold to face the enemy and that the fighting occurred at a narrow place. I have addressed these concerns in detail elsewhere: the Anglo-Saxons at the 'crimp' in their battle lines would have turned half-right, to face the enemy. The 'narrow place' was the ridgeway, across which the main shield wall had been deployed. On page 156: It was a steep slope for Norman attackers to scale, which is the case with the narrow and steep-sided valley now occupied by the Southeastern Railway line. One page 157: The likely Anglo-Saxon use of stakes/spears for a hedgehog defence would apply to my scenario as well. Page 161: The numerous references to a difficult climb up a steep slope for the Normans in early source works are suddenly contradicted, after being cited as correct and pertinent in other parts of their book, and questioned regarding their accuracy. Page 162: In another reversal, the steep slopes and valley are cited. (Again, this mirrors the terrain at the railway valley.) Page 163: The fosse and Malfosse are mentioned as key elements of the battle. I place them at the Southeastern Railway ravine. Page 167: The hill, forest, narrow place and untilled and rough ground are again noted as key contributors to the outcome of the battle, which I again place in the same valley. Page 169: The fosse is mentioned as guarding one side of the Anglo-Saxon army (as the Southeastern Railway valley would so serve). Duke William was able to command and fight from the middle of a slope, which would be on Quarry Hill, behind the present-day Tesco Express carpark. Page 170: The fosse and plain are present (being, in my theory, the narrow valley and the scenic meadows and lower reaches of the Powdermill Lane/B2095 ridge), with the steepness of the hill (or far bank of the valley, in my estimation); and the fact that the Anglo-Saxon flanks were difficult to surround. Page 171: The youths, herdsmen, clerks and priests were able to view the fighting from the hillside (Quarry Hill in my scenario); and the presence of the Malfosse and hillock (where I propose King Harold originally planted his standard and where the surviving Anglo-Saxons made their last stand, a few yards south of today's Marley Lane roundabout.) Page 172: The hilltop and the fact that the Anglo-Saxons could roll stones downslope as the Normans had a rough climb up. Again, this would be the same valley. On page 173 there are references to the report by William of Poitiers that at the battle site was a relatively 'treeless hill' near the thick forests, which coincides with the conical, hill-like peak on the Hastings ridge just south of the Marley Lane roundabout, where I speculate that King Harold originally placed his standard prior to moving to the slighter peak at the Powdermill Lane roundabout and then to the critical sector in the St Mary's tract. There is also a reference to the Anglo-Saxons being on a ridge that contained fewer trees and also meadows, which, again, approximates my view of the Anglo-Saxon main line of resistance being in such terrain, atop the Powdermill Lane/B2095 slight ridge there, adjacent to the steep-sided, narrow valley where the Southeastern Railway is now to be found. On page 186 the Starkeys concede that Senlac Hill/Battle Hill is 9 miles from Hastings and that the battle took place at a valley and narrow place. In fact, Sedlescombe is 5.69 miles away (straight-line), but, if one takes the ridgeway route, it is closer to 9 miles. However, again, the Sedlescombe site is neither at a valley nor a narrow place. On page 187 the authors refer to the rough ground at the battle site and the fact that the Normans approached over rising ground, such as would be the case if they advanced along the ridgeway, then diverged onto Quarry Hill. On the same page they cite the existence of the fosse and King Harold's command to face the enemy, which I dealt with concerning the A2100 and flanking dispositions. On page 188 the Starkeys place King Harold on the hill, with the fosse now behind the Normans; and they also refer to this being a narrow place. On page 189 there is yet another reference to the fosse and a summit of a hill and the Anglo-Saxons rolling stones down. Here they again reverse the comments made on page 161 as they report on the steep slopes. Such slopes exist at the Southeastern Railway ravine. On page 190 the Anglo-Saxons are said to be on a hill near the forest from which they had come and also that the Normans appeared over rising ground and then crossed a valley. This would be the case after they swung left onto Quarry Hill, then attacked across the Southeastern Railway valley. On page 206 the Starkey brothers concede that the future abbey site already had a ridgeway in 1066. On page 221 the Starkeys resort to a natural fosse created by a 'landslip' to create one at their conjectured battlefield. On the same page there is yet another reference to a conical summit, which, again, applies to the highpoint just south of the Marley Lane roundabout. On page 232 the authors write that the slope would have been steep, slippery and untilled. Once more, this would describe the Southeastern Railway ravine. On page 251 the writers print a copy of the Yeakell and Gardner 1770 map, which shows almost continuous woods in the area; but they leave out the part showing the existence of the steep-sided and narrow valley now housing the Southeastern Railway right-of-way.

In Nick Austin's book, again, descriptions of the terrain favour or are equally valid for the Southeastern Railway valley, etc. These are found on page 228, with references to the ditch, stakes and the confined space. On page 230 he cites the report that Norman youths and priests viewed the battle from a slope, which I believe was on Quarry Hill. On page 231 Austin cites the existence of the fosse, which, to me, is the ravine. On page 232 Austin says that the Anglo-Saxons fell back onto rising ground, which would be the case if they were driven back from the narrow valley and retreated onto the slight ridge behind that now hosts Powdermill Lane/the B2095. On the same page he writes that the Normans pursued the retreating Anglo-Saxons by moving across a valley. On page 233 Austin mentions the Malfosse, which I contend was likely either the same valley as the 'fosse' where the Southeastern Railway now runs, or it could possibly be on the opposite flank of the battle area, where the land below Marley Lane and adjacent to Station Approach was a meandering marshland or, more likely, this is the flooded and boggy area below Battle Abbey. On page 250 Austin refers to the rugged and twisting footpath from the Tesco Express on Quarry Hill to Crowhurst, which would, to this writer, hardly accommodate even a force of 500 men and much less so for 5,000 of them. He also refers to Telham Hill as being a key factor in the local real estate with regard to the battle, which would not be the case if his proposed fighting at Crowhurst had occurred. On page 251 he again refers to Telham Hill. He goes on to cite the lack of bodies being found in modern times on the traditional battlefield or anywhere else. In reply I can only say that the absence of evidence is not evidence of absence. On page 272 Austin says the battle was fought on a great field, not in a narrow place. On page 273 the author says the Normans shot their arrows uphill; but I contend they were shot across the valley at the far bank of the grand 'ditch' encompassing the Southeastern Railway line. On page 312 Austin resorts to illustrated terrain features shown on the Bayeux Tapestry that confirm the hill and valley and the sightings of the opposing sides by their scouts, both of which confirm traditional accounts, but without disproving my theories or anyone else's. (My scenario includes a hill, the narrow valley and the scouts sighting each army on Caldbec Hill and Telham Hill.) Page 313 points to uneven ground and a plain beyond and a swamp and stream, which is what we find at Quarry Hill, the narrow valley, the 'plain' where the narrow valley opens out near Battle Abbey Farm and the swampy land with many becks below Battle Abbey. On page 314 Austin indicates that there was rising ground, a plain and more rising ground where King Harold died. This approximates Quarry Hill, the valley between it and the St Mary's tract, with a plain at the extreme right flank of the Anglo-Saxons and left flank of the Normans – once they fought their way across the valley and Harold's end near the ridgetop in the St Mary's tract.

The comparisons apply to the book by John Grehan and Martin Mace. On page 55 they refer to the steep slopes at the battlefield and that King Harold was concerned about securing his flanks, no matter where the battle would be fought. On page 69 they write about when the Normans turned on the Anglo-Saxons who had pursued them 'down the hill'. This, I contend, could just as easily refer not to a hillside but, rather, the bank of a narrow valley. As for the small hillock where Anglo-Saxons were surrounded: that, I believe is the point where the standard had been originally – just a few yards to the south of the Marley Lane roundabout. On page 87 they write of Duke William's men being forced to climb a steep slope, which, again, need not have been on Caldbec Hill but just as well this would describe a difficult charge up the bank of a narrow valley. On page 88 they again report that the Normans had to scale a steep slope; and they remind us that King Harold's infantry could not withstand the Norman cavalry in the open without extreme difficulty and danger; but Caldbec Hill is reckoned to have been largely treeless in 1066, as it is today. On page 89 they refer to reports that the Anglo-Saxons built a fortress at a narrow place. On page 90 the authors write about how the Anglo-Saxons emerged from the forest at a hill with a rough and untilled valley, which describes the area around and at the ravine that now holds the Southeastern Railway tracks. On page 98 they mentioned the Bayeux Tapestry scene of the fighting, which was lush with foliage and that it was on rough ground and the depiction of the Anglo-Saxons facing left and right. This would have been the case if their shield wall had been deployed as I described – along the Powdermill Lane slight ridge, then across the ridgeway and turned back in a crimp as it folded back along the high ground to link with the remainder of their main line of resistance on the wooded slope between Station Approach and Marley Lane. On page 100 they make note of the plain and the fosse and describe how at first the Normans, then the Anglo-Saxons, were driven into the valley, to be followed by being pursued upslope toward the opposing rising ground. This, too, approximates a phase of the battle as I conjecture it to have been – with the Normans attacking from Quarry Hill, then across the Southeastern Railway valley, then up and onto the Powdermill Lane/B2095 slight ridge. On page 101 Messrs. Grehan and Mace recall that the Anglo-Saxons rolled stones down the steep slope, which slope, I contend, was the bank of the valley between Quarry Hill and the Powdermill Lane ridge. On page 104 the writers remind us of reports of a palisade or barrier around the Anglo-Saxons, which could have been thrown up by local Fyrdmen on the day prior to the battle or even early on the morning of the fighting. On page 107 they write: 'We also know that the English forces spent the night before the battle in the immediate vicinity of the eventual battlefield and that the Normans had to travel all the way from Hastings to make contact with their enemy.' In this I note that the Anglo-Saxons are here said to have bivouacked 'in the immediate vicinity' of the next day's combat, which could also mean that they slept on Caldbec Hill, Battle Abbey Ridge or even at the battle line I propose farther forward. Also, I believe the bulk of the Norman army was encamped at Baldslow and/or Beauport Park, to shorten their march so they could either advance along the ridgeway or divert toward Appledore, Dover and Canterbury. On page 114 the authors state that the battlefield was steep and confined, not open, as at Caldbec Hill or on more level ground, as with Mr Austin's postulated battlefield at Crowhurst. On page 123 the authors rightly report that King Harold would have refused his flanks for protection; but to me this meant that the right flank eventually, as the Normans extended their own left flank, ended up on lower and more open ground, according to my reckoning, allowing the Normans to stretch and break and then outflank it, resulting in some Norman knights dying in the boggy lands below Battle Abbey, to be accompanied or followed by the collapse of the Anglo-Saxon right flank. On page 125 Grehan and Mace repeat that the Normans were fighting up a rough and steep hill – or, to me, a slope, such as the bank of the narrow and steep-sided valley. On page 129 they tell us that the hill (or slope?) where the battle was fought was steep and untilled. On page 131 the writers report on the placing of palisades. I observe that the woods at the narrow valley would have provided many young trees to be felled and used as stakes driven into the ground at the lip of the valley's banks on both margins of the ridgeway, especially on the Anglo-Saxon right-hand – at the Southeastern Railway valley. On page 132 the authors remind us of the speech Duke William gave to his troops before the fighting began. This hillside where the duke gave his pep-talk to his troops was located with the Anglo-Saxons 'on the opposite ridge', which describes Quarry Hill and the Powdermill Lane/B2095 ridge across the narrow valley. On page 136 the writers state that Oakwood Gill is generally accepted now as being the site of the Malfosse; but I believe it is too far from the actual battle location to be the Malfosse, which I place as most likely at the lakes and becks at the base of the Battle Abbey grounds – almost the only place where the actual battle bled over onto the historically accepted site. On page 137 we find that in their quoting of him, the authors will find that Rupert Furneaux agrees with my previous observation regarding the site of the Malfosse, at the foot of the traditionally accepted location of the battlefield. I believe the higher ground cited on page 138 is actually the conical hillock or peak just south of the Marley Lane roundabout at Battle Hill/Senlac Hill. On page 139 the report of the Norman scouts spotting the opposing army could just as easily place the Normans at Baldslow and Telham Hill late Friday, 13 October, enabling them to see the Anglo-Saxon standards on and/ or near Caldbec Hill. On page 152 the authors cite Frank Stenton, with whom I agree that the flooded depression between the duke's position and the fighting describes the marshy ground at the lower end of the valley where the Southeastern Railway now runs and flows over onto the lowest edge of the Battle Abbey grounds.

Returning to my tours of the area, the terrain features I discovered began to prove, to me, some of the more likely events in the progression of the Battle of Hastings. Various clues from different locations started to fall together in a way that made sense, despite the evident – and heretofore generally mystifying – probable decisions of the two commanders on the scene on 14 October, 1066 – King Harold and Duke William. These questions were answered by the terrain and the likely vegetation growing upon it in 1066, which were covered in this and the previous section. The final proof, to me, was in my actual survey of the area between the Southeastern Railway line and the lay of the land all around, particularly in the direction toward Hastings, from which Duke William and his Norman and allied conquerors would advance and from which they would deploy before ever reaching the imagined, generally accepted site of the battle on the Battle Abbey estate. Instead of marching left, downhill, crossing and descending from the ridge that now hosts Powdermill Lane/the B2095 into the boggy ground, then wheeling right to confront the Anglo-Saxons on the low ridgetop where Battle Terrace is now located, placing Duke William's men at a greater disadvantage, the Normans were confronted by King Harold's men emerging from the woods to block the ridgeway with a stout shield wall up to five ranks deep where it crosses the narrow valley between Quarry Hill and the Powdermill Lane/B2095 slight ridge. On the other flank, King Harold had his men arrayed on the wooded heights that first face more eastward, bending back toward the high ground between today's Station Approach and Marley Lane. Returning to the narrow valley: the defence lines were of fewer ranks and even clumps of warriors in the initially thick and then ever-thinning woods to the Anglo-Saxon right. To King Harold's left of his initial placing of his standard on the conical hillock at the peak of the Battle Abbey Ridge, there would have been a short, leftward-facing line of warriors wrapping around the steep slope, arcing back toward Marley Lane, where the forward-deployed battle line would continue until anchored at the becks, marsh and woods then there, at the edge of today's Harrier tract.

Finding his army's advance stalled by the stout defence of the ridgeway and by the bogs to his right, Duke William arrayed his men in three lines of attackers – archers in front, then infantry, followed by cavalry – as they moved across Quarry Hill, then shifted their main assault from the ridgeway to the right flank of the Anglo-Saxon battle line. They made repeated attacks downslope, firing arrows then charging across the valley and onto the opposite bank, eventually breaking through at several points with first barrages of arrows, then infantry attacks, followed and accompanied by cavalry charges, which also outflanked the ever-extending Anglo-Saxon right and where some of the charging horsemen came to grief in the becks and swampland below today's Battle Abbey. Then, as King Harold foresaw, all was lost as the Norman mounted warriors and fighters on foot overwhelmed the Anglo-Saxons, King Harold and his brothers were killed and the Normans pursued the then fleeing defenders as the sun settled in the west.

Chapter 12

Aftermath

Immediately following the decisive struggle atop Battle Hill, King Harold's body, along with those of thousands of his fellow Anglo-Saxon and Anglo-Danish comrades, including his brothers, lay as gutted, torn and bloody remains. Despite the fact that Harold's mother, Gytha, offered the weight of his body in gold to William the Conqueror, he refused the offer and instead trusted the royal carcass to one William Malet, ordering him to bury the body near the seashore.[1] Of the earliest accounts, only William of Poitiers tells us that Harold was buried 'by the sea'. [*] This initial observation was later echoed by others.

After the epic battle, fierce struggle and decisive victory at Battle Hill, William the Conqueror advanced on the hapless settlement of Romney, where he took revenge against the people there for the deaths of the Normans who landed close to the town in error while the main invasion force had landed near and at Pevensey. This act of vengeance occurred, according to William of Poitiers' account, just after that writer credited the Conqueror with being a benevolent and merciful victor.[2] This act of retribution and its origin, would seem to further indicate that at least a

---

[*] In eulogizing King Harold, William of Poitiers seems to unintentionally concede Harold's legitimate claim to the English throne: 'Your end proves by what right you were raised through the death-bed gift of Edward'. [Rendered from the Latin: *'Arguunt extrema tua quam recte sublimatus fueris Edwardi domo in ipsius fine'* (*The Gesta Guillelmi by William of Poitiers*, pp. 140, 141).] So, despite the fact that William of Poitiers tried to show that King Harold's death proved the invalidity of his elevation to king, the admission that King Edward had given him the kingship contradicts almost all other assertions by Duke William and William of Poitiers regarding King Edward's supposed intention to place the Norman duke on the throne of England.

minimal Anglo-Saxon military force had remained in the area, possibly from or near Appledore.

As they continued their victorious march, the Normans proceeded to Dover and Canterbury, then advanced on London, where Stigand, the Archbishop of Canterbury, and the remaining nobles of England and the leaders of the city had rallied a large army, which William of Poitiers described as being so large in number that London, 'in spite of its great size, could scarcely accommodate them all'. He also reports that there was, indeed, a successor to King Harold II – the then 10-year-old Edgar the Atheling. William of Poitiers also tells us that a force of 500 Norman knights kept the Anglo-Saxons in check while the majority of the invading force moved westward along the south shore of the River Thames, pillaging and burning before crossing over to the north bank.[3]

The tasks yet ahead for William the Conqueror in becoming the new monarch and then completely subjugating England would take some time and is beyond the scope of this book and requires the production of a separate volume to describe the extended campaign and following events in a respectable manner.

Conclusion

In his summation of his coverage of the brief reign of King Harold II, Tony Robinson observed that had Harold not suffered two separate major invasions of his country within a few weeks, he would be remembered as the great Anglo-Saxon king who ended the Viking depredations of not only England and the British Isles but all of Europe.[1] But the burden of defending his homeland twice within such a short period of time condemned him to be known as the loser of the decisive battle near Hastings instead. C. Warren Hollister is also generous to King Harold II in his wrapping-up of his work *Anglo-Saxon Military Institutions on the Eve of the Norman Conquest* when he asserts that Harold simply had an extraordinary string of bad luck, which no other mortal man would have been likely to overcome.

I agree with the assessments of this television documentary producer and also this scholarly expert. Having been fascinated by this subject since I first found out about it, now 65 years ago, and having also learned at that time that I bear an Old French given name and an Anglo-Saxon surname and that my family's roots extend back into both England and France, it was almost foreordained that I would one day, many, many years later, have the opportunity, the good luck and the cooperation and assistance of so many good people to be able to myself research the circumstances of the Norman Conquest, to write about it; and to concur that King Harold II was both a very capable and yet a very unlucky man. With the defeat of his army and his falling, so, too, fell Anglo-Saxon England.

Endnotes

By Way of Introduction: Prelude and Preliminaries to Investigating the Battle of Hastings

1. 'Time Team Special'. Television Documentary – Season 20 – '1066, The Lost Battlefield', 12 December 2013.
2. *The Battle of Hastings 1066: The Uncomfortable Truth – Revealing the True Location of England's Most Famous Battle* by John Grehan and Martin Mace (Pen and Sword Books, Barnsley, South Yorkshire, 2012).
3. *The Battle of Hastings at Sedlescombe* by Jonathan Starkey and Michael Starkey (Momentus Britain, second edition, third revision, 2010–19).
4. *Secrets of the Norman Conquest* by Nick Austin (Landscape Studios, Crowhurst, East Sussex, second edition, 2012).

Chapter 2: Anglo-Saxon England – the Background

1. Project Gutenberg, *The Anglo-Saxon Chronicle,* by unknown authors (medieval church scribes). Translator: James Henry Ingram. http://www.gutenberg.org/cache/epub/657/pg657.html
2. http://ryemuseum.co.uk/more-on-medieval-rye/
3. *Medieval History,* by Israel Smith Clare, p. 354. http://www.englishmonarchs.co.uk/saxon_15.htm
4. http://www.patriciabracewell.com/2018/10/the-battle-of-assandun/
5. http://www.englishmonarchs.co.uk/vikings_2.htm
6. https://www.britannica.com/biography/Canute-I

7. https://www.britannica.com/biography/Godwine) (http://www.englishmonarchs.co.uk/saxon_16.htm

8. https://www.unofficialroyalty.com/harold-harefoot-or-harold-i-king-of-england/

9. http://www.englishmonarchs.co.uk/saxon_16.htm

10. https://spartacus-educational.com/NORswegen.htm

11. http://www.englishmonarchs.co.uk/saxon_16.htm

12. http://www.englishmonarchs.co.uk/saxon_16.htm

13. David C. Douglas, *William the Conqueror: The Norman Impact Upon England* (Methuen, London, 1990), pp. 412, 413.

14. Project Gutenberg's *The Chronicle of the Norman Conquest*, by Master [possibly known the further identifier as either 'Robert' or 'Richard'] Wace. https://www.gutenberg.org/files/41163/41163-h/41163-h.htm. Hereafter Wace.

15. *The Anglo-Saxon Chronicle* – Avalon Project: Documents in Law, History and Diplomacy. Yale Law School – Lillian Goldman Law Library. https://avalon.law.yale.edu/medieval/ang11.asp

16. Wikipedia article – citing Herbert Thurston, 'St Ælred', *The Catholic Encyclopedia*', vol. 1 (Robert Appleton Company, New York, 1907). 20 September 2012, Bell, 'Ailred of Rievaulx (1110–1167)'. 'Aelred of Rievaulx ; also Ailred, Ælred and Æthelred; was an English Cistercian monk, abbot of Rievaulx from 1147 until his death and known as a writer. He is regarded by Anglicans and Catholics as a saint.' (Naturally, this writer visited the very impressive ruins of the abbey at Rievaulx, Yorkshire, during my stay in England.)

17. Wace, p. 76.

18. Ibid., p. 86, Note 6.

19. Ibid., p. 78.

20. Ibid., p. 77.

21. Ibid.

22. Ibid., pp. 79, 80.

23. Ibid., p. 80.

24. *The Gesta Guillelmi by William of Poitiers*, edited and translated by R.H.C. Davis and Marjorie Chibnall (Clarendon Press, Oxford, 1998), p. 69.

25. Wace, p. 83.

26. Ibid.

27. Ibid., p. 86.

28. *Eadmeri Historia Normanorum in Anglia*, edited by M. Rule, Rolls Series, 1884, p. 7.

29. As reported by Davis and Chibnall in *The Gesta Guillelmi by William of Poitiers*, p. 70, Note 3.
30. Wace, p. 77, Note 3.
31. http://www.englishmonarchs.co.uk/saxon_16.htm
32. https://biography.wales/article/s12-GRUF-APL-1063
33. 'Legends of Power – King Harold'. Television documentary by Tony Robinson.
34. *The Anglo-Saxon Chronicle* – Avalon Project: Documents in Law, History and Diplomacy. Yale Law School – Lillian Goldman Law Library. https://avalon.law.yale.edu/medieval/ang11.asp
35. '*The Gesta Guillelmi by William of Poitiers*, p. 119 and Note 3.
36. Ibid., p. 101, Note 2. Also: https://www.britannica.com/biography/Stigand

Chapter 3: The First Trip to Battle

1. *The Gesta Guillelmi by William of Poitiers*, p. 129.
2. Ibid., p. 133.
3. The Project Gutenberg EBook of *Heimskringla*, by Snorri Sturluson; produced by Douglas B. Killings and David Widger. https://www.gutenberg.org/files/598/598-h/598-h.htm#link2H_4_0615
4. *Heimskringla*, #80.
5. *Heimskringla*, #81.
6. *Heimskringla*, #87.
7. *Heimskringla*, #82.
8. *Heimskringla*, #86, #87.

Chapter 4: The First of the Three Battles of 1066 – Fulford

1. *Heimskringla*, #87.
2. *Heimskringla*, #88.
3. Natural History Museum https://www.nhm.ac.uk/discover/first-britons.html
4. The Project Gutenberg EBook of *Heimskringla*, by Snorri Sturluson; produced by Douglas B. Killings and David Widger. https://www.gutenberg.org/files/598/598-h/598-h.htm#link2H_4_0615
5. *Heimskringla*, #87.
6. Charles Jones, *The Forgotten Battle of 1066: Fulford* (Tempus Publishing Ltd, Stroud, 2006), pp. 137–9.
7. *Heimskringla*, #87.

8. *Heimskringla*, #86.
9. *Heimskringla*, #87.
10. *Cambridge Dictionary*. https://dictionary.cambridge.org/us/dictionary/english/fen.
11. *The Anglo-Saxon Chronicle* - Avalon Project: Documents in Law, History and Diplomacy. Yale Law School – Lillian Goldman Law Library. https://avalon.law.yale.edu/medieval/ang11.asp

Chapter 5: The Second of the Three Battles of 1066 – Stamford Bridge

1. Regia Anglorum Historical Re-enactment & Living History society Members Handbook – Saxon 2007 PDF. https://regia.org/members/handbook/2007%20saxon.pdf, also *Anglo-Saxon Military Institutions on the Eve of the Norman Conquest*, by C. Warren Hollister, pp. 16, 17.
2. The Project Gutenberg EBook of *The Anglo-Saxon Chronicle*; Ingram translation – collation of all nine versions. http://www.gutenberg.org/cache/epub/657/pg657.html
3. *Heimskringla* #89.
4. *Heimskringla*, #90.
5. *Heimskringla*, #92.
6. Historic Britain blog https://mercedesrochelle.com/wordpress/?p=390
7. *The Carmen de Hastingae Proelio of Guy, Bishop of Amiens*, edited and translated by Frank Barlow (Clarendon Press, Oxford, 1999), p. lxxii.
8. *The Anglo-Saxon Chronicle*. Online Medieval and Classical Library Release #17 http://mcllibrary.org/Anglo/
9. Ibid.
10. Ibid.
11. Ibid.
12. *Anglo-Saxon Military Institutions on the Eve of the Norman Conquest* by C. Warren Hollister (Clarendon Press, Oxford, 1962), pp. 134–40.
13. *Science Daily*, https://www.sciencedaily.com/releases/2004/09/040902090552.htm
14. Total War Centre, https://www.twcenter.net/forums/forum.php?s=6c69bb5e605ea44a5fd79f959f25e775
15. Ibid.
16. Ibid.

17. Ibid.

18. 'Archived from the original on 2012-08-23. Retrieved 2016-07-21'. Source copied as 'Cavalry Saddles and Stirrups'.

19. https://www.arild-hauge.com/PDF/New_Iconographic_Interpretations_of_Gotl.pdf – p. four on the PDF, labelled as p. 91 of the text.

20. Anglo-Saxon Narrative Poetry Project. *The Exeter Book* – Maxims. https://anglosaxonpoetry.camden.rutgers.edu/maxims-i/

21. *The Anglo-Saxon Chronicle*. Online Medieval and Classical Library Release #17. http://mcllibrary.org/Anglo/

22. *The Anglo-Saxon Chronicle*. An edition with TEI P4 mark-up, expressed in XML and translated to XHTML1.1 using XSLT. http://asc.jebbo.co.uk/ Manuscript D.

23. Bosworth-Toller Anglo-Saxon Dictionary. http://bosworth.ff.cuni.cz/

24. *The Anglo-Saxon Chronicle*. An edition with TEI P4 mark-up, expressed in XML and translated to XHTML1.1 using XSLT. http://asc.jebbo.co.uk/ Manuscript D

25. 'History and Hardware of Warfare – Anglo-Saxon Military Organization, Part III, posted 10 February 2019 (https://weaponsandwarfare.com/2019/02/10/anglo-saxon-military-organisation-part-iii/).

26. *Heimskringla*, #90.

27. Ibid.

28. Ibid.

29. Ibid.

30. *Heimskringla*, #91.

31. *The Anglo-Saxon Chronicle*. Online Medieval and Classical Library Release #17. http://mcllibrary.org/Anglo/

32. Ibid.

33. *Heimskringla*, #91.

34. *Heimskringla* #92.

35. *The Anglo-Saxon Chronicle*. Online Medieval and Classical Library Release #17. http://mcllibrary.org/Anglo/

36. *Heimskringla*, #92.

37. *Scandinavian Studies*, Vol. 60, No. 1 (Winter 1988), pp. 13–29.

38. *Heimskringla*, #93.

39. *Heimskringla*, #94.

40. Axes, Blades & Shield | Ancient armour, Horse armour, Bronze Age. January 2020. https://www.pinterest.com/pin/675751119058698711/

41. *The Vintage News* (https://www.thevintagenews.com/2016/05/17/rare-surviving-period-examples-barding-medieval-armor-horses/).
42. Ibid.
43. *Heimskringla,* #94.
44. *Heimskringla,* #95.
45. Ibid.
46. Ibid.
47. Ibid.
48. Ibid.
49. *Heimskringla,* #97.
50. https://www.distancefromto.net/
51. *Heimskringla,* #97.
52. The Project Gutenberg EBook of *The Anglo-Saxon Chronicle,* by 'Unknown' (various scribes).
53. *Heimskringla,* #86.
54. The Project Gutenberg EBook of *The Anglo-Saxon Chronicle,* by 'Unknown' (various scribes). http://www.gutenberg.org/cache/epub/657/pg657.html
55. Ibid.
56. Ibid.
57. Ibid.
58. Ibid.
59. Ibid.
60. Ibid.
61. Ibid.
62. Ibid.
63. *Heimskringla,* #97.
64. The Project Gutenberg EBook of *The Anglo-Saxon Chronicle,* by 'Unknown' (various scribes). http://www.gutenberg.org/cache/epub/657/pg657.html
65. Ingram translation – collation of all nine versions: The Project Gutenberg EBook of *The Anglo-Saxon Chronicle,* by Unknown. http://www.gutenberg.org/cache/epub/657/pg657.html)
66. *Heimskringla,* #99.
67. *The Chronicle of the Norman Conquest* by Master Wace.
68. *Heimskringla,* #99.
69. *Heimskringla,* #99.
70. The Project Gutenberg EBook of *The Anglo-Saxon Chronicle,* by 'Unknown' (various scribes). http://www.gutenberg.org/cache/epub/657/pg657.html

Chapter 6: The Battle of Hastings – What Others Have Had to Say About its Actual Location

1. https://www.distancefromto.net/
2. https://www.google.com/search?q=driving+distance+from +Hastings%2C+UK%2C+to+Battle%2C+UK&rl z=1C1CHBF_enUS837US837&oq=driving+distance+from+ Hastings%2C+UK%2C+to+Battle%2C+UK&aqs= chrome..69i57.18336j0j7&sourceid=chrome&ie=UTF-8
3. https://www.distancefromto.net/
4. https://battleofhastingsnewsite.wordpress.com/2019/01/15/ netherfield-a-place-to-defend/
5. Ibid.
6. Seabed Mapping: Dungeness to Selsey. Reference: TR64. Status: FINAL. Date: 22 December 2014. Project Name: Sussex IFCA Seabed Mapping. Authors: A. Colenutt & J. Evans. Checked By: A. Colenutt. Approved By: T. Mason. https://assets. sussexwildlifetrust.org.uk/Files/schip-seabed-mapping- dungeness-to-selsey.pdf
7. Ibid.
8. Ibid.
9. *The Battle of Hastings at Sedlescombe,* by Jonathan Starkey and Michael Starkey, p. 155.
10. The Project Gutenberg EBook of *The Anglo-Saxon Chronicle,* by 'Unknown'. http://www.gutenberg.org/cache/epub/657/pg657. html)
11. *The Anglo-Saxon Chronicle.* An edition with TEI P4 mark-up, expressed in XML and translated to XHTML1.1 using XSLT. http://asc.jebbo.co.uk/ Manuscript D.
12. The Project Gutenberg EBook of *The Anglo-Saxon Chronicle,* by 'Unknown' (various medieval scribes). http://www.gutenberg. org/cache/epub/657/pg657.html
13. *The Gesta Guillelmi by William of Poitiers,* pp. xxiv, 107.
14. Ibid, p. xxv.
15. Ibid, p. xxxv, note 55.
16. Ibid, p. xxxvii, note 99.
17. Ibid, p. 111.
18. Wace, pp. 122, 123.
19. *Anglo-Saxon Military Institutions on the Eve of the Norman Conquest* by C. Warren Hollister, p. 124.

20. *The Anglo-Saxon Chronicle* – Avalon Project: Documents in Law, History and Diplomacy. Yale Law School – Lillian Goldman Law Library. https://avalon.law.yale.edu/medieval/ang11.asp

21. *The Gesta Guillelmi by William of Poitiers*, p. 121.

22. Ibid, p. 121.

23. Ibid, pp. 123, 125, Note 1.

24. Ibid, p. 123.

25. Ibid, p. 125.

26. Wace, p. 128.

27. *The Anglo-Saxon Chronicle*. An edition with TEI P4 mark-up, expressed in XML and translated to XHTML1.1 using XSLT. http://asc.jebbo.co.uk/ Manuscript D.

28. Wace, p. 154.

29. *The Anglo-Saxon Chronicle*. An edition with TEI P4 mark-up, expressed in XML and translated to XHTML1.1 using XSLT. http://asc.jebbo.co.uk/ Manuscript D.

30. *The Anglo-Saxon Chronicle* Online Medieval and Classical Library Release #17. http://mcllibrary.org/Anglo/

31. Ibid.

32. https://www.oldenglishtranslator.co.uk/

33. *The Carmen de Hastingae Proelio of Guy, Bishop of Amiens*, p. 21.

Chapter 7: The Composition of the Anglo-Saxon Army – Of Fyrdmen, Hidesmen, Huscarls and Thegns

1. https://spartacus-educational.com/MEDFyrd.htm

2. Wace, Chapter XVIII. How The Men of England made Ready and Who They Were'. https://www.gutenberg.org/files/41163/41163-h/41163-h.htm

3. Regia Anglorum Historical Re-enactment & Living History Society Members Handbook – Saxon 2007. https://regia.org/members/handbook/2007%20saxon.pdf

4. https://www.english-heritage.org.uk/learn/1066-and-the-norman-conquest/the-weaponry-of-1066/

5. *Anglo-Saxon Military Institutions on the Eve of the Norman Conquest* by C. Warren Hollister, p. 26.

6. http://www.medievalwarfare.info/weapons.htm#guisarmes

7. Bosworth-Toller Anglo-Saxon Dictionary http://www.bosworthtoller.com/006460

8. *Anglo-Saxon Military Institutions on the Eve of the Norman Conquest* by C. Warren Hollister, p. 81.
9. Ibid, p. 40.
10. Ibid, p. 24.
11. Ibid, p. 73.
12. *Webster's New World College Dictionary*, 4th Edition. https://www.collinsdictionary.com/us/dictionary/english/soke Word origin: ME < ML soca < OE socn, jurisdiction, prosecution < base of secan (< sokjan), to seek'.
13. WordSense.eu | Dictionary https://www.wordsense.eu/hus/
14. Britannicawww.britannica.com › ... › Sociology & Society
15. https://regia.org/research/warfare/Huscarl.htm
16. Ibid.
17. Ibid.
18. Ibid.
19. Ibid. For sources, the Regia Anglorum article cites: Abels, R.P., *Lordship and Military Obligation in Anglo-Saxon England*; Hollister, C. Warren, *Anglo-Saxon Military Institutions on the Eve of the Norman Conquest*; Larson, L.M., *The King's Household in Anglo-Saxon England*; Stenton, F., *Anglo-Saxon England*.
20. *Anglo-Saxon Military Institutions on the Eve of the Norman Conquest* by C. Warren Hollister, pp. 9 and 10.
21. 'The Deadliest Blogger: Military History Page, The historical writing of Barry C. Jacobsen', 'Military History Blog of "Deadliest Warriors"', https://deadliestblogpage.wordpress.com/2017/05/03/elite-warrior-of-the-dark-ages-anglo-saxon-Huscarl/
22. Ibid.
23. Ibid.
24. 'Household Men, Mercenaries and Vikings in Anglo-Saxon England', by Richard Abels, in John France (ed.), *Mercenaries and Paid Men – The Mercenary Identity in the Middle Ages* (Brill, 2008), p. 143.
25. Ibid.
26. 'Mercenaries, Mamelukes and Militia – Toward a Cross-Cultural Typology of Military Service', by Stephen Morillo, History Department, Wabash College, pp. 244, 245, as cited in 'Mercenaries and Paid Men – The Mercenary Identity in the Middle Ages. Proceedings of a Conference held at University of Wales, Swansea', 7th–9th July, 2005, edited by John France.
27. 'Mercenaries and Paid Men – The Mercenary Identity in the Middle Ages'. Proceedings of a Conference held at University

of Wales, Swansea', 7–9 July, 2005, edited by John France, p. 144.

28. Ibid.

29. Medievalists.net. https://www.medievalists.net/2011/05/household-men-mercenaries-and-vikings-in-anglo-saxon-england/

30. https://deadliestblogpage.wordpress.com/2017/05/03/elite-warrior-of-the-dark-ages-anglo-saxon-huscarl/

31. *The Gesta Guillelmi by William of Poitiers*, p. 127, note 6.

32. Project Gutenberg's *The Chronicle of the Norman Conquest*, by Master Wace. 'How The Men of England Made Ready and Who They Were', pp. 173, 174. https://www.gutenberg.org/files/41163/41163-h/41163-h.htm

33. Regia Anglorum Historical Re-enactment & Living History Society Members Handbook – Saxon 2007. https://regia.org/members/handbook/2007%20saxon.pdf

34. *Anglo-Saxon Military Institutions on the Eve of the Norman Conquest* by C. Warren Hollister, pp. 131–3.

Chapter 8: Where the Forests End and Begin – Today and in 1066

1. 'Old Maps of East Sussex' https://www.oldmapsonline.org/en/East_Sussex

2. As shown by Stephen Charnock, in 'On Certain Geographical Names in the County of Sussex' – a report to the forty-second meeting of the British Association for the Advancement of Science, p. 177.

3. www.archiuk.com › cgi-bin › build_nls_historic_map http://www.archiuk.com/cgi-bin/build_nls_historic_map.pl?search_location=,%20Battle,%20East%20Sussex&latitude=50.907943&longitude=0.487751

4. 'Battle Extensive Urban Survey report and maps' site, https://www.westsussex.gov.uk/media/1716/battle_eus_report_maps.pdf

5. Ibid.

6. *The Carmen de Hastingae Proelio of Guy, Bishop of Amiens*; map of the Battle area, on p. lxxviii.

7. Wace, pp. 173, 174.

8. 'Time Team', Special. Television Documentary – Season 20 – '1066, The Lost Battlefield', 12 December 1 2013.

9. Project Gutenberg's *The Chronicle of the Norman Conquest*, by Master Wace. https://www.gutenberg.org/files/41163/41163-h/41163-h.htm

10. Wace, p. 239.

11. https://www.english-heritage.org.uk/learn/1066-and-the-norman- conquest/the-weaponry-of-1066/

12. *Anglo-Saxon Military Institutions on the Eve of the Norman Conquest* by C. Warren Hollister, p. 132.

Chapter 9: Who Were the Men Who Fought in the Norman Army?

1. *Lordship and Community: Battle Abbey and its Banlieu, 1066-1538*, by Eleanor Searle (Pontifical Institute of Mediaeval Studies, Toronto, 1974), pp. 21–3. (file:///C:/Users/Robert/Downloads/3584-7311-5-PB.pdf

2. 'The history of Battle'. https://www.sussexlife.co.uk/out-about/places/the-history-of-battle-1-5179629

3. F. Stenton, *William the Conqueror and the Rule of the Normans* (Putnam, London, 1907), p. 198.

4. *The Gesta Guillelmi by William of Poitiers*, p. 77, Note 2.

5. *The Carmen de Hastingae Proelio of Guy, Bishop of Amiens*, pp. 21 and 23.

6. Ibid., p. 23.

7. Ibid.

8. 'Old Sussex Mapped – Yeakell and Gardner's Sussex 1778-1783'. http://www.envf.port.ac.uk/geo/research/historical/webmap/sussexmap/Yeakelllarge42.htm

9. Wace, p. 172.

10. https://www.english-heritage.org.uk/learn/1066-and-the-norman-conquest/the-weaponry-of-1066/

11. https://britishheritage.com/military-history/weapons-normans-battle-hastings

12. https://www.english-heritage.org.uk/learn/1066-and-the-norman-conquest/the-weaponry-of-1066/

13. https://britishheritage.com/military-history/weapons-normans-battle-hastings

14. Ibid.

15. https://www.english-heritage.org.uk/learn/1066-and-the-norman-conquest/the-weaponry-of-1066/

16. *The Gesta Guillelmi by William of Poitiers*, p. 129.

17. Ibid., p. 127.

18. https://www.english-heritage.org.uk/learn/1066-and-the-norman-conquest/the-weaponry-of-1066/

19. Ibid.

20. https://britishheritage.com/military-history/weapons-normans-battle-hastings

21. *The Gesta Guillelmi by William of Poitiers*, p. 133.
22. Wace, p. 175.
23. 'William's Army', at 'The Engliscan Gesithas' – 'The English Companions'. https://www.tha-engliscan-gesithas.org.uk/education/the-norman-military-system
24. *The Gesta Guillelmi by William of Poitiers*, p. 129, Note 3.
25. *Anglo-Saxon Military Institutions on the Eve of the Norman Conquest* by C. Warren Hollister, p. 140.
26. *The Battle of Hastings 1066: The Uncomfortable Truth – Revealing the True Location of England's Most Famous Battle* by John Grehan and Martin Mace, p. 55.
27. Ibid., pp. 133, 135.
28. 'William's Army', at 'The Engliscan Gesithas' – 'The English Companions'. https://www.tha-engliscan-gesithas.org.uk/education/the-norman-military-system
29. Spartacus Educational. https://spartacus-educational.com/MEDprimogeniture.htm#:~:text=Primogeniture%20was%20the%20custom%20of,William%20the%20Conqueror%20in%201066
30. 'William's Army', at 'The Engliscan Gesithas' – 'The English Companions'. https://www.tha-engliscan-gesithas.org.uk/education/the-norman-military-system
31. Ibid.
32. Ibid.
33. *The Gesta Guillelmi by William of Poitiers*, p. xxvi.
34. Ibid.
35. Wace, p. 114.
36. Ibid., pp. 109–11.
37. Ibid., pp. 112–14.
38. Ibid., p. 115.
39. Ibid.
40. Ibid, p. 117.
41. *Anglo-Saxon Military Institutions on the Eve of the Norman Conquest* by C. Warren Hollister, p. 87.
42. Ibid, p. 117.
43. Ibid, p. 109.

Chapter 10: The Final Trips to Battle

1. *Secrets of the Norman Conquest* by Nick Austin, p. 52.
2. Definitions from Oxford Languages. https://www.google.com/search?q=%22hurst%22+meaning&rlz=1C1CHBF_

enUS837US837&oq=%22hurst%22+meaning&aqs=chrome..
69i57j0i324j0l7j0i22i30.4697j0j4&sourceid=chrome&ie=UTF-8

3. *The Battle of Hastings, 1066*, by C.K. Lawson (Tempus Publishing, Ltd., Stroud, 2002).
4. *The Carmen de Hastingae Proelio of Guy, Bishop of Amiens*, p. 23.
5. Ibid, p. 23.
6. Ibid, p. 25.
7. Ibid.
8. Wace, p. 190.
9. *The Carmen de Hastingae Proelio of Guy, Bishop of Amiens*, p. 25.
10. *The Gesta Guillelmi by William of Poitiers*, p. 131.
11. *The Carmen de Hastingae Proelio of Guy, Bishop of Amiens*, p. 27.
12. Ibid.
13. Ibid., p. 26.
14. Ibid.
15. Wace, p. 44.
16. *The Gesta Guillelmi by William of Poitiers*, p. 133.
17. *The Carmen de Hastingae Proelio of Guy, Bishop of Amiens*, p. 27.
18. *The Gesta Guillelmi by William of Poitiers*, p. 133.
19. Ibid.
20. Ibid., p. 129.
21. *The Carmen de Hastingae Proelio of Guy, Bishop of Amiens*, p. 27.
22. Wace, p. 191.
23. Ibid, p. 193.
24. *The Carmen de Hastingae Proelio of Guy, Bishop of Amiens*, pp. 27 and 29.
25. Ibid, p. 29.
26. Ibid, p. 31.
27. *The Gesta Guillelmi by William of Poitiers*, p. 135.
28. *The Carmen de Hastingae Proelio of Guy, Bishop of Amiens*, p. 31.
29. Ibid, p. 33.
30. Wace, p. 181.
31. Ibid, p. 183.
32. *The Carmen de Hastingae Proelio of Guy, Bishop of Amiens*, p. 33.

Chapter 11: The Bayeux Tapestry, and the End of the Battle of Hastings

1. 'The Viking Age Compendium – citing Dawson, Fowke, Hicks'. http://www.vikingage.org/wiki/wiki/Reproductions_of_the_Bayeux_Tapestry

2. Bayeux Tapestry - From Dot To Domesday http://www.dot-domesday.me.uk/bayeux2.htm

3. Ibid.

4. Ibid.

5. Ibid.

6. 'The Viking Age Compendium', http://www.vikingage.org/wiki/wiki/Reproductions_of_the_Bayeux_Tapestry

7. Ibid.

8. Ibid.

9. https://www.history.org.uk/primary/resource/2530/the-strange-death-of-king-harold-ii-propaganda-an

10. Wace, p. 253.

11. Ibid., p. xxiii.

12. Ibid., p. 254.

13. Ibid.

14. Ibid.

15. *The Gesta Normannorum Ducum of William of Jumièges, Orderic Vitalis and Robert of Torigni Vol. II*, edited and translated by Elisabeth M.C. van Houts (Clarendon Press, Oxford, 1995), p. 169 – Dennis' citation.

16. As cited by Dennis, ibid., p. 198.

17. Ibid.

18. Ibid.

19. *Aimé du Mont Cassin, Storia di Normanni*, edited by V. de Bartholomeis (Rome, 1935). (*The Gesta Guillelmi*, p. 136, Note 3.)

20. https://www.history.org.uk/primary/resource/2530/the-strange-death-of-king-harold-ii-propaganda-an

21. Ibid.

22. *The Carmen de Hastingae Proelio of Guy, Bishop of Amiens* – Dennis' citation in: https://www.history.org.uk/primary/resource/2530/the-strange-death-of-king-harold-ii-propaganda-an

23. Ibid., p. 229 and pp. 262–4 – Dennis' citation in: https://www.history.org.uk/primary/resource/2530/the-strange-death-of-king-harold-ii-propaganda-an

24. https://www.history.org.uk/primary/resource/2530/the-strange-death-of-king-harold-ii-propaganda-an

25. *The Gesta Guillelmi by William of Poitiers*, p. 129.

26. Ibid., pp. 131, 135.

27. Ibid., p. 131.

28. Ibid., p. 137.

29. Ibid., p. 139.

Chapter 12: Aftermath

1. *The Gesta Guillelmi by William of Poitiers*, p. 141.
2. Ibid., p. 143.
3. Ibid., p. 147.

Conclusion

1. 'Time Team' Special. Television Documentary – Season 20 – '1066, The Lost Battlefield', 12 December 2013.

Bibliography

Principal Sources

Anglo-Saxon Military Institutions on the Eve of the Norman Conquest, by C. Warren Hollister (Clarendon Press, Oxford, 1962).

Battle Abbey: The Eastern Range and the Excavations of 1978-1980, by J.N. Hare. Historic Buildings and Monuments Commission for England (Alan Sutton Publishing, Gloucester, 1985).

English Historical Documents, Volume II – 1042-1189, general editors David C. Douglas and George W. Greenway (Oxford University Press, Oxford, 1953–81).

Heimskringla: Or, the Lives of the Norse Kings, by Snorri Sturluson. https://www.gutenberg.org/files/598/598-h/598-h.htm

King Harold and the Bayeux Tapestry, The Manchester Centre for Anglo-Saxon Studies, Volume III, edited by Gale R. Owen-Crocker (The Boydell Press, Woodbridge, 2005).

Lordship and Community – Battle Abbey and its Banlieu, 1066-1538, by Eleanor Searle (Pontifical Institute of Medieval Studies, Toronto, 1974).

Secrets of the Norman Invasion, by Nick Austin (Ogmium Press, Crowhurst, 2011).

The Anglo-Saxon Chronicle – Avalon Project: Documents in Law, History, and Diplomacy. Yale Law School – Lillian Goldman Law Library. https://avalon.law.yale.edu/medieval/ang11.asp

The Anglo-Saxon Chronicle, by unknown authors [scribes]. Translator James Henry Ingram. http://www.gutenberg.org/cache/epub/657/pg657.html

The Battle of Hastings at Sedlescombe, by Jonathan Starkey and Michael Starkey (Momentous Britain, 2010–19).

The Battle of Hastings, 1066, by M.K. Lawson (Tempus Publishing Ltd, Stroud, 2002).

The Battle of Hastings, 1066: The Uncomfortable Truth, by John Grehan and Martin Mace (Pen & Sword, Barnsley, 2012).

The Bayeux Tapestry, The Bayeux Museum.

The Bayeux Tapestry Edition Ville de Bayeux, 2007.

The Carmen de Hastingae Proelio of Guy, Bishop of Amiens, edited and translated by Frank Barlow (Clarendon Press, Oxford, 1999).

The Chronicle of Battle Abbey, edited and translated by Eleanor Searle (Clarendon Press, Oxford, 1980).

The Chronicle of the Norman Conquest, by Master [Possibly known the further identifier as either 'Robert' or 'Richard'] Wace. https://www. gutenberg.org/files/41163/41163-h/41163-h.htm

The Gesta Guillelmi of William of Poitiers, edited and translated by R.H.C Davis and Marjorie Chibnall (Clarendon Press, Oxford, 1998).

The Gesta Normannorum Ducum of William of Jumièges, Orderic Vitalis and Robert of Torigni, Volume II, edited and translated by Elisabeth M.C. Van Houts (Clarendon Press, Oxford, 1995).

The Norman Conquest – Its Setting And Impact, by Dorothy Whitelock, David C. Douglas, Charles H. Lemmon and Frank Barlow (Eyre and Spottiswoode, London, 1966).

The Norman Conquest of England – Sources And Documents, by R. Allen Brown (The Boydell Press, Woodbridge, 1984 and 1995).

The Norman Conquest of the North – The Region And Its Transformation, 1000-1135, by William E. Kappelle (University of North Carolina Press, Chapel Hill, NC, 1979).

Other Sources Consulted

Ashley, Maurice, *The Life and Times of William I* (Weidenfeld and Nicolson, London, 1973).

Barney, Stephen A., *Word-Hoard: An Introduction to Old English Vocabulary* (Yale University Press, Newhaven and London, 1977).

Bede, *A History of the English Church and People* (Barnes & Noble, New York, 1993).

Douglas, David C., *William the Conqueror: The Norman Impact Upon England* (Methuen, London, 1990).

Dupuy, Colonel Trevor N., *The Evolution of Weapons and Warfare* (Boobs Merrill, New York, 1980).

Ganeri, Anita, *Focus on Vikings* (Shooting Star Press, New York, 1993).

Gravett, Christopher, *Hastings, 1066: The Fall of Saxon England* (Osprey, London, 1992).

Hinde, Thomas (ed.), *The Domesday Book: England's Heritage, Then & Now* (CLB International, Godalming, 1997).

Hollister, C. Warren, *The Impact of the Norman Conquest* (John Wiley and Sons, New York, 1969).

Howarth, David, *1066: The Year of the Conquest* (Barnes and Noble, New York, 1993).

Jones, Charles, *The Forgotten Battle of 1066: Fulford* (Tempus Publishing Ltd, Stroud, 2007).

Le Goff, Jacques, *Medieval Civilization – 400-1500* (Barnes & Noble, New York, 2000).

Lacey, Robert, and Danziger, Danny, *The Year 1000* (Little, Brown, New York, 1999).

Mason, Antony, *Viking Times* (Simon and Schuster, New York, 1997).

Norman, A.V.B., *The Medieval Soldier* (Barnes & Noble, New York, 1993).

_____, and Pottinger, Don, *English Weapons and Warfare 440-1660* (Barnes & Noble, New York, 1992).

Owen, Gale R., *Rites and Religions of the Anglo-Saxons* (Barnes and Noble, New York, 1981).

Palgrave, Sir Francis, *History of the Anglo-Saxons* (Dorsey, New York, 1989).

Savage, Anne, (translator and collator), *The Anglo-Saxon Chronicles* (CLB International, Godalming, 1984).

Sawyer, P.H., *From Roman Britain to Norman England* (St Martin's, New York, 1978).

Trevelyan, G.M., *A Shortened History of England* (Penguin, New York, 1965).

Walker, Ian W., *Harold: The Last Anglo-Saxon King* (Sutton, Stroud, 1997).

Whitlock, Ralph, *The Warrior Kings of Saxon England* (Barnes and Noble, New York, 1993).

Index